GREAT RIVALRIES

Cycling and the Story of Italy

GREAT RIVALRIES

Cycling and the Story of Italy

Kevin Andrews

Connor Court Publishing

Published in 2019 by Connor Court Publishing Pty Ltd

Copyright © Kevin Andrews 2019

All rights reserved. No part of this book may be reproduced or transmitted in any form or by any means, electronic or mechanical, including photocopying, recording or by any information storage and retrieval system, without prior permission in writing from the publisher.

Connor Court Publishing Pty Ltd
PO Box 7257
Redland Bay QLD 4165
sales@connorcourt.com
Phone 0497-900-685

Printed in Australia

ISBN: 9781925826456

Cover design: Maria Giordano

Cover Photo: Gino Bartali and Fausto Coppi

Photos in the book are, to the best of our knowledge, from the public domain or the copyright has expired. However, if any photos have copyright ownership, please contact the publisher and this will be rectified in subsequent editions of this book.

To Benjamin

Follow your road . . .

Lying on a featherbed will not bring you fame, nor staying beneath the quilt. . . get up; defeat your breathlessness with a spirit that can win all battles if the body's heaviness does not deter it.

-- Dante Alighieri, The Divine Comedy

This book tells the story of the great rivalries that shaped both the country and cycling during the first one hundred years of modern Italy. These rivalries that were – and are still – debated with such animation and enthusiasm in local bars throughout the entire country of Italy.
-- Simon Gerrans[1]

---

[1] **Simon Gerrans** *was a champion Australian cyclist, winning two of the monuments of cycling, Milan-San Remo and Liege-Bastogne-Liege; two stages of the Giro d'Italia; stages of the Tour de France and the Vuelta a España, and finishing second in the World Championship Road Race. He won the Australian Championship twice, the Tour Down Under four times, the Herald-Sun Tour twice, and the Melbourne to Warrnambool Classic amongst many other victories. Simon retired from the professional peloton in 2018.*

Foreword

As with many cyclists, Italy holds a very special place in my heart.

My first trip abroad was to Italy. It was the year 2000 and I was a fresh-faced 19-year-old with a passion for cycling. I boarded a plane without a clue of what to expect, but I was excited for the adventure. The fact I spoke no Italian and didn't even know exactly where in Italy I was headed was of no concern.

I arrived in a small village in the northern Italian region of Veneto and joined a 'squadre dilettanti', a local under 23 team. I was placed in this team by Cycling Australia to gain my first taste of international racing. Shortly after arriving and before I had even recovered from the long travel, I discovered I had landed exactly the right place, a country full of people who shared my passion.

In the years to follow, Italy not only happened to be the country where I made my international debut, it was also where I won my first Tour de France stage in the 2008 Tour and in 2012 my first classic, *La Primavera*, the Milano – San Remo. I also had the honour of winning stage 14 of the 2009 *Giro d'Italia* and wore the converted *maglia rosa* in 2015, as a result of leading a winning Orica-GreenEDGE team across the line at the opening team time trial.

One thing I'll never forget from my first trip to Italy was listening to the locals at the bar in our village passionately debate, in the way that only Italians can, everything cycling. Was Pantani the best climber of all time? How many stages of the upcoming Giro was Cipollini going to win? But what the Italians loved to debate the most of all was the *great rivalries* in the sport of cycling.

Contents

Foreword	9
Introduction	11
Acknowledgements	12
Prologue	13
1. Modern Italy and the Bicycle	17
2. The Birth of the Giro	33
3. Pedaling out of Poverty	53
4. Pedals and Politics	71
5. The Changing Order	87
6. Changing of the Guard	101
7. Triumphs and Tensions	117
8. The March to War	135
9. A Star is Born	143
10. A Shifting World	155
11. The Descent into Darkness	171
12. The Resumption of Hostilities	185
13. Great Rivalries	203
14. A World Made New	225
15. The Transition Years	243
Epilogue	259
Australian Cyclists in Italy	269
Time line	277
Glossary	281
Bibliography	285
Index	287

Introduction

Ever since learning to ride my mother's old postal delivery bike as a child, cycling has fascinated me. Growing up at Rosedale in rural Gippsland, I learnt that some of Australia's best cyclists had lived in the region. Keith Rowley, the winner of the inaugural *Herald Sun* Tour, was born at Rosedale. John Trevorrow, a winner of many of Australia's greatest races, was born at nearby Morwell; and Jim Taylor, a champion cyclist of the 1950s, later lived at Rosedale. I recall vivdly the flash of the multi-coloured jerseys as the *Herald Sun* tour peloton sped past our farm.

My family was involved in horse racing and I subsequently became a sports commentator, calling many sporting events for more than a decade, and writing for a number of publications about sport.

Athletics was popular at the time, and I competed during school and university. It was while studying at Melbourne University, where I trained with the renowned athletics coach, Franz Stampfl, that I learnt of Nino Borsari, a prominent figure in nearby Carlton. Nino had won a gold medal for Italy in cycling at the 1932 Olympics. He later raced in Australia before settling here, becoming a leading figure in the Italian, business and sporting communities in Melbourne. He was instrumental in sending the first Australian team to compete in the Giro d'Italia in 1952, and influential in attracting the Olympic Games to Melbourne in 1956. A neon sign celebrating his 1932 gold medal remains a Carlton icon almost a century after his victory in the Los Angeles Olympic Games.

My interest in the southern European nation piqued while working as an Associate to Sir James Gobbo, a prominent Australian of Italian heritage; and subsequently representing in the Australian Parliament many constituents who emigrated from Italy.

My wife, Margaret, and I, together with our chidren, have been keen recreational cyclists. We have attended the Tour Down Under in Adelaide regularly as well as some major international races. Our youngest son, Ben, has progressed through the junior cycling ranks, and curently rides for a UCI Continental team on the Oceania circuit as well as in Australia and Europe. As a consequence, I became more interested in the history of the sport.

Anthony Cappello from Connor Court, suggested this book after learning of the wartime exploits of the champion Italian cyclist, Gino Bartali. As I researched the topic, I realized that the tale of the great Italian cyclists is interwoven with the story of Italy itself; hence this book. While this account revolves around Bartali and his great rival, Fausto Coppi, it is more than about than the two competitors. It is a tale about great rivalries, both sporting and political, and an account of Italy in the second half of the 19th and the first half of the 20th centuries. I hope you enjoy it.

-- Kevin Andrews, May 2019

Acknowledgements

I am grateful to a number of people for reading the manuscript and offering many helpful comments, including Professor Robert Pascoe, and Anthony Moate.

I thank Emily Andrews for Italian translations and her observations on the draft chapters.

I thank Stephen Hodge, one of Australia's best cyclists of the 1990s, for the photograph of Alfredo Binda, which is part of the Opperman Collection of historic photographs: (www.cyclinghistory.com.au).

I am grateful to John Beasley for the information about his father's races in Europe and the photograph of the 1952 Nilux team.

Finally, I am indebted to Simon Gerrans, one of Australia's most successful cyclists, for generously writing the Foreword.

Prologue

Rivalry, which is the very soul of sport, reveals itself almost immediately
-- Gino Bartali.

You may have the universe if I may have Italy
-- Giuseppe Verdi.

Two riders appeared through the mist towards the top of the Passo Rolle, the high road linking the Fiemme and Primiero Valleys in the Dolomites. Although lower than the famed Stelvio Pass, the 1989 metre high Rolle was a brutal climb on a rough gravel road. Side by side they struggled to reach the summit, lactic acid stabbing their legs with each pedal stroke. The older, shorter man, with a crushed nose from a fall, bounced on and off the saddle. His younger challenger climbed fluidly. Stroke by gruelling stroke they grasped for oxygen as they fought their way to the apex of the climb. Individually, they were two of the greatest cyclists Italy ever produced. Together, they were the stuff of legend – Gino Bartali and Fausto Coppi.

It was stage 17 and the last major climb of the 1946 Giro d'Italia. With World War II at an end, hostilities had resumed between the two champion cyclists. When the climb over the high pass was first added to the Giro d'Italia route in 1937, the then much younger Tuscan had prevailed against the best of the pre-war cyclists. Bartali crested the ascent ahead of Coppi a decade later, but his rival claimed the stage at Trent by nine seconds after the dangerous, winding drop into the valley below. They had finished together after crossing the Passo della Mauria from Udine to Auronzo di Cadore on stage 15. The next day, Coppi rode with eagles' wings, distancing Bartali on the Passo Falzarego. With 35 kilometres to ride, he had opened a five minute break. But Bartali, with the assistance of team mate, Aldo Bini, who surprisingly regained time after appearing to have been dropped by the leaders, was just over a minute behind Coppi as they charged towards Bassano del Grappa, the town of the famed covered bridge over the Brenta River, where in the years before, fierce battles had been fought. The older man held his overall lead and retained the leader's jersey, the *maglia rosa*, for the final three-day cross-country charge to the conclusion of the event at Milan.

Bartali had triumphed in the first great three-week duel since the war. He had won the Giro d'Italia twice before, in 1936 and 1937, as well as the 1938 Tour de France, but the younger Coppi was victorious in the last great contest for many years, the 1940 Giro. Emerging from the scars and privations of World War II, Italians had two heroes to champion. It lifted their spirits – and separated the *tifosi*, the delirious fans of the sport. The country was divided between the *Bartaliani* and the *Coppiani*. From Prime Minister and Pope to peasant farmer, Italians took sides. No-one was exempt. It was at the heady intersection of sporting rivalry and political agitation that prevailed in post-war Italy. It echoed the troubled evolution of the nation, and revealed the longing for a restoration of national pride. Indeed, the 1946 race was referred to as the *Giro della Rinascita* – the revival tour. And it made two great cyclists more than champions; it created legends that persist until today.

Great sporting rivalries are based on superb athletic achievements and an intense competitive spirit, but they expose much more. The background, experience and character of the contestants are revealed with all their strengths and flaws. In the spotlight of public attention, every action and behaviour is amplified and scrutinised. Nuances are obscured and caricatures created. Divisions are intensified. The contestants become greater than they are which in turn spurs more interest and attention. Narratives are exaggerated. Such is the story of Gino Bartali, Fausto Coppi and Italian cycling.

Behind the legend of *Bartali e Coppi* were two driven men, with different backgrounds, experiences and outlooks, who at a given time encountered each other on and off the bike. They shared hardships and privations as children, and a burning desire to succeed. One was a pious Catholic who couriered counterfeit travel documents across Italy as part of operations to rescue Jews from fascist persecution. The other a quietly intense individual who was conscripted to fight in Africa before capture by the British forces and becoming a prisoner-of-war, and who later scandalised conservative Italy by leaving his wife and having an affair and a child with a married woman. They rode as teammates and against each other. They were the yin and yang of Italian cycling, opposites bound together by circumstance and history.

Like all legends, the stories retold over the decades are part truth and part fiction, part explanation and part exaggeration. Discerning one from the other after 70 years of retelling is a challenge. The writer can attempt it, but, as when they competed, Bartali and Coppi were the subject of contrary understandings and passionate opinions. With the passing of years, the intensity may diminish, but the different accounts remain.

Great Rivalries is the story of Gino Bartali, Fausto Coppi and the champion riders who preceded them. It is also about the place of cycling in a nation emerging from division, its agrarian past, widespread impoverishment, and competing visions about creating a modern state. It is interwoven with the story of Italy itself, which began a century earlier – and continues to play-out today.

Giovanni Gerbi, Italy's first professional cyclist.

1

Modern Italy and the Bicycle

Beyond the Alps lies Italy

-- Livy.

I offer neither pay, nor quarters, nor food; I offer only hunger, thirst, forced marches, battles and death. Let him who loves his country with his heart, and not merely with his lips, follow me

-- Giuseppe Garibaldi.

Visitors to modern Italy delight in the history of a vibrant nation. The home of three great civilizations, the Hellenic, the Roman and the Western, it exudes the history of millennia. From the ancient artifacts of the earliest Greek settlements in the south, to the eternal city of Rome and beyond, Italy is a treasure trove of archaeological relics, historical settlements and cultural surprises, all linked together by the modern infrastructure of fast trains and an extensive autostrade. But this wasn't always the case. The modern Italian state is a recent invention; and that invention is foundational to this story, as both Italy and the bicycle were created over a similar time. Indeed, the increasing capacity for people to travel longer distances for work and pleasure was critical to the development of the modern industrial state.

Following the collapse of the Roman Empire, the Italian peninsula gradually formed around a series of city-states, often in conflict with each other, but gradually more engaged in trade and social intercourse. By the 1800s, seven distinct states existed: the Kingdom of Sardinia; the Kingdom of Lombardy-Venetia; the Duchy of Parma; the Duchy of Modena; the Grand Duchy of Tuscany; the Papal States; and the Kingdom of the Two Sicilies. A longing for a unified Italy and a rejection of foreign domination was the long-held dream of many people over the centuries. Famous Italians, Dante, Petrarch and Machiavelli amongst others, aspired to a united nation. This came to be known as the *Risorgimento* – meaning the revival of a united Italy. The era of Napoleonic rule and the subsequent domination by the Austrian Empire, which restored the regional rulers deposed by the Frenchman, spurred the desire for a united nation.

In the Napoleonic era, many – especially the educated and intellectuals – aspired to a new style of government free of some of the ancient constraints of the aristocracy and the old order. This desire for a new order could not be contained. But there were many currents and divisions. Vague ideas about desired outcomes and regional divisions countered any pathway to a nation-state. Competing interests of the Church and the liberal movements, and regional rivalries punctured any sense of unity. Countless revolts ended in defeat.

The economy in Europe stagnated for decades, a downturn that particularly affected agricultural Italy. Population growth compounded the economic impact on the poor, rural class, while epidemics cut a swath through the populace. Tariff policies depressed grain prices, state-sponsored development of railways stalled and reliance on foreign investment grew.

These characteristics – regional loyalties and antagonisms, and a weak economy – were to restrain national unity for a long time. And the same factors were to arise periodically for decades into the future.

Above all, modern Italy is the product of three men: Guiseppe Mazzini, a romantic nationalist who fervently believed in a God-ordained, united country; Giuseppe Garibaldi, the sailor and later South American guerrilla fighter, who became the military champion of the nationalist cause; and Count Camillo Benso di Cavour, a Piedmontese nobleman who shaped the Parliament of the new nation. Mazzini's 'Young Italy' society attracted strong support, and became an influential vehicle for unification.

Between 1820 and 1861, a series of revolutions and wars eventually led to the Proclamation of the Kingdom of Italy on March 17 with the king of Piedmont, Victor Emmanuel, the new monarch. The Catholic Church had mixed views about unification. Pius IX, who was pope from 1846-1878, was at first sympathetic to political liberalism, but ended his papacy at odds with the new secular order and the unification of Italy. In 1870, Rome became the capital of the new nation after the defeat of the Papal armies. Even then, parts of modern Italy were separate, in particular the region surrounding Trieste in the northeast that was not incorporated in the new nation until the end of the Great War. It would be another decade in 1929 before the issue of the Papal States was resolved with Mussolini entering into the Lateran Treaty with the Church.

Although Italy was largely united geographically, there remained many divisions about the direction of the nation that continued to play out for the next century. The revolutionary changes that had occurred across Europe resulted in uncertainty, competing visions for the future, and even further revolutionary change. Social Darwinism, projected by intellectuals such as Herbert Spencer, Thomas Malthus and Francis Galton, became increasingly popular, and had links to the totalitarian practices that evolved on both the left and right in the 20th century: collectivism, both socialist and communist, gained widespread support. New conflicts between capitalism and labour arose as the industrial revolution progressed. Anarchy reared its head from time to time, while defenders of traditional values and structures, such as the Church, perceived challenges to their central tenets from various quarters.

While a united Italy was achieved in the 1860s, the following two decades witnessed considerable turmoil, compounded by an economic depression in 1873. The moderate secular liberal society that Mazzini and others fought for was under threat from various forces, including Anarchists, who grew in numbers and strength from the 1870s onwards, unleashing terror in Italy and elsewhere across Europe.

By the 1890s, the fault-lines of the new nation were evident: the absence of a national narrative and the continuing regional divisions and rivalries; the vast economic gulf between the North and the South; a Parliament that continued to reflect regional interests at the expense of the national; and an ongoing antagonism between the secularists and the Church of whose property, vast parcels had been confiscated and sold by the State, and whose adherents had been banned from participating in the political process. All this was happening as the industrial revolution commenced, spluttering at first, but slowly transforming the country. Concurrently, the political establishment had fractured, especially on the Left, into competing groups and interests. National progress and prosperity was hostage to a weak economy, and political and economic cycles that were out of balance.

Italians faced a critical challenge: how to create a united, democratic state. The *Risorgimento* had been designed to achieve unity and national purpose, but it was in danger of disintegration by the 1880s. A banking scandal that implicated many of the political leadership further undermined the faltering trust in parliamentary government.

The Crispi-Giolitti era

Two men, Francesco Crispi and Giovanni Giolitti, largely shaped the direction of Italy over the next three decades. Both had been implicated in the banking scandals, but survived politically to shape the nation, for better or for worse. Between them, they served as prime minister of Italy for nearly 20 years.

Crispi was a complex character, a man of the Left who had fought with Garibaldi. He insisted on defined party lines and strong executive government. He also extolled patriotism, and believed that military success would generate national pride. The ties between government and the military had a long history in many parts of Italy, especially in Piedmont. Crispi longed to recreate the sense of unity and purpose that military victory engendered.

This authoritarian sentiment was never far below the surface at various times – and was to emerge in a more virulent form following the Great War. Cavour had implemented his program without much reference to Parliament. Garibaldi was at ease with the use of emergency powers. The late Engligh historian, Christopher Duggan, observed:

> To this tradition Crispi added a juridical justification: nations he asserted (in what was really just a logical extension of Mazzini's idea of the nation as divinely ordained), had an existence prior to individuals composing them (*natio quia nata*, in his rather cryptic Latin phrase), and thus had rights of their own – in particular the right to self-preservation. Hence, recourse to dictatorship was acceptable if 'the nation' were in danger.

Crispi used this justification to crush riots in Sicily, and sought to engage the German Chancellor, Otto von Bismark, in a war against France. His militaristic bent resulted in an Italian foray into Africa. The death of 5,000 Italian soldiers who were routed in the Battle of Adwa by the Ethiopian forces was an unmitigated disaster. Crispi lost office. While he had made important reforms to the governing process in his first term as Prime Minister, his preoccupation with foreign affairs, and his increasing authoritarianism, while the country was experiencing dark economic times, left a divided nation as the end of the 19th century beckoned.

It was a period of political and social ferment. Crispi's appeal to militaristic patriotism had failed. The system of government itself was under siege. King Umberto, who came to the throne after the death of his father Victor Emmanuel II in 1878, introduced martial law and used the army to quash riots in Milan in 1898. Two years later he was assassinated by an anarchist, Gaetano Bresci, in revenge for the shooting of demonstrators in Milan. As the century ended, the 'Italian question' was still a work in progress.

Italians entered the new century amidst political and social turmoil, but change was already underway. From the mid 1890s, the economy was finally reviving. Industrialisation had reached the peninsula. The portents for a more stable economic and political cycle were good. The political beneficiary of the economic upturn was Giovanni Giolitti, who became Prime Minister in 1901, and remained in office for most of the period until 1914. He was the first Italian leader who had not been an active participant in the *Risorgimento* and was less confined by the ideas of his predecessors. Although a liberal from the left, Giolitti governed from the centre, adjusting his policies to favour conservatives and progressives as the case required. In doing so, he became the nation's longest serving Prime Minister to date.

Giolitti recognised the changing nature of the economy. He supported industrialisation through a series of measures, such as re-organising the banking sector and investing in hydro-electricity, rather than continuing to rely of agriculture as his predecessors had done. However, agriculture also benefitted as textile manufacturing boomed.

Whereas Italy had lagged behind other industrialising nations in the 1880s and 90s, it outperformed most between 1896 and 1914. GDP growth per capita averaged 2.1 per cent in Italy, just behind the United States at 2.4 per cent, but ahead of other European nations. The country also benefitted from increasing tourism of the *Belle Époque* era in Europe and the large inflow of remittances as millions of Italians emigrated to the new world, especially the US.

The consequence was a relatively golden era for the country. While agriculture remained the most significant employer, new jobs opened up in manufacturing. Productivity increased in the early years of the new century, as did wage growth. However, the economic gulf between North and South remained, while industrial disputes and strikes beleaguered the nation. The economy suffered a down turn in 1907 and again in 1912, but it was a different country that entered the Great War to the one a generation before.

A wonderful new invention

As the convulsions that led to modern-day Italy occurred during the 1800s, technological progress was advancing rapidly. The industrial revolution – essentially the energy and technological evolution of the 18th and 19th centuries – swept aside centuries of experience within generations. Modern transport was a critical factor. The impact of the steam engine cannot be underestimated, but it was a more simple invention, the modern bicycle, that had a significant impact on mobility, mores and modernity. In 1800, few people were wealthy enough to own a horse (and carriage). The great majority of the population had no independent means of transport beyond walking. Hence their usual journey was limited to a small number of kilometers from home – whether for work or pleasure. Hence the prevalence of regional and sub-regional dialects throughout the nation. A century later, the bicycle had revolutionized that reality. Ordinary people could journey many kilometers from their home, either for work or joy. The experience of life had been revolutionized in an unanticipated way by the modern bicycle. Not since the invention of the wheel itself had a technological advance had such an impact. The revolutionary impact of the bicycle faded as subsequent vehicles such as the car and the aeroplane were invented.

Cycling and the Story of Italy

Although it has been argued that the Italian Leonardo da Vinci had drawn a sketch of a bicycle in the 1400s, the claim is of doubtful veracity. It would appear that the forerunner of the bicycle was made in Germany in 1817. A Scottish blacksmith, Kirkpatrick MacMillan, invented the first mechanically propelled bike in 1839. Over the next few decades, various advances were made, the most notably being the chain drive, the pneumatic tyre and the rear freewheel hub. By the end of the 1800s the bicycle as we now understand it had been developed.

Hundreds of thousands of bikes were built and sold from the 1880s onwards as manufacturers sprung up across Europe. In 1885, a 21-year-old Milanese medical instrument maker, Edoardo Bianchi, seized on the business opportunity of manufacturing the recently invented and increasingly popular bicycle. Bianchi's bicycles, with their distinctive celeste paint and a crowned eagle badge, attracted a large market. Two years later, he started manufacturing motorcycles, and later, automobiles. One of Italy's best-known brands had been created. By the turn of the century, his factory in Milan was producing 45,000 bicycles and 1,500 motorbikes a year. When Giovanni Tommasello, a rider sponsored by Bianchi, won the Grand Prix de Paris in 1899, the company's products attracted additional prestige. It was the beginning of a long partnership with some of Italy's greatest cyclists – Costante Girardengo, Fausto Coppi, Marco Pantani and Mario Cipollini amongst them. Bianchi also became a sponsor of major events.

A few years after Edoardo Bianchi established his manufacturing business in Milan, another enterprising craftsman, Pietro Dal Molin, opened a small workshop on the banks of the Brenta River at Bassano del Grappa. Dal Molin was fascinated by the bicycle, especially reports of the sporting achievements of riders in England, France and his native Italy. The local Veloce Club of Bassano had been founded in 1892, reflecting the growing interest in the sport. Dal Molin purchased a little known English brand, Wilier, and commenced manufacturing in a building near the famous Bassano bridge in 1906. His bikes were soon in demand and Dal Molin expanded production with a new factory. Despite heavy fighting in the region, especially on Mount Grappa to the north of the town, manufacturing continued during the war, with many of the machines used by the famed Italian Rifle Regiment.

Other bicycle manufacturers set up in the era. Vittorio Rossi was established in 1902 and began producing bikes in 1908. Teaming up with Franco Tosi, a businessman from Legnano, they produced bicycles based on patents he had purchased from the English manufacturer, Wolsit. Following the war, the brand name was changed to Legnano. Like Bianchi, Legnano saw the commercial advantage of sponsorship. The Legano professional team was soon established, attracting some of the greatest Italian riders, including Alfredo Binda, Gino Bartali and Fausto Coppi. Fausto eventually switched to Bianchi, adding to the intense rivalry between Italy's greatest cyclists in the late 1940s and early 1950s.

Of the manufacturers that started in the early days of cycling, few remain today. Many of the other famous Italian brands, such as Cinelli, Colnago, De Rosa, Masi and Pinarello, were established after World War II.

Bicycling clubs sprung-up across Italy from the late 1800s as enthusiasts enjoyed the novel freedom of the new machine. Soon feats of endurance and races were organised. Across Europe – and in the new world – velodromes attracted thousands of spectators, where mounted contestants provided a thrilling new sporting spectacle. Like the arenas of old, these amphitheatres became the home to a fresh breed of daring rivals.

The birth of Italian racing

By the late 1800s, Milan was becoming a major trading hub, connecting eastern and central Italy with France, as the rail system spread rapidly. An industrial, working class city, with a long heritage, Milan was a vibrant place. Like elsewhere in Europe, the new cycling craze had taken hold of popular imagination. For the first time, relatively cheap transport was available to the masses. The new invention provided unprecedented mobility for all classes. It wasn't long before man's natural desire to go faster and further than anyone else emerged.

Cycling has a long, proud history amongst Italians. From the earliest days, large sections of the populace fell in love with the sport, creating a culture that is unique. With the exception of the French and the Belgians, no other people had such a compelling, at times fanatical, engagement with their local and national heroes. A whole language developed around the sport on the Italian peninsula.

The association with local champions reflected the recent history of Italy. Fiercely proud and competitive, the regions of Italy championed their own riders with alacrity. This passion spurned great rivalries and an intense competitive spirit that at times consumed the nation. Proud, passionate and persistent, the Italians placed the Kings of the Road on a new pedestal. Across the country, the *tifosi* – the passionate fans of the sport – would line the roads to urge on their favourite riders, running beside them, shouting, waving, encouraging even greater effort on gravel strewn mountain paths, or rolling plains.

The epicenter of this activity was in the northern regions of Lombardia, Piedmont and Liguria, and the triangle of Italy between the great cities of Genoa, Turin and Milan. It was here that some of Italy's greatest cyclists trained and raced. In the little towns of Novi Ligure and Cittiglio, the *campionissimo* – the champion of champions – Costante Girardengo, Alfredo Binda, and Fausto Coppi, were born and raised.

The success of the great races in France spread across the border to northern Italy in the first decade of the 20th century. The political unification of Italy enhanced the power and prestige of Milan as the prosperous commercial focus of the new nation. As a major rail hub, and the centre of a rich industrial region, the capital of Lombardy grew in stature as the home of culture, art and sport. In 1876, an enterprising group of local business and sporting identities organised a test of endurance, a 200-kilometre ordeal from Milan to Turin.

Milan-Turin (1876)

Among the ten cyclists who lined up at the start on a cool Spring morning was the 22-year-old Paolo Magretti, later to become a noted entomologist, whose studies of wasps, bees and ants in his native Lombardy and in Africa was of world renown. A large throng of people cheered off the intrepid band of riders as they headed from Milan towards the Ticino River and the town of Asti on gravel and dirt roads before climbing the Colle di Superga and the final sweeping descent into Turin. It was Magretti who triumphed before large crowds waiting in the capital of Piedmonte, then also the capital of the nation.

Cycle racing had been born in Italy, but it had a chequered progress for the next two decades. Milan-Turin was only conducted twice more before the end of the century, in 1894 and 1896. Dominated by Italians and Europeans – the Australian Phil Anderson was the first non-European to win it in 1987 – the race remains the oldest Italian Classic, and one of the oldest in the world. Since 1987, it has been conducted in the northern autumn.

It was in Milan two decades later that a young journalist, Armando Cougnet, joined the sporting paper, *La Gazzetta dello Sport (The Sporting Gazette),* first published in 1896 to coincide with the opening modern Olympic Games. Observing that newspapers in other countries had began promoting cycling races, Cougnet and his colleagues at the paper proposed a similar program. Over four years from 1905 to 1909, they established the three most prestigious races in Italy, the Giro di Lombardia, Milan-San Remo and the Giro d'Italia.

Giro di Lombardia (1905) – La classica delle foglie morte (The race of the falling leaves)

Situated between the great Po River valley to the south and the Italian Alps to the north, the expanding city of Milan offered a topographic variety for enthusiastic cyclists. Riders could pedal south over rolling hills or turn north towards Lake Varese and Lake Como. It was on these roads that the first major Italian race was organised, starting and finishing in the capital of Lombardia.

The origins of some of the greatest races in the world can be found in rivalry between newspapers for readership. The Giro di Lombardia was no different. Facing a threat from a new paper which had organised a race to attract readers, the *Gazzetta dello Sport* editor, Tullo Morgagni, asked the leading cyclist, Giovanni Gerbi to assist him to organise a rival event. The result was Milan-Milan, renamed the Giro di Lombardia in 1907.

Conducted in autumn, it was described as *La classica delle foglie morte*

– 'the race of the falling leaves'. As one of the five monuments of cycling – the original great one-day races – the Giro di Lombardia traditionally wraps up the long European road season.

Giovanni Gerbi

The victor of the inaugural Giro di Lombardia, Giovanni Gerbi, was one of the first great stars of the sport in Italy. As an 18-year-old amateur, Gerbi burst onto the cycling scene by winning the Coppa del Re at Novara in his native Piedmont in 1902, a feat he repeated the following year, then riding for the Maino team. Gerbi had an explosive temperament from his youngest days. His father purchased a bike after he was expelled from school for his rebellious behaviour. It proved to be the perfect antidote for the young Gerbi who many contend was the first real professional cyclist in Italy.

Gerbi quickly stamped his authority on the roads of northern Italy. In 1903, he won Milan-Turin. Known as *Il Diavolo Rosso* – the Red Devil – for the colour of his jersey, and his explosive nature, Gerbi became the first Italian to ride the Tour de France in 1904, but abandoned the race after being attacked by a mob of fans and breaking his fingers!

It was from 1905 onwards that the rider from Asti dominated road racing. Over the next few years, he claimed most of the major races of the era, including the Giro del Piemonte, the Corza Nazionale and the Rome-Naples-Rome thrice. Asked how he won the first Giro di Lombardia, Gerbi replied:

> I won it as the other races, using my best quality: I was a great finisher. Once I gained two or three hundred metres, it was done: nobody was able to catch me back. The race was mine . . . Obviously I always needed time to study a detailed plan. So for me it was very important in the preparation to study the route. Every time I scheduled in advance the moment of my attack, and often I was able to perform it as planned. Obviously choosing the right moment depended on some calculation, some adjustment.

Gerbi's prescience to reconnoitre the course was a feature of his shrewd approach to races, a value shared with many later successful cyclists. It was an aspect of his 'win-at-all-costs' mentality that has infected most sports, including cycling. Gerbi was also prepared to exploit the rules – or lack thereof – to his advantage. He may not have been the first cheat in the sport, but he was definitely one.

In the initial Giro di Lombardia, Gerbi's inspection of the course revealed a rail crossing intersection where the riders would have to dismount to avoid falling from their bikes. To take-up the story, told in 1952 by the *Gazzetta dello Sport* writer, Ulisse Corno:

> Gerbi, fifty metres before the intersection placed some mud on the side of the rail in order to find the way to get out. Then, once in the race he gained the lead of the bunch and led it in the middle of the rails. At the right time he left the prepared way and started to pedal with desperation. The others, proceeding between the rails crashed all together in a tremendous way. Giovanni Gerbi, clever devil, baptized in such a way the Giro di Lombardia: he won by 45 seconds.

This trick paled into insignificance compared with his behaviour the following year. According to cycling folklore, Gerbi or his supporters, ahead of the peloton, tied up a signalman at a level crossing before riding away to claim the victory. He was banned for two years as a consequence, a penalty that was reduced because of his enormous popularity.

Gerbi's best placings in the Giro d'Italia were third in 1911 and 1912. In 1913, he broke the world six-hour record, riding 208.161 kilometres. His career thereafter was in descent. He gave away racing in the early 1920s, made an unsuccessful comeback in 1926, before retiring from the professional ranks. Gerbi kept riding, winning the Italian Masters Championship in 1932 and 1933. Long before Girardengo, Binda, Bartali and Coppi, Gerbi was the king of cycling.

Although the route has changed many times, 'Il Lombardia', as the race is now known, traditionally includes a number of long, steep climbs. The most famous is the Madonna del Ghisallo, a 10.6 kilometre climb above Lake Como. Although not the longest climb, nor the steepest – the much shorter 1.7 kilometre Muro di Sormano at an average gradient of 17 per cent and topping out at 25 per cent is three times as steep – it is the signature ascent of the Giro. This is partly because of its commanding position over Lake Como, and partly because of the small church that stands at the summit. The shrine of the Madonna del Ghisallo includes a cycling museum and an eternal flame for riders who have died. Amongst the photos and artifacts is the crumpled frame of the bike ridden by Fabio Casartelli, the local cyclist, who suffered fatal head injuries after crashing into a concrete pillar on the descent of the Col de Portet d'Aspet in the Pyrenees in the 1995 Tour de France. Outside the small church, overlooking beautiful Lake Como are the statues of Italy's two greatest riders and fiercest rivals, Gino Bartali and Fausto Coppi, along with the first World Road Race Champion, Alfredo Binda.

Milan-San Remo (1907) - La Classicissima di Primavera (The Spring classic)

The automobile had been invented in the late 1800s, but a decade later the new vehicles were still very unreliable. It was this undependability that led to the establishment of the other great northern classic, Milan-San Remo. From the middle of the 18th century, the Côte d'Azur - known by the British as the French Riviera – became the playground of the rich and famous. From Monaco, which built a famous casino in the renamed Monte Carlo, to St Tropez, tourists flocked to the balmy Mediterranean coast. Across the border, San Remo blossomed as a popular seaside tourist attraction, with a series of grand hotels attracting visitors from far and wide. In competition from other coastal cities for tourists, the enterprising city fathers engaged the famous French architect, Eugène Ferret, to design a grand casino. Constructed in the prevailing art nouveau style, the Casinò Municipale di San Remo was opened in 1905.

With the establishment of the casino, city officials began searching for a major sporting event. The *Gazzetta* responded with plans for a major car rally, a two stage event from Milan to the Ligurian coastal city. A field of 31 cars departed Milan on the rally, but only two survived the rough roads to drive into San Remo. Instead of a crowning glory for the city, it was an embarrassing flop. The municipal leaders of San Remo still wanted a major attraction. Understanding the success of the Giro di Lombardia, Armando Cougnet, by then half owner of the *Gazzetta* decided another one-day cycling race would work. The San Remo officials were prepared to offer a significant amount of prize-money if Cougnet could assemble a first class field including French riders who would attract the French press. This would provide welcome publicity for San Remo and attract visitors who otherwise flooded to attractions on the Côte d'Azur like Monte Carlo.

Understanding that this was probably his last chance to be successful with the enterprising San Remo community, Cougnet set about assembling the best field he could find. Knowing that the San Remo municipal leaders were anxious to attract widespread publicity in the Parisian papers, the *Gazzetta* owner looked across the Alps for willing contestants. The huge prizemoney on offer, and further inducements from the San Remo casino, attracted four French riders, including Lucien Petit-Breton and Gustave Garrigou who were to become two of the dominant riders of the pre-war era.

Lucien Petit-Breton

The French rider, Lucien Petit-Breton, won the first Milan-San Remo, before going on to win the Tour de France in 1907, and again in 1908. Born in Brittany, he lived his early life in Argentina, before returning to France with his parents in 1902. The dapper, moustached Petit-Breton had already won the Argentinean track championship before returning to France where he quickly demonstrated his talent, winning the famous 24-hour Bol d'Or endurance race and breaking the World Hour Record on the velodrome. Named Lucien Georges Mazan, he changed it to Lucien Breton and then Petit-Breton to deceive his father, who had wanted him to pursue a more respectable career.

The early tours were conducted on a points system that favoured Petit-Breton in his first attempt in the Tour de France following victory at San Remo. Although he had lost considerable time on the third stage over the Col de la Porte, he remained in second placing behind Emile Georget on points. When the leader was relegated to last for illegally changing bikes on the tenth stage, Petit-Breton, assumed the lead, winning the 1907 event from Gustave Garrigou. Petit-Breton became the first rider to win back-to-back Tours the following year as a member of the strong Peugeot team.

Petit-Breton was to return to Italy for the 1910 and 1911 Giro, but his best days were behind him. He finished fifth in a stage in 1911, but failed to complete both editions. In 1917, he was killed in a car accident near the front during the Great War.

Cycling and the Story of Italy

Gustave Garrigou

After winning Paris-Amiens and Paris-Dieppe as an amateur, Garrigou turned professional as a 22-year-old in 1907. Milan-San Remo was to be one of his first major races in the open class. It was to bring him into conflict with Giovanni Gerbi, the Italian 'Red Devil'. Although 62 riders registered for the race, only 33 braved the cold, windy start at 4.00 am in Milan.

Departing from central Milan, the riders travel about 100 kilometres across the rolling Lombarian plains before reaching the Turchino Pass.

Conducted at the beginning of the road season in early spring, Milan-San Remo has been raced in various conditions, ranging from glorious days of sunshine, through to rain and snow. In some years, the Pass has been under heavy snow, adding to the challenge of the the *Primavera* – opening classic of the season.

For many years, riders who established a break on the climb over the Turchino could maintain their lead on the long descent to Savona and the rolling coastline into San Remo. Riding through sleet, Gerbi attacked on the dangerous climb of the Turchino, gaining three minutes on the peloton. Gerbi was caught by Garrigou, who waited for Lucien Petit-Breton – also riding for the Bianchi team in the race – to join them, setting-up a three-way finish in San Remo. As many cyclists have discovered, a two-on-one showdown usually favours the two. But Gerbi, who had agreed to help Petit-Breton in exchange for sharing the huge monetary reward, took no chances. Riding into the coastal town, Gerbi shoved Garrigou off his line, allowing Petit-Breton to attack and claim victory by 35 seconds after the 288- kilometre slog from Lombardy. The next two riders, Luigi Ganna and Carlo Galettti, were more than half an hour behind.

Garrigou protested the result and was promoted to second placing ahead of the 'Red Devil.' The close result and the controversial finish generated publicity in excess of what the San Remo fathers could have anticipated. One of the world's greatest one-day races had been created.

Garrigou went on to become one of the best riders of the era.

He finished second in the Tour de France in 1907 and 1909, fourth in 1908 and third in 1910 before winning both Milan-San Remo and the Tour de France in 1911. That Tour attracted great controversy when another French rider, Paul Duboc, collapsed in the Pyrenees after drinking from a poisoned bottle. Duboc's supporters, believing Garrigou responsible, incited the crowds on a following stage at Rouen to attack the race leader. Garrigou was protected by official cars as he departed the town amidst jeering crowds. It was later believed that Garrigou was innocent, and an assistant for a rival team had spiked the drink. Duboc recovered to finish second in that Tour. Garrigou finished on the podium in Paris in both the 1912 and 1913 Tours, marking himself as one of the best pre-war cyclists in Europe.

By the outbreak of the Great War, six foreign riders had won the nine editions of the *Primavera*, although only one non-Italian was to win it between the wars. Foreign riders also successfully contested the Giro di Lombardia in the early years, including Henri Pélissier who won twice, in 1911 and 1913.

The success of both the Giro di Lombardia and Milan-San Remo reflected the growing prosperity of the northern Italy in the early years of the 20th century. The growing interest in these races would lead to an even more challenging event – a grand tour of Italy.

2

The Birth of the Giro

Italy owes you an undertaking which has merit of the applause of the whole universe
-- Guiseppe Garibaldi.

Cycling is suffering
-- Fausto Coppi.

Despite the success of the two one-day races, *La Gazzetta dello Sport* was suffering from faltering sales as it competed for readership with its rival publication, *Corriere della Sera (Evening Courier)*. With the automobile becoming more popular, the idea of promoting a motor race had also occurred to the Milanese newspaper proprietors, as it had elsewhere in Europe. However, bitter experience of the Milan-San Remo car race and the success of the Tour de France promoted the sports journalists at *La Gazzetta* to propose a Tour of Italy.

The Giro d'Italia was born of intrigue, rancour and an intense competition for readership between two Milanese newspapers, a very similar story to the beginnings of the Tour de France six years earlier. In Paris, a fierce rivalry between the proprietors of two papers, *Le Velo* and *L'Auto,* the falling circulation of the latter; and the brilliant idea to replicate the popular six-day track races on the road, led to the creation of the Tour de France. Driven by the editor of *L'Auto*, Henri Desgrange, the Tour was an outstanding success. Desgrange, a leading endurance rider before turning his attention to journalism, was to guide the Tour for the next four decades, building it into one of the

GREAT RIVALRIES

La Gazzetta dello Sport announces the inaugural Giro d'Italia.

Luigi Ganna, winner of the first Giro d'Italia (1909).

most well-known and popular sporting events in the world.

In 1908, the proprietors of *Corriere della Sera* had discussions with Edoardo Bianchi and the Touring Club of Italy to establish an Italian version of the French stage race. Although the Touring Club was promoting automobile events by then, it was regarded as best placed to make the necessary arrangements for a national tour. Bianchi had become one of the biggest bicycle manufacturers in Italy and a major sponsor of events.

The idea of a national tour had been discussed on the Mediterranean peninsula after news of the *Grand Boucle* – the Tour de France – reached Italy. Armando Cougnet, the cycling writer for *La Gazzetta dello Sport*, and a keen cyclist himself, had witnessed the impact of the month-long French event – and the public clamour for daily stories of feats of endurance by the contestants – when he reported on the Tour in 1906 and 1907. From the very beginning, cycling and the media formed a symbiotic relationship.

Had it not been for personal antagonism and quick thinking, the Giro d'Italia would have been organised by the *Corriere della Sera* and the famous *maglia rosa*, the pink jersey worn by the race leader since 1931, would never have eventuated.

In August 1908, Angelo Gatti, a disgruntled former employee of Bianchi, who had started a rival company, Atala, learnt from Bianchi's manager, Gian Fernando Tomaselli, that the *Corriere della Sera* and Bianchi were planning a Grand Tour of Italy to rival the Tour de France. Gatti passed on the information to Tullo Morgagni, editor of the struggling *Gazzetta dello Sport*. Morgagni was decisive. On August 5, he sent a telegram to Armando Cougnet, who was in Venice, and the paper's owner, Emilio Costamagna: 'Without delay, necessity obliges *Gazzetta* to launch an Italian tour, Return to Milan. – Tullo.'

It was an audacious step. *La Gazzetta* was nearly broke, and had no capacity to fund a grand tour. Yet Morgagni and the owner, Emilio Costamagna, understood that public fascination with a three-week long tour would drive circulation for the struggling journal. Meeting in the Milan office of Costamagna, who had returned from Mondovi, the three men discussed Morgagni's proposal. They didn't know how they would stage such a race, but to delay would allow the *Corriere* to claim the event. There was no time to lose. Cougnet began to compose the announcment.

The following day, a headline boldly proclaimed that a national Giro d'Italia would be conducted the following May:

> The *Gazzetta dello Sport*, pursuant with the glory of Italian cycling, announces that the next spring will see the first 'Giro d'Italia', one of the biggest, most ambitious races in international cycling.

La Gazzetta had gazumped *Il Corriere*, but it had little to offer beyond the daring announcement. Cougnet acknowledged this, writing that it was a poor child of honest parents "and like all babies that you hear, it squealed its way to life in the columns of *La Gazzetta*."

For months, it appeared that the adventurous idea for a grand tour would die in its infancy. Despite constant promotion in the pages of the *Gazzetta*, the stream of funding was dry. By September, the paper noted with sadness that the venture was on hold. It seemed to Costamagna and Cougnet that their child would suffer a premature death.

It was a friend and accountant at the Cassa di Risparmio bank, Primo Bongrani, who solved the problem by suggesting widespread sponsorship for the event. Bongrani was secretary of the Italian Olympics Committee and an influential businessman in Milan. Taking time from his job, Bongrani raised the necessary funds to stage the race and offered prize money appropriate for such a contest. In addition to the Italian Cycling Association, commercial sponsors were attracted, including the San Remo casino and Lancia. Bongrani had a major breakthrough when the *Corriere*, having been beaten to the race by their rival newspaper, agreed to offer 3,000 lire for the first place prize money. The rival paper had missed the event, but could still prosper from involvement. The Giro d'Italia was to become a reality in May 1909. The race received Royal Endorsement when the King of Savoy offered a gold medal for the victor. This imperial *imprimatur* opened the doors to further financial support.

On March 26, 1909, six weeks before the scheduled event, the *Gazzetta* published the schedule for the Giro d'Italia. Although less than the first announced 3,000 kilometres, the race was to be over a daunting 2,500 kilometres from Milan through Bologna and Chieti to Naples before returning via Rome, Florence, Genoa and Turin. The thought for most Italians, who had never ventured more than 20 kilometres from their home, of riding 2,500 kilometres around Italy in eight stages, was mind-boggling. Many of the roads, especially in the south of the nation in 1909, were rough gravel and dirt tracks, almost unpassable in some places. The superhuman effort required to complete such a ride, let alone win, was unimaginable for most Italians. One-day races like Milan-San Remo and the Giro di Lombardia had raised awareness of cycling and elevated a group of new sporting heroes like Giovanni Gerbi and Luigi Ganna. The idea of repeating the effort of the great one-day races eight times with just a day or two of rest between each stage captured the imagination of the nation.

In truth, Cougnet had been cautious in planning the first Giro. By 1908, the Tour de France, upon which he had modelled his event, was a ridiculous 4,488-kilometres, 14-stage enduro. The Tour de France director, Henri Desgrange, was almost manic in staging his event, once quipping that "the ideal Tour would be a Tour in which only one rider survived the ordeal." A fitness fanatic, he perceived the event as a test of character and strength in which the cyclist who had endured the most suffering would triumph. The attitude was reflected in the rules that Desgrange imposed and arbitrarily enforced. Unlike some other endurance races, there would be no assistance from pacers. Riders would have to carry their own spares, and do their own repairs if their bike was damaged. They could not even accept food from others. These rules caused considerable controversy in the second Tour, and almost led to the demise of the event after just two editions.

The second Tour de France was organised on the same route as the first edition. Desgrange had increased the daily payments to attract more participants, including the 50 year old Henri Paret, the oldest cyclist to ever contest the event. Before the first stage, the 467-kilometre slog from Montgeron on the outskirts of Paris to Lyon had concluded, the Tour was engulfed in controversy and intrigue. Riders fell, bikes suffered fractures, and the leaders, Maurice Garin and Lucien Pothier, were attacked by four masked men in a car! Other riders, including one of the favorites, Hippolyte Aucouturier, were fined or disqualified for cheating. Garin, the winner of the first Tour, also riled the fanatical crowds when it was revealed that he had been given food by the race director, Géo Lefèvre, contrary to the rules.

As news of the race was telegraphed to the papers in Paris, and spread across the country, sections of the public became more agitated. The second stage turned into open warfare between cyclists and the supporters of their rivals. When Antoine Faure established a lead heading into the Alps, a crowd from his region attempted to disrupt the following peloton. Riders were thrown off their bikes and injured. Maurice Garin could only ride with one arm, and another rider was knocked unconscious. The tyres on Géo Lefèvre's car were slashed. An official had to fire a pistol above the crowd to disperse the melee. Later nails and glass were spread along the road, causing more chaos for the riders.

Further troubles followed in the third stage, as riders were stopped and set upon by partisan crowds. Barricades and other obstructions were becoming commonplace as the race continued on the circle around France. "I'll win the Tour de France," said Maurice Garin, "Provided I'm not murdered before we get to Paris."

Garin was finally declared the winner, ahead of Pothier, his brother, César Garin and Aucouturier, when the race finished in Paris, but the controversy continued. Nine riders had been disqualified for cheating, including catching rides by car and train. Henri Desgrange believed that was the end of the matter, but the governing body of the sport, L'Union Vélocipédique de France (UVF), had other ideas.

Five months later, after its own inquiry into the race, the UVF announced dramatic penalties. The first four finishers were disqualified, as were nine other riders. Ferdinand Payan and Charles Prevost were banned for a year, Garin for two, and Chaput, Chevallier and Pothier for life. The fifth placegetter, 19-year-old Henri Cornet became the youngest ever winner of the Tour. He too was warned for taking a lift in a car, as was Aucouturier.

Desgrange and the UVF became engaged in a bitter dispute, for which the historical records were lost during the Second World War. The whole story will never be known. *L'Auto* editor Desgrange lashed out in his publication:

> The Tour de France has just finished and its second edition will, I fear, be the last. It will have died of its own success, of the blind passions which have been unleashed, of the abuse and of the suspicions that have come from ignorant and ill-intentioned people. And yet, however, it seemed to us and it still seems that we had built, with this great event, the most durable and the most imposing monument to cycle sport. We had hoped to each year bring a little more sport across the greater part of France. The results of last year showed that our reasoning was correct and here we are at the end of the second Tour de France, sickened and discouraged, having lived through these three weeks of the worst slander and abuse.

Desgrange's despair did not last long. The following year, the third Tour was conducted, but the events of 1904 had a lasting impact. More, shorter stages were added and riding through the night was eliminated. The overall winner was also decided on a points system for the first time, with one point for a stage win, two for second etc. The rider with the lowest number of points at the end of the race would be the victor – a system that endured until the eve of the Great War in 1913.

By contrast, Cougnet wanted a competitive event that would enchant the Italian population and provide further impetus for his business. He copied the Tour points system which had been introduced by Desgrange to reduce cheating but allowed riders to receive mechanical assistance, which the dictatorial Desgrange prohibited.

The first grand tour of Italy

In the early hours of May 13, 1909, 127 riders assembled in the Piazzale Loreto outside the offices of the *Gazzetta dello Sport* for the start of the grand tour of Italy. It was to be the richest race in the world. Ahead of them lay a 397-kilometre race to Bologna, the first of the eight stages. A quarter of the original entries didn't front for the race, including a number of international riders. Several French riders on the Alcyon team were ordered to ride the Tour of Belgium instead of crossing the Alps to Italy.

Amongst the throng of riders, supporters and fans gathered in the Piazzale were five foreigners. The most attention was focused on Lucien Petit-Breton, who with the assistance of Gerbi had won the inaugural Milan-San Remo. Petit-Breton started the race as the winner of the past two Tour de France. Alongside him was Louis Trousselier, who had burst to attention when he won the grueling Paris-Roubaix followed by the Tour in 1905. The year before the inaurgural Giro, he claimed the prestigious Bordeaux-Paris race, adding to his attraction for the Italian organisers. Three other international riders also started the Giro: the Frenchmen André Pottier, the third place-getter in the 1908 Milan-San Remo, Maurice Decaup who had placed in Tour de France stages; and the Austrian, Henry Heller, whose professional career seems to have commenced and finished that year!

The starters were a mixture of professionals, aided by their teams, and independent amateurs. There were those who rode for a living, and the poor adventurers who had seized the chance of fame and fortune. Having to carry their own food, drink and supplies, as well as find a bed at the end of each stage, the chances of these amateurs being successful was remote.

At 2.53 am, a large crowd cheered off the riders in the torchlight for their epic journey. If the *Gazetta* and the *Corriere* had hoped for high drama with which to entice and excite their readers, it came from the very outset. The peloton was barely two kilometres along the via Monza when a mass crash occurred, badly damaging Giovanni Gerbi's bike. The 'Red Devil' searched out a local Bianchi shop where a mechanic repaired his damaged fork and rear wheel while his opponents pedalled towards the first checkpoint at Bergamo more that 70 kilometres away. Gerbi had lost some three hours on the field. He was in good form that year, winning the Rome-Naples-Rome race, and placing in a series of other events. With a punishing effort, Gerbi rejoined the field, keeping alive his chances.

If the Italian *tifosi* were disappointed by Gerbi's misfortune, it was the French supporters who would next be displeased. Approaching an ascent near Lake Garda, Luigi Galetti and Lucien Petit-Breton crashed. The Frenchman was reportedly munching on a chicken when the disaster occurred. He stuck the rough ground heavily, suffering concussion and probably a broken collar bone. Nonetheless, he remounted to chase the peloton, catching them and attacking, but to no avail. He was later to drop off the lead group.

Cycling and the Story of Italy

Viewers of the modern Giro d'Italia observe the peloton racing along smooth roads and sealed mountain passes. In the beginning, it was very different: rough gravel and dirt tracks. The closest modern race is the Strade Bianche – a race over the white gravel roads of Tuscany. First conducted as a professional contest in 2007, the gravel sectors around Sienna approximate the best roads of the early decades of the Giro.

Luigi Ganna suffered a flat tyre with 70 kilometres to ride on the intitial stage of the inaugural Giro, but caught the leaders when they were forced to stop at a train crossing. With just 12 riders left at the front of the race as they neared Bologna, the large crowd was set for an exciting finish at the city's Zappoli racecourse. It was appropriate that the sprinter, Dario Beni, claimed the victory, but a sudden rainstorm had caused so much chaos as the crowd rushed for cover, that confusion reigned about the placings amongst officials. Beni, one of the best pre-war cyclists, who won two national road titles, was to bookend the Giro by also winning the final stage into Milan.

The exhausted riders had a three-day rest after the opening stage before tackling the next leg, a 381-kilometres journey southward along the Adriatic to Chieti. Petit-Breton was too injured to start. Giovanni Cuniolo won the stage, but Gerbi led at the end of the stage on points. Three riders who were caught hitching a train ride during the stage were disqualified, although two were permitted to continue.

As the peloton rested again, interest in the Giro was reaching fever point. Encouraged by stirring reports in the *Gazzetta* and other newspapers, the *tifosi* came out in their thousands. The swarm was so large that they threatened the orderly conduct of the event as tens of thousands crowded the start and finish of each stage. Even in the mountains, for the next three stages, crowds lined the roads, forcing Cougnet, the race director, to swing a whip to clear the roadway ahead of the cyclists. The pandemonium was to grow all the way to Milan.

The French rider, Louis Trousselier, was a particular target of the fanatical Italians. Sitting in second place after the arduous climb over the Apennines from Chieti to Naples, his path was sabotaged by nails on the road during the long stage to Rome. Some 20,000 people cheered as Luigi Ganna outsprinted his compatriot Carlo Oriani in the eternal city. Trousselier suffered more misfortune in the following hilly stage to Florence, flatting a number of times before his rear hub fell apart on the rough roads. One way or another, an Italian was going to win the inaugural Giro!

Ganna led by just two points over Galetti when the stage finished on the Florence velodrome before an uncontrollable crowd who flocked onto the arena after just one of the two scheduled final laps. Trousselier knew his chances of winning had been dashed, leading the Frenchman to withdraw and return home. The only other challenger to Ganni and Galetti, Giovanni Rossignoli, lost time – and more importantly points – leaving the leading pair in a two-man fight for overall victory at Milan.

Rossignoli, who was to finish on the podium thrice in the Giro, was not done. He defeated Galetti in the tough uphill finish at Genoa, distancing Ganna, who survived as leader by just one point. The *Gazzetta* editors could not have planned a more exciting race. But success had its own challenges. Despite the very early morning starts, tens of thousands of fans crowded the riders, making it difficult for them to assemble, let alone ride off for the stage. And in the afternoons, even larger crowds – which had been buoyed by the breathless coverage of the race in the newspapers – converged on the finishing point, impeding riders and officials. Courgnet's baby had grown into an unruly teenager.

The penultimate stage from Genoa to Turin almost ended the race. Cougnet solved the challenge of the start by organising an orderly neutral zone for the first few kilometres before the actual race start. This allowed fans the space to see their heroes riding along the city roads together instead of the chaos that had developed in the previous stages. But the finish was still a problem. With reports that 50,000 people were expected at the finish in Turin, Cougnet moved the finish six kilometres closer to the start. The plan appeared a master stroke, but the race director forgot to inform his officials, resulting in chaos. To add to the confusion, Cougnet's car broke down in a hailstorm towards the end of the stage. Eventually officials determined that Ganna had defeated Rossignoli with Galetti in third placing. With three points separating Ganna and Galetti, the scene was set for an exciting finale in Milan.

Cycling and the Story of Italy

To emerge as the victor of the Giro, Ganna could not afford to finish more than two places behind Galetti. Once again Cougnet decided to alter the finish line, but would make the decision as the race progressed, leaving riders unaware until towards the end of the stage. The final charge across the rolling hills of Piedmont and Lombardy involved all the chicanery and skullduggery that had been associated with the race. Two of Ganna's teammates, who had dropped out of the race previously, rejoined to assist their captain until discovered and ejected. Then Ganna flatted with 70 kilometres to ride. Knowing that he was chasing back onto the peloton, the leading group dashed through a closed train crossing as they approached Milan. When they tried the dangerous move at a second crossing, Cougnet stopped them, allowing the race leader to rejoin.

The presence of mounted police had the huge crowd at the finish more or less under control. But as the leading bunch sprinted towards the finish, one of the horses was spooked and fell over in the path of the cyclists, bringing the Giro to an end in a tangled confusion of bikes, riders and fans. Beni was awarded the stage victory. Ganna had finished third, behind Galetti, securing victory and fame as the first winner of the Giro d'Italia. He had averaged 27 kilometres per hour, an amazing feat considering the weight of the bikes, the weather and the state of the roads. Asked by Cougnet at the conclusion of the 2,500-kilometre grand tour what could he say about the feat, his reply was one that has resonated down the years with cyclists: "Me bursa el cu" – my butt is on fire!

Luigi Ganna

Fortune favoured Ganna in the inaugural Giro, especially the points system. Had the race been determined by the total elapsed time, as it is now, Giovanni Rossignoli would have been victor, as he had ridden the race 37 minutes faster than Ganna. It turned out to be the apex of Ganna's professional career.

Born into a large farming family at Induno Olana, a small village near Varese, in 1883, the young Luigi was destined for a life as a farmer or labourer. At the age of eight, he took a job as a bricklayer in Milan, a 100-kilometre round trip by bike! The young Ganna soon started riding in local races, proving him to be one of the best amateurs in the region. By 1905, Ganna was confident enough of his ability to abandon his job and cycle full time. He was rewarded by a third placing in the Giro di Lombardia three years running from 1905-1907 and second in Milan-San Remo the next season before claiming the *Primavera* in 1909. He also rode a new one-hour record on the velodrome at Milan, pedalling 40.045 kilometres in 60 minutes. His impressive performances caught the eye of the team managers at Bianchi, who offered him the substantial sum of 200 lire a month. Later Atala would increase the offer to 250 lire, more than most professionally qualified Italians could earn.

As the ninth child of peasant farmers, Ganna's childhood experiences grounded his dream: to get married and buy a house. The 5,325-lire first prize for winning the Giro set up Luigi for life. By the end of the cycling season, he had won more than 20,000 lire. He later recalled:

> 1909 was the year that marked a turning point in my life. I won the first Tour of Italy cycling, I got married and I bought the house and a small workshop that was to eventually create the machine for new cycling champions. Even today [close to 70] . . . I go to look at frames, to experience first hand dumbbells and forks . . . The most beloved symbol of my existence.

Luigi launched the Ganna brand bike in 1912. Carlo Oriani, who had finished fifth in the first Giro d'Italia, won the Giro di Lombardia on one of Luigi's bikes, creating welcome publicity for the new manufacturer.

Ganna retired in 1915, but his name lived on as a manufacturer into the early 1950s. In the era of Bartali and Coppi, the so-called 'third man', Fiorenzo Magni, rode a Ganna to victory in the 1951 Giro d'Italia.

Consolidating the Giro

The 1909 Giro not only set-up Ganna for life, it consolidated the future of the *Gazzetta dello Sport* and its owners. At last Cougnet could draw a regular salary. The audacious chance he and Morgagni had taken resulted in a national institution, soaring sales, and financial success.

The second edition in 1910 was guaranteed prize money, intense interest, and an international field of riders. Few changes were made, including better measures to control the excitable *tifosi*. Equal points were awarded after 50th placing on each stage in an attempt to avoid some of the confusion of the first tour. Two additional stages, adding another 500 kilometres, were included on a route that followed a similar circumnavigation of northern and central Italy as the first tour.

While Luigi Ganna was to win the first Giro, the disappointed Carlo Galetti was to stamp his presence on the subsequent races. Luigi Ganna's preparation suffered a set back in the April running of Milan-San Remo. The French cyclist Eugène Christophe mastered the terrible snow covered Turchino Pass to win by over an hour from Ganna. But the Giro hero was later disqualified for having accepted a ride in a car during part of the race. The conditions were so appalling that Christophe was hospitalised for a month at San Remo recovering from frostbite and took two more years to fully regain his health.

Lucien Petit-Breton returned for the second edition, along with Jean-Baptiste Dortignacq, who had finished on the podium at the 1904 and 1905 Tour de France. The field of 101 riders also included the first Germans, Karl Dittenbrandt and Arno Ritter.

Ganna lost so much time – and so many places on the points system – after flatting on the first marathon stage from Milan to Udine that his chances of repeating his 1909 triumph were dashed. The French pair, Petit-Breton and Dortignacq, immediately posed a threat to the local Italian champions, finishing first and third in the second stage to Bologna. Stirred up by the angry *tifosi*, some of whom had physically attacked the French riders, the Italians put their regional loyalties aside to combine against the foreign challenge.

By the end of the next stage, Galetti, who had worked with his Atala teammates, Ganna and Eberardo Pavesi had a stranglehold on the race. Petit-Breton abandoned, and Dortignacq was forced out through illness. With national pride restored, the Italians resumed their regional rivalries.

Despite a bad fall in the final stage, Galetti prevailed in Milan to win the Giro, making him the most decorated Italian cyclist before World War I. Pavesi was second while Ganna managed third placing despite his disastrous opening stage.

GREAT RIVALRIES

Carlo Galetti

Born in 1882 at Corsico near Milan, Galetti began work in a printing works at age eleven. Starting work at a young age was common in Italy at the time. Only half the population was literate and regional dialects prevailed. Italy was a poor country by European standards, especially the impoverished South. Industrialisation was developing in the North, opening up new opportunities for young people who were prepared to work hard in the burgeoning factories.

Good fortune smiled on the youngster from the poor outer southwestern suburbs of Milan. The Azzini family, who were keen cyclists, owned the printing works. Luigi, Ernesto and Giuseppe Azzini all rode at the professional level in Italy, winning a series of major races. A bicycle was a necessity to travel to work for many people, the young Carlo amongst them.

Only two more editions of the Giro were contested before Italy entered the Great War. Although they may not have realized it, the *tifosi* lining the roads for the 1913 Giro witnessed the debut of a talented young rider, Costante Girardengo, who was to become their great post-war hero. At just 20-years of age, Girardengo had already won the Italian Championship, and had been signed for the strong Maino team. He was to finish sixth behind his team-mate, Carlo Oriani.

The last Giro before the War was brutal: the eight stages averaged almost 400 kilometers each, with the shortest being 328 kilometres and the longest 430 kilometres! Only eight of the 81 starters finished the 3,170-kilometre slug which was won by the little-known Alfonso Calzolari by almost two hours, the biggest winning margin in the history of the race.

A year later on May 23, 1915, Italy joined the Allied forces in the Great War. It would be four long years before a sense of normalcy returned to the nation, as a generation of young men were sacrificed to the conflict that enveloped Europe.

Nicknamed *Il Scoiattolo dei Navigli* – the squirrel of the canals – after the Milanese suburb in which he lived, Galetti soon developed into one of the cycling stars of the era. His potential was displayed with an impressive win in the 1906 Rome-Naples-Rome Classic and a second placing to Cesare Brambilla in the 1906 Giro di Lombardia.

Following further podium places, he was signed to the powerful Atala team in 1908.

The Three Musketeers

Although Galetti was to win the Giro three times, including the 1912 edition which was conducted as a team's race, he was a controversial figure, changing teams often, and gaining the reputation as a wheel-sucker amongst his competitors. Galetti attracted great friendships and greater rivalries.

Luigi Ganna was both friend and rival. Together with Eberardo Pavesi, Galetti and Ganna became known as The Three Musketeers, a trio of friends who trained together on the roads of Lombardy. They were also fierce rivals. Devastated by his loss to Ganna in the inaugural Giro, Galetti redoubled his efforts in subsequent years. The 1910 Giro was a classic example of the need for riders to work together, as Galetti, Ganna and Pavesi combined to defeat their French rivals before challenging each other for ultimate victory.

To the uninitiated, road cycling may appear to be an individual contest. Modern television viewers of the grand tours observe the concentration on the leader – the wearer of the *maglia rosa* or the *maillot jeune* – as if his sole efforts carry the day. Alone however, few riders, even champions, can succeed. From the earliest days, riders found that by co-operating, they could ride faster, longer and more effectively. Hence the birth of the *gregario* (the *domestique* in French) – the support riders who sit on the front saving their leader from the wind, collecting water bottles from the team car, or drafting their rider back onto the peloton after a mishap. The use of support riders was more readily accepted in Italy than it was in France where the Tour de France director, Henri Desgrange, forbid the practice, even disqualifying Maurice Brocco from the 1911 race for colluding with other riders. Desgrange believed that the Tour should be an individual competition. His term of abuse for Brocco – a *domestique* – subsequently became the favoured description for the all-important support riders. To be regarded now as a 'super domestique' is a term of great praise!

GREAT RIVALRIES

Before teams were formally arranged, professional cyclists learnt the advantages of assisting each other. A favour given could become a favour repaid. A disastrous day in the saddle could be saved by other competitors drafting, encouraging and assisting. A breakaway might succeed if the group worked together – especially if they split the prize money!

The Three Musketeers – Galetti, Ganna and Pavesi – became a feared combination. In 1910, they shared the stage victories after seeing off their French challengers. Galetti was to prevail again in 1911, after being paid a fortune to move from Atala to Bianchi. At stake was more than a bike race. The contract to supply thousands of bicycles to the Italian military was also to be decided. Bianchi wanted the best team to show-off their product, and were prepared to pay for it.

The third iteration of the Giro was truly the first Tour of Italy. Armando Cougnet had purchased the sole ownership of *La Gazzetta dello Sport* from Emilio Costamagna. He decided to mark the 50th anniversary of the reunification of the peninsula by starting and finishing the race in the national capital, Rome. For the first time, the riders ventured south of Naples, to Bari on the Adriatic Sea. The event was also extended in length to an extraordinary 3,500 kilometres, including a climb to Sestriere, now a 2,000-metre high ski resort in the Alps between Turin and Grenoble, but then a narrow goat track through the snow.

The professionals rode in five teams: Atala, Bianchi, Fiat, Legnano and Senior. Each had four riders, including three French entrants riding for Fiat. Heading them was Lucien Petit-Breton, one of the finest riders of the era. He was joined by Maurice Brocco and Omar Beaugendre, winner of Paris-Tours in 1908 and runner-up in the Giro di Lombardia a year later.

Petit-Breton, returning for the Giro, was widely considered the favourite to win the marathon challenge. However, the Italians were not for having an interloper win their tour. Galetti claimed the first stage to Florence and then duelled with Giovanni Rossignoli on the next three legs to Mondovi. By the time they faced the first great mountain stage of any Grand Tour, the climb to Sestriere, the two Bianchi riders led the Frenchman, with Gerbi in fourth position.

Cycling and the Story of Italy

Entering the Chisone Valley for the massive climb, the peloton experienced what riders down the decades have learnt: one great difference between the Tour de France and the Giro d'Italia is the weather. Conducted in spring, when snow still covers the Alps, and rain is frequent, the Giro presents a very different challenge to the hot dry days of July.

Only 41 of the original 100 starters faced the wet, muddy struggle through the snow. Petit-Breton set off to conquer the mountain, but he struggled on the climb, and was passed by other riders, many of whom were pushing their bikes through the almost impassable terrain. Reaching the summit well behind, the French champion threw caution to the wind on the treacherous descent, catching the leading riders before Turin and defeating Galetti in a two-up sprint. It was a courageous ride. Emilio Costamagna later wrote in *La Gazzetta:*

> In the Mondovi-Turin stage he learned he was up against a coalition of the best Italian climbers. In one stage he also knew his defences had come undone, going from first to last and had then in the final moment triumphed with a sprint worthy of a track champion.
>
> His elegant silhouette, an attractive figure of a lord competing with dignity on the field of professional glory and money was saluted everywhere with true sporting enthusiasm.

Petit-Breton became the first foreigner to lead the Giro after the ninth stage, but found himself in a break with five Bianchi riders in the following stage. He confronted an iron law of cycling: a team of riders will invariably defeat a lone competitor, even a great champion. Described by the journalist, Emilio Colombo, as "a man who pedalled with a wonderful speed and suppleness," Petit-Breton crashed in the penultimate stage whilst in second placing. He was not to finish a grand tour again, despite numerous subsequent attempts. He was later to die in the Great War.

Galetti won the 1911 Giro from his team-mate, Giovanni Rossignoli, the second of his three victories. Once again Rossignoli, whose \best result was victory in the 1905 Milan-Turin, had ridden a faster overall time, but lost under the points system. Only 24 riders finished the gruelling circle of Italy.

GREAT RIVALRIES

The Red Devil, Giovanni Gerbi, who made the last step of the podium in 1911, was desperate to win the following year. For reasons not entirely clear, Armando Cougnet decided to make the 1912 Giro a team's race. Perhaps it reflected the fact that the previous race had been dominated by the Bianchi squad. Under the new, complex rules, teams of four riders would contest the race, with three having to finish for the team to remain in the event.

Gerbi encouraged the two leading Bianchi riders, Galetti and Rossignoli to defect to his squad for the event. Both agreed to the transfer, but Galetti changed his mind after urging from another of the Three Musketeers, Eberardo Pavesi, to remain with the celeste team. An angry Gerbi lashed out at Galetti, challenging him with a 10,000-lire wager, a winner-takes-all, 300-kilometre race.

Galetti refused the challenge, but *La Gazetta* recognised the enormous opportunity for publicity and stumped up the prize money. The 300-kilometres time trial saw Gerbi depart Milan an hour before Galetti. In the end, the Squirrel – as Galetti was known – prevailed over his challenger by less than 5 minutes. Gerbi was determined to turn the tables in the Giro, which had been reduced to just 2,443 kilometres, with eight stages averaging over 300 kilometres each.

The race attracted just 54 entrants. Despite Gerbi's burning desire to claim the endurance crown, the strong Atala team of Galetti, Ganna, Pavesi and Giovanni Micheletto dominated the race. Only the Peugeot team came near them. If 8 stages of more than 300 kilometres each wasn't enough, a 9th stage was added – over the Giro di Lombardia route after the stage from Pescara to Rome was annulled when the peloton was directed more than 50 kilometres off course. The riders abandoned the stage and took a train to Rome, causing a riot amongst the thousands of spectators who had paid to witness the finish in a local stadium.

In the end, Atala won the Giro easily from Peugeot and the Gerbi team, but the much criticised teams format was abandoned in favour of the previous arrangements. The return to the individual points system favoured Carlo Oriani, who had finished fifth in the inaugural Giro, but had been conscripted to fight in the Italo-Turkish War, a costly foray into Libya by the Italians. Although off the bike during the conflict, Oriani joined the Maino team in 1912, winning the Giro di Lombardia. Oriani was supported by a strong team in the Giro. He also benefited from the bad luck of his rivals: Gerbi had to retire with an injury; Pavesi crashed when leading the race; and Ganna rode off the route for more than 80 kilometres. Despite not winning a stage, Oriani joined the Giro victors when the race finished in Milan. It was to be his greatest and final victory. A year later he was dead, having contracted pneumonia after trying to save a fellow soldier who had fallen into a river in the Italian alps.

The tour was notable for another reason; the emergence of the young Costante Girardengo, who would dominate Italian cycling after the Great War. The young rider from Novi Ligure finished sixth in his first attempt. He started in the 1914 Giro, undoubtedly the most arduous grand tour ever. Only eight of the 81 starters completed the eight-stage, 3,170-kilometres race. Just finishing was a feat in itself. Armando Cougnet also abandoned the points system in favour of a general classification based on elapsed time, placing more pressure on the riders to perform. If that wasn't enough, he introduced a time-limit for each stage.

The stages of the 1914 Giro averaged almost 400 kilometres! One stage was a massive 430 kilometres, and two others just short of that distance. The race included the freezing climb to Sestriere through mud and snow. The weather was appalling for most of the journey, already poor roads were flooded and, at one stage, the peloton was sabotaged by tacks strewn across their path. In a feat never repeated since, Lauro Bordin rode solo for an impressive 350 kilometres before being passed in the 430 kilometres Lucca to Rome stage. Most of the favoured riders, including Petit-Breton, Doboc, Rossignoli, Galetti, Ganna, Oriani, Pavesi and Girardengo abandoned. Alfonso Calzolari won the race by the biggest margin ever – 1 hour 57 minutes and 26 seconds – in the slowest Giro on record. The brutal race was designed to boost the sales of *La Gazetta dello Sport*, which was then published daily.

A 1915 Giro d'Italia was planned, but the outbreak of hostilities in Europe eventually dragged Italy into the Great War. The conflict would devastate parts of Europe, claim millions of lives, and set in train events that would lead to yet another war two decades later.

Costante Girardengo, the first *campionissimo* (champion of champions).

3

Pedalling out of Poverty

Ti chiamerò Campionissimo (I will call you the champion of champions)
-- Emilio Colombo about Costante Girardengo.

It would be dangerous to follow Ottavio Bottecchia up a mountain pass. It would be suicidal. His climbing is so powerful and regular that we would end up asphyxiated
-- Nicolas Frantz, winner of the 1927 and 1928 Tour de France.

The Giro d'Italia was just a few years old when the war that would ravage much of Europe and decimate a generation of young men broke out. Although gaining in prestige, the race would be interrupted for five years during the terrible conflict that engulfed the continent. Six hundred thousand Italians would die in the Great War and many more would be injured.

When Henri Desgrange surveyed the Western Front in 1919, he was shocked by the devastation of the conflict. The destruction of great swathes of northern France and Belgium was a stark reminder of the brutal annihilation of a generation of young men, most in the prime of their lives. As Desgrange's party progressed north, the countryside was increasingly devastated, wrecked by poverty and despair. Nothing would prepare them for the scene they encountered when they entered the battlefields of the Somme:

> We enter into the centre of the battlefield. There's not a tree, everything is flattened! Not a square metre that has not been turned

upside-down. There's one shell hole after another. The only things that stand in this churned earth are the crosses with their ribbons of blue, white and red. It is hell.

The description *l'enfer du Nord* – the Hell of the North – thereafter became associated with the Paris-Roubaix race, a lasting memorial to the millions who lost their lives in the bloodiest battles in history. For Italy, that hell was Caporetto. Of the bloodiest and horrible human tragedies of the Great War – Gallipoli, Verdun, the Somme and Caporetto – it is the least recalled, partly because of the disastrous cost of victory, and partly because of the subsequent fascist claim to it for propaganda.

In early June 1914, Italy suffered a series of violent strikes and uprisings – the 'Red Week' – leading to the use of the army to restore order. Italy abandoned its support for Austria and Germany, and the Foreign Minister, at the urging of the Military Commander, General Luigi Cadorna, turned on its former allies. Cadorna, a staff officer with little frontline experience, led an offensive against Austria-Hungary at the Isonzo River. One of the loveliest valleys of Europe became the scene of a terrible series of battles in which more than a million Italians and 650,000 Austrians were either killed on injured, and some 600,000 Italians deserted or surrendered. Ernest Hemingway, who served as an Italian ambulance driver in the war, described the awful shelling, anguished screams and mangled bodies on the front lines in *A Farewell to Arms*. After two and a half years, as the war was coming to an end, the Italians finally crossed the Isonzo in November 1918.

Few groups were spared the terror of the Great War. The dead included Carlo Oriani, who triumphed in the 1913 Giro after finishing fifth in the first edition of the race. Lucien Petit-Breton, the victor in the 1907 and 1908 Tour de France, and the first foreigner to lead the Giro in 1911, was another casualty of the horrific conflict, as were François Faber and Octave Lapize. Others were injured, or had the best years of their lives squandered by the 'war to end all wars'. The consequences were as indiscriminate as the shrapnel that shredded millions of young lives.

In his *Short History of the World,* the Australian historian, Geoffrey Blainey writes:

Of the 8,500,000 soldiers and sailors who died in the First World

War, Germany lost the most, followed by Russia, France, Austro-Hungary and then Britain and its empire. These five powers, along with Italy, which entered the war in 1915, lost nine out of every 10 soldiers killed in the war. In addition, more than 20,000,000 soldiers were wounded, and this list of the slain and maimed did not include maybe five million civilians who died as a direct result of the war. Hundreds of thousands of the dead had no known grave. To see at Verdun the war memorial commemorating 130,000 dead French soldiers who have no known grave, is to catch a glimpse of the grief felt in all those houses and tenements out of whose doors these man had cheerfully stepped away to war. From crowded apartments in Moscow to sheep farms in New Zealand there were millions of mantlepieces on which stood framed black-and-white photographs of earnest or smiling young men, killed in the war which everyone now called the Great War, not realizing that a greater war was barely 20 years ahead.

When the war finally ended, 16 million were dead and another 20 million injured. Parts of Europe were devastated. A generation of young men had been decimated. Economies were in ruin. Poverty was widespread. The old order was crumbling. New radical ideas were being pressed. It was a time of continuing turmoil as revolutionary movements gained traction. A new contest between anarchy, authoritiarism and democracy was playing out in many nations: just as the continent was recuperating from the 'war to end all wars', the seeds of another global conflict were being planted.

Yet people yearned for a return to the normal, to forget the horrors of conflict, and resume their ordinary lives. There is a human spirit that can overcome almost all obstacles, and this character was on display as Europe recovered from the four-year war. Within months of the ceasefire on November 11, 1918, the first great post-war cycle race was staged. Now largely forgotten, the seven-stage, 2,000 kilometre Circuit des Champs de Bataille (the Tour of the Battlefields) passed through the scenes of some of the bloodiest battles of the Great War. The race, which was organised by *Le Petit Journal*, was conducted in late April and May 1919. The Belgian rider, Charles Deruyter, eventually won the gruelling slog through the wartorn battlefields, with many of the original 87 starters abandoning the race.

Less than a year after the Armistice was signed at Versailles on June

28, 1919, the three great northern classics of the era, Liege-Bastogne-Liege, Paris-Roubaix and the Ronde van Vlaanderen (the Tour of Flanders), were run again. Life in Italy had not been affected by the war as badly as on the Western Front. The two one-day classics, Milan-San Remo and the Giro di Lombardia, had been run each year with the exception of the Milan race in 1916.

For the group of riders who had emerged as leaders of the peleton prior to the war, few would remain dominant after the conflict. Like any great athlete, it takes years of constant training and endeavour to reach the top as a cyclist. A break of four to five years from regular competition can be very difficult, if not impossible, to overcome.

Of the riders who dominated the pre-war era in Italy, including Luigi Ganna, Carlo Galetti, Giovanni Rossignoli, Carlo Oriani, Eberardo Pavesi and Alfonso Calzolari, few were prominent after the conflict. Instead, it was the 26-year-old Costante Girardengo who emerged as the first great endurance champion of the nation. His story, and the story of the great riders who emerged in the 1920s and 30s, predates to the subsequent appearance of Gino Bartali and Fausto Coppi a generation later.

Costante Girardengo

Girardengo's prodigious talent had begun to flower prior to the war. Born in 1893 into a family of seven children on a farm near the village of Novi Ligure, Piedmont, Girardengo was a diminutive child. Like most rural children of the era, he helped his parents, Carlo and Gaetana, on their small farm while attending primary school. The family later moved a few kilometres to Bettole de Scrivia, where they opened a shop selling salt and tobacco and operating an adjoining inn. With little education beyond the customary primary years, the teenage Girardengo had few prospects beyond a labouring job. Industrialisation had been growing in the North, especially around the major cities like Milan, and farm work was waning, yet remained the major source of work. Much of the country was still mired in poverty at the time of the Great War. Prospects for a young man like Costante were limited.

Girardengo obtained an apprenticeship in a tannery at Lecco before finding work in an ironworks. He eventually obtained work at the Alfa

Romero workshops at Tortona, necessitating a 40 kilometre ride each day on his father's old bike.

Cycling was becoming increasingly popular in the north-western region of Italy. Long before the car had become affordable for the average person, the bike was an increasingly common mode of transport. Bicycle manufacturers sprang up across the north – Bianchi at Milan, Maino at Alessandria and Wilier at Bassano del Grappa amongst them. Track racing was popular from the 1890s onwards, but the lure of long endurance events on the roads caught the imagination of the populace in the new century. Newspapers like *La Gazzetta dello Sport* and the *Corriere della Sera* in Milan quickly recognized that promoting cycling races would boost readership and advertising.

The young Costante was aware that the two great one-day races, Milan-San Remo and the Giro di Lombardia were contested in the north-west of the nation. Indeed the former race travelled close to his childhood village of Novi Ligure. The announcement in 1908 of the inaugural Giro d'Italia fuelled the growing interest in the sport. Cycling races were springing up in various towns, including at Novi Ligure, where a youthful Costante Girardengo, participated.

Lining up alongside Costante at Novi was another young rider who would have a profound impact on Italian cycling. Born the same year as Girardengo at Novi, Biagio Cavanna often defeated his companion in their local contests. Cavanna was a sports fanatic who studied the human body long before modern day physiotherapists and sports scientists. Despite his enthusiasm, his cycling ability was limited to early victories in local events. By 1915, he had given up the bike for boxing, where he became the Piedmontese champion. It was his subsequent role as a masseur, coach and talent spotter that connected Cavanna to two subsequent champions, Learco Guerra and Fausto Coppi, and the rise of the village of Novi Ligure as the breeding and training ground of some of Italy's greatest cyclists.

At first Cavanna defeated Girardengo in the Novi championships, but a year later, Costante dominated, winning or placing in almost every race he contested. Challenges beyond the region beckoned the teenager. In 1912, the Maino professional team offered the 19-year-old Costante the opportunity to ride with them after he fell foul of regulations prohibiting amateurs from carrying a sponsor's advertising. Girardengo's role at Maino was to support the team's star rider, Carlo Oriani.

A stonemason by trade, Oriani had finished fifth as an independent rider in the inaugural Giro. Two years after the first Giro, Oriani was conscripted into the military to fight in the Italo-Turkish war – an Italian invasion of the Ottoman Empire in Northern Africa, particularly Libya. The war, which lasted for a year, stirred resentments in the Balkans against the Turks, and the outbreak of the conflict that resulted in the Great War.

Returning to Italy, Oriani resumed racing, joined the Maino team and won the Giro di Lombardia in 1912. Girardengo was mostly a *gregario* for the team, but did win a race in his first season as a professional, the since defunct Coppa Bagni di Casciana. The following year, he would challenge the existing order in the peloton and give notice that he would be a force to be reckoned with in the future.

Girardengo's precocious talent was on display at the Italian National Championships, conducted that year along a familiar route for the 20-year-old near Alessandria in the region of Piedmont. Costante had skipped military service at Verona, taken a train to Alessandria, where he borrowed a bike and defeated the best riders in the nation. It was the first of nine national road race championships in which he was to claim victory. He repeated the performance in 1914, and wore the tricolour Italian champion's jersey every year from 1919 to 1925, when the championship was conducted over a series of races.

By the time the field had assembled in Milan for the Giro, Girardengo had shaken-up the leading riders. Carlo Galetti, who had won the second and third Giri, and led the winning Atala team in 1913, called him 'Girarbaldengo', a pun on his name as if talking to a pet. In the end, neither the 'Head of State', Galetti, nor the neo-pro, Girardengo, finished the race. Although he eventually abandoned the tour, Girardengo made his mark on what was probably the toughest tour ever conducted.

The growing realisation that the young Girardengo was a force to be reckoned with was cemented in the third stage of the 1914 Giro, a colossal 430 kilometre ride from Lucca, north-west of Florence, to

Rome. The sixth edition of the race was perhaps the most brutal ever. It had just eight stages, averaging 396 kilometres each. The shortest stage was a mere 328 kilometres, longer than any stage in a modern Grand Tour. Much of that year's tour was conducted in chilly rain. Not only were the dirt roads wet and muddy, the stages started at midnight, causing the riders to contend with rough and slippery surfaces in virtual darkness. The sixth stage from Bari on the southern Adriatic coast to L'Aquila in the central Italian region of Abruzzo took almost 20 hours for the winner, Luigi Lucotti, to complete. If any grand tour ever came close to Henri Desgrange's idea that it should be so tough that no-one would finish, it was the 1914 Giro d'Italia.

By the end of stage two, just 37 of the 81 starters at Milan remained in the race. Girardengo was in second place, one-hour, four-minutes and seven-seconds behind the leader, Alfonso Calzolari, riding for the Stucchi team. In addition to its length, the third stage was notable for two reasons. First, Lauro Bordin established a record, never beaten, for the longest break-away in the Giro. The Bianchi rider surged ahead of the other 36 cyclists for an incredible 350 kilometres before being caught towards the end of the marathon journey. Secondly, the victor of the massive stage was Costante Girardengo, who passed Bordin towards the end of the day. Although he didn't complete the tour – only eight of the original 81 starters made it back to Milan – Girardengo had made his mark in the peloton. The remainder of his season was unremarkable. He rode for the Automoto team in the Tour de France two months later, but crashed a number of times before abandoning the race. It was his only start in the Tour. In 1915, he won Milan-Turin, but was disqualified in the Milan-San Remo after crossing the finish line in first placing for going off the course during the race. Within months, Europe was at war.

Girardengo continued to work as well as ride. While cycling was becoming increasingly popular, generally it did not pay sufficiently to allow competitors to support themselves. Being an industrial worker, Giarardengo was not conscripted into the military in the Great War. Although unscathed by the fighting, he contracted the Spanish Flu. The pandemic, which was first noted in Spain, infected as many as 500 million people worldwide, leaving between 20 and 50 million – if not more – dead. It has been estimated for example, that more US servicemen died from the flu than were killed in the Great War. Many, otherwise healthy young men and women were struck down by the infectious disease. The virus weakened the victim's bronchial tubes and lungs, opening the way for bacterial pneumonia to take hold. At one stage, Costante's manager refused to renew his racing licence, believing he had been weakened too much to race. But he recovered, and returned to racing as the war ended.

If Giaradengo's pre-war performances had shown potential, his post-war cycling fulfilled that promise. It commenced before the war ended when he won Milan-San Remo, the first of an unprecedented six editions of the famous monument of cycling. Only the great Belgian Eddy Merckx, eclipsed that record when he won his seventh *Primavera* in 1976. Girardengo was on the podium at San Remo every year from 1917-1926 and won again in 1928. His record speaks for itself: nine Italian road race championships; six Milan-San Remo; three Giri di Lombardia; two Giri d'Italia and 30 stage wins. He also won the Grand Prix Wolber, then the unofficial World Championship, and finished second in the first official world title. But it was the manner of the wins that made the cyclist from Novi Ligure such a commanding figure in the sport.

Physically, 'Gira' was diminutive. He was nicknamed the Novi Runt by his fellow riders. But his small frame disguised a powerful body suited to the enormous endurance required for success. His 1919 victory cemented his standing as Italy's best cyclist. As the 61 starters departed Milan, Girardengo was not necessarily favoured to triumph. Indeed the young Gaetano Belloni had burst onto the scene by winning the Giro di Lombardia in 1914 while still an amateur. He had turned to cycling after losing a thumb in a textile machine at work, being unable to effectively continue his chosen sport, Greco-Roman wrestling. Ruled out of the military, he won a number of the races that continued during the war including the Milan-San Remo and the Giro di Lombardia.

The field assembled for the 1919 Giro d'Italia in Milan also included the Belgian ace, Marcel Buysse, who had won stages of the Tour de France and claimed the 1914 Ronde van Vlaanderen. His brother, Lucien, who was to win the 1926 Tour de France, was also amongst the

61 starters, as was the 1914 Giro d'Italia victor, Alfonso Calzolari, who had easily claimed the pre-war edition, despite being penalized three hours for accepting a tow.

Girardengo won the first stage in a sprint from Calzolari. He won seven of the ten stages, and was never headed on General Classification, finishing the 3,000-kilometre journey almost 52 minutes ahead of Belloni. Only Alfredo Binda, Eddy Merckx and Gianni Bugno were to repeat the performance of leading throughout the entire tour. *La Gazzetta* editor, Emilio Colombo, deployed the expression *Campionissimo* – Champions of Champions – to describe the victor. Only two other riders, Alfredo Binda and Fausto Coppi, have been accorded the title.

Tano Belloni finished second, a position that he was to occupy more often than not throughout his long career that included many successful seasons of the very popular six-day track racing in America prior to his retirement at age 42 in 1934. Despite a reputation for being the eternal runner-up, Belloni won the Giro d'Italia in 1920 after Costante withdrew in a fit of pique after being penalized for an illegal wheel change. Tano was also one of the oldest winners of the Giro di Lombardia, when he prevailed in the 1928 'race of the falling leaves' at the age of 36.

Girardengo's daring tactics, especially his willingness to surge ahead of the field in long, solo breakaways, enthralled the *tifosi*. In his first Milan-San Remo, a race he made his own for almost a decade, Gira arrived at the Ligurian city 13 minutes ahead of Belloni after a 180-kilometre breakaway. He won another Giro d'Italia in 1923, having quit the race the previous year in protest at a decision to allow the Legano team to continue after illegal wheel changes. Fifth in that 1923 Giro was another of the greatest Italian riders of the 1920s, Ottavio Bottecchia, who achieved most of his significant victories in France.

Ottavio Bottecchia

He appeared at the crest of a mountain pass, small and swarthy, his hollow face framed by large ears, sticking out beyond a crop of black hair, as his long skinny legs pounded on the pedals. It was the Col d'Izoard in July 1924. Dirt and mud encased rider and bike, as he fought for traction on the loose, stony surface of the steep mountain track. High above the clouds that surrounded the valleys below, there were no spectators, just the car that accompanied him across the Alps.

For the past nine days, he had led the Tour de France. He would never surrender the leader's yellow jersey, the first man to lead the Grand Tour for every stage, although, for reasons that can only be speculated upon, he chose not to wear the famous yellow jersey during the stage from Toulon to Nice, the closest to his native Italy.

Ottavio Bottecchia, the eighth child of a poor family, was born near Treviso in the Veneto. After just a year at school, he worked as a bricklayer and a wood collector before becoming a member of the famous Bersaglieri corps during World War I. Carrying a heavy machine gun on a bicycle, Bottecchia fought in the northern mountains, earning a gallantry medal for his exploits.

Like many of his fellow countrymen and women, the 25-year-old Bottecchia had little prospects in war-torn Italy after the conflict that had raged in the north of his country, so emigrated to France to find work as a builder, before returning to Italy a year later, having converted his wartime role into a passion for the great endurance races.

He won three major races in 1920, the Giro del Piave, the Coppa della Vittoria and the Duca d'Aosta, and three others the following year, the Coppe Gallo a Osimo, the Circuito del Piave and the Giro del Friuli. Like many other riders of the era, cycling was a pathway out of poverty for Bottecchia. Married, and almost illiterate, Bottecchia had few other prospects of escaping the oppression many experienced as Europe tried to rebuild itself. Despite his later success, the experience of his poor origins remained with the Italian.

Henri Pélissier, the French rider who won the 1923 Tour, noticed Bottecchia's successes in the early twenties. Employed as a *domestique*, the 29-year-old almost stole victory from the Frenchman, winning stage two, wearing the yellow jersey for six days, and finishing second, just over 30-minutes behind. Pélissier predicted correctly that his helper would win the following year.

Bottecchia had quickly gained prominence, finishing fourth in the Giro di Lombardia, and fifth in both the Giro d'Italia and Milan-San Remo. But few expected the domination of the Tour that unfolded in 1924.

Cycling and the Story of Italy

At almost 30-years of age, the Italian won the 381-kilometre first stage from the capital to Le Havre in just over 15 hours, gaining a time bonus as a result. After the second 371-kilometre stage to Cherbourg, Bottecchia held a two and a half minute lead. Two stages later, Pélissier, his brother, Francis, and another French rider, Marurice Ville, withdrew from the Tour after clashing with race director Henri Desgrange. Pélissier had been penalised in the third stage for discarding one of the jerseys he wore to shield him against the cold, pre-dawn start, and had been stopped by officials a number of times on the colossal 405-kilometre third stage from Cherbourg to Brest. Disgusted by the treatment, the French star abandoned the event, leaving his Italian rival the undisputed leader of the Automoto team.

Holding a three-minute lead after the 19-hour marathon 482-kilometre stage from Les Sables d'Olonne to Bayonne, Bottecchia dominated the mountains, leading over each of the Aubisque, the Tourmalet, the Apsin and the Peyresourde. Thereafter, he was able to cruise to victory, returning to Paris after 226 hours of racing more than 35 minutes in advance of the field. Bottecchia completed a unique double: the first rider to carry the yellow jersey throughout the Tour, and the first Italian to win the famed race.

His win excited great enthusiasm in Italy. *La Gazzetta dello Sport* launched an appeal for him at home, raising over 61,000 lire, including the first lira from Mussolini, although Bottecchia was alleged to be a socialist sympathiser. His success and relative wealth did little to erase his humble beginnings. The cyclist wore old clothing and shoes, and travelled third class by train to save money. He even wore the yellow jersey all the way back to Milan! The opportunity to escape poverty was a powerful motivation for many of the pioneering cyclists of the era.

Bottecchia returned to France as the reigning champion in 1925 where he again won the first stage. Assisted by Lucien Buysse, who would go on to claim the 1926 Tour, the Italian gained time on his rivals in the mountains, and was able to claim an easy victory. The following year, he abandoned the race in a thunderstorm, never again to contest the event.

A year later, Bottecchia was dead, mysteriously murdered near his home at Peonis after a training ride. He had gone for a ride alone after his long-time training partner, Alfonso Piccini, had decided not to join him. His skull had been crushed, and bones broken. His body was found in a paddock some distance from his undamaged bike. His younger brother had also died after being hit by a car a year earlier. Speculation about the circumstances of his death abounded. Had he been hit by a car? Had the fascists murdered him? The questioning continues today, but no-one knows the real cause, although many suspect that he had been killed by fascist thugs for his support of socialism.

By winning the Tour de France, Bottecchia cemented one of the great rivalries of European cycling between the French and the Italians. It continues to this day.

Following after Girardengo and Bottecchia was the greatest rider of the era, the first official World Champion, Alfredo Binda.

Alfredo Binda

There are occasions in great sporting eras that mark the end of one epoch and the beginning of another. One of these was the 1925 Giro d'Italia in which the undoubted star of the era, Costante Girardengo, was ultimately defeated by a young challenger, Alfredo Binda.

Binda was born at Cittiglio near Varese in 1902, the tenth of fourteen children. Unable to support him, his parents arranged for the young man to move to Nice where he lived with an uncle and worked as a plasterer. It was at the seaside city that he followed in the footsteps of his brother, Primo, competing on both the track and road. In 1922, Binda joined a local team before being selected for the La Française squad the following year, where he won a number of races, including the Tour du Sud-Est and the Nice-Mont Chauve hillclimb. Lining up in that event were the stars of the era, including Costante Girardengo and Henri Pélissier. By the time the race reached the summit of Mont Chauve, these two Grand Tour champions had been bested by the 23-year-old neo-pro. It was an auspicious debut for the young rider, and an early indication of his signature strengths of seemingly effortless pedaling and phenomenal climbing.

Observing his early success, Eberardo Pavesi, the manager of the prominent team, Legnano, signed Binda for his squad after he journeyed back to Italy at the invitation of the rider who was to be his nemesis, Girardengo. It was in the prominent green jersey of Legnano that Binda was to begin his domination of the sport in the Mediterranean nation.

Legnano had won the 1924 Giro with Giuseppe Enrici, the first non-European to win the tour. Enrici had been born in Pittsburg, Pennsylvania, to an emigrant family who later returned to their native Italy. (The Italians claimed Enrici as their own, meaning that it was not until 1988 when the US rider, Andy Hampsten, was victorious that it was officially conceded that someone from the New World had claimed the *maglia rosa*.) The 1924 race had also featured the only woman to contest the famous Tour, Alfonsina Strada, who had registered under the name Alfonsin, and was only revealed as a woman later. She finished the Tour when the majority of the entrants failed to do so, but was banned from competing again the following year.

The 1925 Giro was shaping as another victory for Girardengo, who opened the new year by winning his fourth Milan-San Remo from Giovanni Brunero. But by the time the fourth stage finished in Rome, the *campionissimo* was neck and neck with a new challenger for his title, the 23-year-old Binda. Although the younger man had been used to riding on the paved roads of France, he adapted quickly to the poor, rough, dirt and gravel tracks of Italy that still criss-crossed the southern country. Part of his success involved the insightful decision to use extra heavy tyres for the Giro, a choice that resulted in not one puncture during the 3,520-kilometre journey.

Binda was also the beneficiary of intense rivalries that wreaked the peloton. After Girardengo – riding for the Wolsit team – helped his *gregario*, Pierino Bestetti, to win the third stage when another teammate, and former Giro winner, Gaetano Belloni, had punctured, Binda – riding for the rival Legnano squad – found himself the unexpected beneficiary of Belloni's assistance, when Girardengo flatted on a subsequent stage. The young challenger pedaled to almost a minute lead over his rival, setting-up one of the great Giro contests. To the astonishment of the Italian champion, Binda extended his lead into Benevento to five minutes, leaving just five stages for the *campionissimo* to rein-in the fearless, strong young leader.

Girardengo threw everything at Binda over the final days of the Grand Tour, but the young man remained glued to his wheel. The champion won three of the stages, but he could not drop his 23-year-old challenger. By the final stage to Milan, Girardengo had all but given up regaining the lead. He was out-sprinted by Gaetano Belloni in the final charge to the line. Binda finished third in the stage to stand atop of the final podium in his debut tour. It was the beginning of a long ascendency as Italy's most dominant cyclist of the era, and one of the greatest of all time.

Expectations of an exciting rematch between the two protagonists in the following Giro grew as the year passed. Binda claimed the last major race of the season, the Giro di Lombardia – the first of three in a row from which he would emerge victorious. However, Girardengo stamped his authority with his fifth win in the Milan-San Remo at the beginning of the new season, setting-up the long awaited match-race in the 1926 Giro d'Italia.

The boisterous crowd was at fever-pitch as the large 204-rider peloton rolled out of Milan on May 15, 1926. But the cycling loving *tifosi* were to be quickly disappointed: Binda crashed on a treacherous gravel descent between Milan and Turin on the first stage, losing 30 minutes on the leaders. Convinced to continue by his team-mates, he rejoined the race riding as a *gregario* for Giovanni Brunero, the 1921 and 1922 victor.

Born south of Turin at San Maurizio, Brunero obtained employment in a bike shop at the age of 18. Within a short time, he had demonstrated his prowess on the road, winning the regional championships. Like many others, his life was interrupted by the Great War when he was conscripted into the Italian military. In the early 1920s, the Canavese cyclist emerged as one of the best performers in Italy.

His first win in the Giro d'Italia came in just his second season as a professional. Although not the fastest on the flat, Brunero was an exceptional climber. Backing up from his 1921 Giro win, he defeated Girardengo in the *Primavera* after his rival crashed into an official with two kilometres to race. The following Giro turned into a farce when Brunero was first disqualified, but later penalised 25 minutes for borrowing a wheel from a team-mate. The teams of his main rivals –

Bianchi (Girardengo) and Maino (Belloni) – withdrew from the race in protest, leaving Brunero's Legnano team to dominate the placings.

Giovanni Brunero subsequently became the first individual three-time winner of the Giro d'Italia when he returned victorious to Milan after racing to Naples and back, one of only 40 riders to complete the muddy event. The fans were left wondering what might have been, had Binda not crashed on that fateful first stage. Girardengo had looked the winner by the time the tour reached Naples, but a sprained wrist forced him out of the event. Despite misfortune – he lost more time on the second stage – Binda subsequently rode a superb tour, taking two solo victories before leading Brunero home in the final three stages, and climbing back onto the podium for second placing.

Nicknamed 'Giuanin' – Little John – because of his short stature, Brunero never attracted the same acclaim as some of his rivals of the era, partly because he tended to win on the climbs rather than the more popular sprints, and partly because of his shy, retiring nature. Sadly, he died at just 39 from tuberculosis, the first thrice winner of Italy's great race.

By the mid 1920s, the format of the Giro had changed to shorter stages over alternative days, a strategy designed to sell more copies of *La Gazzetta dello Sport*. In 1927, it was further refined to even shorter stages, coming to proximate the modern tour. Whether the stages were shorter or longer, Binda dominated the race. On the final stage of the 1927 Giro, he stormed up the Madonna del Ghisallo, the famed climb of Lombardia, with such authority, that no-one could stay near him.

In 1927, the Union Cycliste Internationale (UCI) decided to conduct a World Road Race Championship. In the inaugural race on the famous motor racing circuit at Nurburgring, Germany, the Italian team, headed by Binda filled the first four placings. Girardengo had finished second to his younger rival. The following year at Budapest, the bad blood between them was such that both abandoned the race towards the end, allowing the Belgium rider, Georges Ronsse, to win, a feat he repeated the following year in Zurich.

Binda reclaimed the winner's rainbow jersey at Liege in 1930, but was to fail to stand atop of the podium the following year in what was the most unusual World Championship ever. Instead of the normal one-day road race, the cycling authorities decided on an incredible 172-kilometre time-trial at Copenhagen. Learco Guerra won by over five minutes after riding the flat course with just one gear to reduce weight. Binda was nine minutes behind the winner, who looked like he was to replace him as Italy's best cyclist. But Binda was not done for. In 1932, he triumphed in the Worlds at Rome before winning a remarkable fifth Giro d'Italia in 1933. He had truly replaced Girardengo as *campionissimo*.

Binda was more than a bike rider; he became a superstar of the era. With matinee idol good looks, Binda understood that his performances were worth a fortune to the media and sponsors. He was idolised and books and articles were written about him, as he capitalised on his sporting ability like none before. But his ascendency was counterproductive for the sport, especially the Giro. The sporting public became bored by his total domination of the event. He could be as tough as he was shrewd. When *La Gazzetta* encouraged him to ride the 1930 Tour de France, and promised 22,500 lire not to ride the Giro that year, but failed to pay, he abandoned the French race. Leaving Guerra alone of the Italians to battle on against the might of France and eventually finish second, Binda earnt the wrath of Italy after the Tour organisers claimed that he had withdrawn from the race to prepare for the World Championships.

Binda's *palmeres* provides a snapshot of his dominance over the next few years: Four Italian Championships from 1926-1929; five Giro d'Italia, including an amazing 12 of 15 stage wins in 1927, which he led from start to finish; three World Road Race Championships; two more Giro di Lombardia; and two more Milan-San Remo! In total, Binda won 41 stages of the Giro d'Italia, including 8 consecutively in 1929. Only the flambouyant sprinter, Mario Cipollini, secured one more stage win in the Giro. He was the leader of the Giro on 61 days, only bettered by Eddy Merckx (with 79 days in the *maglia rosa*). So dominant was *il Trombettiere di Cittiglio* – the trumpeter of Cittiglio – nicknamed so because he played the musical instrument – that the Giro directors promised his Legnano team the equivalent of the winning prize money in 1930 – 22,500 lire – for Binda not to race! Instead he contested his only Tour de France.

Binda's fifth and final Giro victory in 1933 was an awesome display of speed, strength and endurance. That year's Giro was perhaps the first truly European contest. French riders, such as Lucien Petit-Breton, had been regular competitors in Italy, but the 1933 Giro attracted perhaps the best quality field in either of the two Grand Tours until then.

After winning the opening 288-kilometre stage to Turin, Binda never relinquished the *maglia rosa*. No rider since has dominated the race like the 32-year-old Binda did that year. Only Coppi and Merckx equalled his five victories, but neither did it in the style of the three-time World Champion.

Binda subsequently managed the Italian National Team, overseeing some of the greatest riders of the next era, including Gino Bartali and Fausto Coppi.

Ottavio Bottecchia, first Italian to win the Tour de France (1924).

4

Pedals and Politics

To race a bike, you need to be a poor man
-- Biagio Cavanna.

I go to church, and have liberal tendencies, but I was a fascist when everyone was
-- Alfredo Binda.

There was very little popular clamour for Italy entering into the Great War. Public sentiment was as best neutral, and generally opposed to the idea. The small group in favour saw involvement in the conflict as the completion of the *Risorgimento*, a patriotic cause that would purify the nation and result in a glorious future. Antonio Salandra, who had replaced Giolitti as Prime Minister in 1914, had committed the nation to involvement in the deadly conflict, unbeknown to Parliament and most of his colleagues. Italy had courted both sides of the conflict in the hope of securing sovereignty over the territories sought by the *Italia Irredenta*, especially Trieste and Istria. It had first negotiated with Austria, but subsequently entered into a secret treaty in London against Germany and Austria. The conflict would cost hundreds of thousands of lives, many of them the six million poor peasants and labourers from the South who were conscripted to fight in the Isonzo Valley and in the rugged, snow covered Alps of the North.

The major Italian objective was to claim the areas in the north-east of the country held by Austria. For Italian nationalists, the objective of the *Risorgimento* for a united country remained incomplete while the provinces of Trieste and parts of what is known as Friuli Venezia Giulia remained in foreign hands. So strong was the sentiment in the north that the Wilier Cycle Company renamed their famous brand Wilier Triestina as an indication of national identity with the region, although it could have also had a commercial advantage: by then bicycles were a significant part of the armed forces.

The humble bicycle had played a significant role in the conflict through the bicycle corps. The mobility, economy and adaptability of the bicycle were quickly recognized by military commanders eager to move troops and equipment in and around war zones. Not only could a soldier on a bicycle carry messages, lay communications lines, and scout the terrain, he could transport more equipment and travel more quickly than a man on foot. Following their use in the Second Boer War (1899-1902) by both British and Boer forces, other armies quickly incorporated the new machines into their establishment. By the outbreak of the Great War, most nations involved in the conflict had bicycle units, including the Italian *Bersaglieri* – the light infantry. Even though the bike was more suited to the flat terrain of France, Belgium and Germany, they were also used on the Italian front, including in the northern Alps. Indeed, winning the contract to supply the military forces was a major achievement. Bicycle manufacturers vied with each other to win the coveted contracts, with achievements in the major races a significant endorsement of the maneuverability and durability of their machines.

By October 1917, the objective of embracing the north-eastern provinces appeared doomed, as the Veneto was captured by the Austrians and some 300,000 Italian soldiers taken prisoner. Morale was low and desertion high. Eventually the Italians repelled their adversaries from the Veneto, and drove them back across the Isonzo.

If the war had finally united most of the provinces under the green, white and red tricolour, the aspiration for a shared approach to the future remained elusive. The war had involved a massive industrial expansion to meet the country's military needs. Factories manufacturing equipment and commodities required for the defence of the nation flourished. These businesses were designated as 'auxiliaries', and had their production and prices fixed by the government, as were the wages and conditions of the workforce. Within three years, output had grown substantially, but when the war came to an end, the level of production was excessive. Government orders declined, businesses were under pressure and worker militancy rose. A new age of anxiety encompassed the nation.

Italy had regained Trentino, Friuli and Istria in the peace resolutions, but failed to obtain Rijeka and Dalmatia on the eastern side of the Adriatic, much to the disgust of the government. It would be the limit of the national boundaries, as following the Second World War, the confines of Italy excluded most of Istria, apart from the area surrounding Trieste.

The pre-war Liberal settlement was under pressure as various political groupings sought supremacy. The Socialists were on the nose, the Pope regarded as an enemy by many in government for condemning the slaughter, and the Parliament treated as meaningless by those who supported the military involvement, including the army. Many thought that the country had been sold-out by the allies in the peace arrangements. A succession of governments followed the resignation of Vittorio Orlando, who became Prime Minister after the disastrous defeat at Caporetto in the Veneto, and who saw victory against the collapsing Austro-Hungarian Empire, only to lose support over the perceived sell-out of the Kingdom of Italy in the peace arrangements. Six governments under four different prime ministers ensued, ranging from the Radical Party, the Liberal Union and the Reformist Socialist Party. Having fought on the side of the victorious democracies, Australia, Britain, Canada, New Zealand, and the United States, against the old empires – Austria and Germany – Italy could not continue to deny greater popular involvement in government. Under Vittorio Orlando, universal male suffrage and proportional representation were granted. The number of voters jumped from 3 million to more than 8 million.

Amidst this turmoil, the seeds of fascism slowly took hold. Central to the ascendency was a Milanese journalist, Benito Mussolini. Dazzling but volatile, Mussolini had been expelled from the Socialist Party in 1914 for supporting intervention in the war. Raised in a Marxist household,

Mussolini became "one of the most effective and widely read socialist journalists in Europe." He had written: "Marx is the father and teacher ... He is a magnificent philosopher of working-class violence" and, reflecting Marx's endorsement of 'revolutionary terror', that "I wish to prepare my country and accustom it to war for the day of the greatest bloodbath of all, when two basic hostile classes will clash in the supreme trial."

After spending a period of time fighting on the front, Mussolini set up a new paper in Milan, *Il Popolo d'Italia (The People of Italy)*. Unlike his socialist comrades, Mussolini had supported the Lybian engagement, and urged national involvement again in 1914. Writing in his paper he proclaimed:

> This appeal, this cry, is a word that I would never have uttered in normal times, but which I give out today clearly and vigorously, without reservations, and with full confidence: that one forceful and fascinating word – WAR!

Politically, he was in no-man's land, rejected by the socialists whose cause he still believed in, but distrusted by the Nationalists and others on the right. When he started to form the *Fasci di Combattimento (Beams of Combat)* in 1919, there was nothing inevitable about the subsequent rise of fascism in Italy. Mussolini had no political program, apart from justification for intervention in the war and a dislike of the Italian Socialist Party, the only one in Europe to remain opposed to the military involvement. The vague nature of his program was reflected in the 1919 elections, when both Mussolini and his movement failed to win any positions in the Parliament.

Responding to the outcome, Mussolini gradually jettisoned his left-wing positions. The historian, Paul Johnson writes:

> Mussolini now wanted to use and exploit capitalism rather than destroy it. But his was to be a radical revolution nonetheless, rooted in the pre-war 'vanguard elite' Marxism and syndicalism (workers rule) which was to remain to his death the most important single element of his politics.

Other events conspired to increase the prominence of his movement. Economic and political turmoil engrossed Italy at the end of the second decade. As the wartime effort became redundant, production fell, unemployment skyrocketed, and inflation rose. Peasants demanded the land that had been promised during the war. And looking to the rise of the Bolsheviks in Russia, militants led a series of strikes and occupations that resulted in civil unrest and open conflict. When Giolitti failed to use troops to end widespread occupation of the factories for weeks on end in 1920, the seeds of more radical change were planted. As worker militancy increased, and local areas declaring revolutionary independence were created during the period known as the 'red biennium', a countervailing force quickly obtained political legitimacy. As a severe recession hit the country in 1920, para-military squads, often formed and supported by former military officers and the local police, began to organise across northern and central Italy. The fascist movement gained widespread support across the Po Valley and in Tuscany. Students and small landholders were prominent amongst the membership of the 'new Patriots'. Neither Giolitti, nor his two successors, Ivanoe Bonomi and Luigi Facta, openly opposed the fascist movement, as it gained strength across the country. Even then Mussolini was in part a captive to the forces at work. The squads were more local fiefdoms than part of a centrally coordinated party. When Mussolini tried to make peace with the socialists in 1921, he was in danger of ceding his authority over the party.

While Mussolini, at that stage, may have preferred an orderly rise to authority as part of a coalition government, his power was built on the brutal regime of the *squadristi*, of which there were at least 300,000 members by 1922. While he approved violent change, he risked losing control of the movement he headed. The issue came to a head in October 1922, when a ragged force of some 40,000 marched on Rome, occupying some public buildings and seizing prefectures. Refusing to order troops to fire on the rebels and disperse the assembly, the King instead summoned Mussolini to Rome from Milan, and appointed him Prime Minister. At 39, he became the youngest to hold the office. In three short years, the direction of the country had completely changed.

While these fateful events were taking place, most Italians witnessed little change in their daily lives. The wants caused by war had been replaced by the deprivations resulting from the conclusion of the war. Severe recession had added to the uncertainty of the era, a factor that had been manipulated by all political interests in the years after the armistice. If anything, Mussolini's appointment brought about less travail and optimism that greater peace and security would eventuate.

The resumption of racing

Italians desired a return to normalcy following the Great War, and the resumption of the Giro d'Italia was a welcome antidote. A number of classics had continued during the conflict, including Milan-San Remo (except in 1916) and the Giro di Lombardia. The grand tour resumed with its past format, but most of the stars of the previous era were no longer racing. Costante Girardengo was the hero of the new era, leading the first Giro after the war from start to finish, a feat only repeated by Alfredo Binda, Eddy Merckx and Gianni Bugno. Described by race director, Emilio Colombo, as *campionissimo* – the champion of champions – after winning the final stage, he ushered in a new era of superb cyclists.

Another great rider, Gaetano Belloni, who gained a reputation for finishing second in major races, won the 1920 Giro after Girardengo abandoned, Gerbi was disqualified for an illegal tow behind a motorbike and the early race leader, Guiseppe Oliveri tore a tendon. The intersection of cycling a politics was evident at the end of the third stage at Rome when a disruptive crowd interfered with the leading cyclists. Whether they were or not, the *Corriere della Sera* described them as 'Bolsheviks' – although there was no apparent reason why militants or radicals would disrupt the race. More likely than not, they were the excitable *tifosi* protesting one perceived infringement of the rules or another!

Despite his *campionissimo* status, Girardengo abandoned again in 1921 after crashing whilst leading the race. The tour turned into a great contest between the defending champion, Gaetano Belloni, and another rising star, Giovanni Brunero. Only 27 riders completed the journey – an advance on the ten the year before. At the finish in Milan, Brunero held on by just 41 seconds to defeat the previous champion. He was to win again in 1922 after both the Legnano and Maino teams withdrew from the race in protest over alleged infringements of the rules.

A return to normalcy?

The first few years after the appointment of Mussolini as Prime Minister marked an uneasy return to more normal political, economic and social conditions in Italy. The new leader craved acceptance and respectability. This echoed the sentiment in much of the country, which having been through a turbulent decade, longed for a new stability. Mussolini reflected these strands in his new government, with ministers drawn from various parties. He sought to centralise control – in himself – over the previously loose groupings of the *squadristi*; reached out to the Church by repairing buildings, restoring crucifixes in public places and making religious instruction compulsory in primary schools. He also opened the Fascist Party to the Nationalists, many of whom were the influential military, civil service and business leaders of the nation. While many of the fascists were paramilitary thugs, Mussolini's embrace of a wider circle, such as the Nationalists and the Syndicalists – who sought a state built on strictly regulated syndicates or corporations – and who all opposed the Socialists, provided him legitimacy amongst many of the public and the political elite.

History rarely provides absolutely definitive answers, as judging the motives and reasons for the actions of the various participants to any set of events is always challenging in retrospect. At best, it involves peering through an often-opaque glass, in which there are patches of clarity. Why didn't the King order the dispersal of the ragbag columns that matched on Rome in 1922? Did he fear the power of the fascists, or the outbreak of civil war? Or did he believe that a peaceful solution was possible by bringing them into the structures of government?

Similar questions can be asked about the extraordinary legislative decision the following year to decree that the party winning the most votes at an election, provided it was more than 25 per cent of all votes, would obtain two-thirds of the Parliamentary seats. Was the fact that the Liberals, such as Giolitti and Salandra, supported the legislation a reflection of their trust in the fascists, despise of the Socialists, a desire for stable government, a naive belief in sufficient checks and balances in the system, or something else? Only the *Partito Popolare* (Popular Party), formed in 1919 by Don Luigi Sturzo, opposed the proposal, which led to a split between the Pope and the party leadership, and a diminution of their political force.

Mussolini remained captive to the *squadristi*, whose murderous brutality still ravaged many parts of the country. When a Socialist Deputy, Giacomo Matteotti, was murdered after condemning fascist violence at the recent elections, Mussolini was ensnarled in a conflict between his ambitions and his supporters. While he had sought to gain control over the loose groupings, many of their powerful regional leaders, like Roberto Farinacci in Cremona, and similar characters elsewhere, retained the control and loyalty of their squads. Many had become part of the militia and local government as the wings of fascism spread. Whether Mussolini had been party to the murder became moot, as he had declared himself the supreme leader. In any event, allegations in the press implicated Mussolini more directly, leading previous coalitionists such as Giolitti, Orlando and Salandra to distance themselves from him.

Faced with calls to resign, Mussolini called the bluff of his opponents in January 1925, challenging them to indict him. Neither King nor Parliament responded. Mussolini's fascist regime had begun. A one-party state was only a matter of time.

Like many dictators, Mussolini craved approval and status. He was also a clever and cunning politician, who understood the force of demagoguery and the human yearning for stability and order. The latter he exploited to the hilt in his rally against the Socialists – and subsequently – the Liberals. In order to achieve his aspirations, Mussolini also knew he had to effectively control or destroy the *squadristi*, the base that underpinned his rise to power, but which threatened his future. His cunning was displayed in his ultimate control of the *squadristi*. Having appointed the leading figure, Roberto Farinacci, to reform it, Mussolini was able to remove him from the organisation when the murderous activities continued. He then expelled tens of thousands of members, replacing them with public servants. In one stroke, he had removed the threat and commandeered the public service. Membership of the party became obligatory for employment and promotion. The press was censured. The one-party state had consumed not only the Parliament, but the organs of government and the media. Mussolini had done so with widespread support. He was truly *Il Duce*.

Sport and the State

National leaders from the earliest days of Greece and Rome often associated themselves with major sporting events and champion athletes. Modern Italy was no different under Mussolini. The fascists regarded both sport and the arts as a means of promoting their vision and restoring the glorious myth of ancient Rome. Mussolini's mistress, Margherita Sarfatti, a patron of the arts, was at the forefront of this movement, creating a Ministry of Popular Culture, as were his brother, Arnaldo, many journalists and other spruikers of *Il Duce*. The press had become a propaganda machine for the regime. Mussolini's speeches were reported positively in great detail. Criticism of the national project was absent from the pages of the media.

At the heart of the fascist regime was a vision for a new, glorious Italy in which all worked together for a grand future. In his *Concise History of Italy*, Christopher Duggan concludes:

> The attempt to forge a new national community struck a chord with those many critics of the liberal state who had long been concerned about the emotional gulf separating the masses from the political institutions. Fascism set out to bridge this gulf. It aimed to replace Italy's flacid parliamentary system with a more vital regime built around myths and symbols, leadership cults, and the deliberate orchestration of collective hopes, fears and insecurities. However this experiment in cultural engineering was somewhat half-baked. Fascism was never a 'totalitarian' system, and in practice was forced to compromise with a variety of value systems, many of them highly conservative. By the 1930s 'fascist man' was no longer a young barbarian. He was a patriotic, hard working, church-going father.

For a movement with an emphasis on the active building of a new glorious nation, and the desire to motivate an involved and committed youth wing, sport and leisure became a critical pursuit. Youth organizations were a vital interest of the regime as sports and recreational clubs were established across the country. Mussolini himself exemplified this goal, often appearing in the press on horseback, swimming, playing tennis or driving a fast car. Motor sports and flying, both viewed as the epitome of the modern world, were popular with *Il Duce* and his sons. But other, more traditional sports, including soccer, boxing, fencing and cycling, were also encouraged and supported. Winning a Grand Prix or the World Cup was highlighted as outstanding sporting achievements and evidence of Italy's superiority in the world.

Mussolini had less interest in cycling, describing it at one stage as 'plebian'. When an appeal was launched for Ottavio Bottecchia after winning the Tour de France, Mussolini gave just one lira, although this may have reflected the belief that the Tour winner was a socialist sympathizer. However, *Il Duce's* two sons were enthusiasts. Mussolini also understood the widespread, often excitable, interest in cycling, amongst the populace, and was content for it to continue.

It is doubtful that many of the cycling stars of the era were active fascists, but along with much of the population, their attitude to the regime was often benign. A notable exception was Pietro Chesi, the winner of the 1927 Milan-San Remo, who was one of the infamous 'blackshirts' – the *Milizia Volontaria per la Sicurezza Nazionale* (Volunteer Militia for National Security). Chesi was shot dead by anti-fascist partisans at Florence in 1944.

It has long been speculated that Ottavio Bottecchia's mysterious death was at the hands of fascists. By contrast, both Costante Girardengo and Alfredo Binda were more sympathetic to the regime. Girardengo was a friend of Mussolini's sons, both cycling enthusiasts, and he was often seen in the company of leading members of the regime. Binda was even more closely associated. A photograph of the champion rider during the era features a bronze relief of Mussolini on his desk. Binda was the political secretary of the Fascist Party at Cittiglio for five years, stating that he was an anti-communist who joined the party to take care of his own interests. The historian, John Foot, writes:

> Binda always claimed to be uninterested in politics, but he was a 'good fascist'. In fact, politics *was* an important part of Binda's life – and is largely ignored by the hagiographies which have appeared in print. . . Binda not only embraced the regime, but also represented the fascists in local politics and thus benefitted from the largesse of the dictatorship.

Yet it was another champion cyclist of the era, Learco Guerra, who became most associated with the ruling regime.

Learco Guerra

Whether it was his broad smile and good looks, his powerful pedalling, or his engaging personality – in contrast to the taciturn Binda, Guerra quickly won the admiration of his fans – and the support of the regime. Even his name, Guerra – meaning 'war' in English, appealed to the fascists. Not that Guerra was ideologically committed to their political pursuits; he was a cyclist who reveled in the sheer excitement of racing. But he became the darling of fans and fascists alike.

Guerra was a late-comer to the sport. Born into a poor family at San Nicolò Po in 1902, Learco Antenore Giuseppe Guerra and his brother Ivano joined their father as bricklayers and labourers. Married at twenty to Letizia Malavasi, they soon had two children. A strong young man, Guerra was passionate about football, playing as a left winger with the local team. Like many workers of the era, the bicycle was his means of transport to and from work. In his mid-twenties, Guerra became interested in bicycle racing, training on a track that had been built around the local football pitch.

Guerra's youthful experiences hardly endeared him to the fascists. The Po Valley was the scene of much socialist activity, including widespread civil unrest after the Great War. Clashes between the socialists and the fascists resulted in riots in Mantova, violent confrontations with the *carabinieri* in which participants were killed, and the jailing of many people. As a labourer, Guerra was reported to be sympathetic to the socialists, who had considerable support in the region. By the time Guerra was conscripted for military service, the war was over. His 18 months in the cycling division was an escape from the toil and troubles of everyday life.

Returning to Mantova, labouring and a new family, Guerra became more interested in racing, entering local events as an amateur, and gradually progressing to the semi-professional ranks as an *isolato* – an independent competitor. Guerra's strength didn't immediately lead to success. A lack of tactical skills against younger and more experienced competitors hampered his early races. Over time, Guerra gained experience and an insight into the nature of competitive cycling, racing as an 'independent' – or semi-professional – in the beginning.

By the age of 26, with a wife and two children, Guerra began to make his mark in the sport. According to contempory accounts, he formed his own cycling club, of which he was the only member, and was given a frame by a local manufacturer. News of his early efforts riding for the local militia team soon spread. His lucky break came when the ageing Girardengo, who was looking for new talent in his quest to defeat Binda, recruited him to his cause. The *campionissimo* arranged for his masseur and trainer, Biagio Cavanna, to attend to Guerra, and urged the Maino team to add him to their riding list.

Guerra's proficiency on a bicycle flowered in 1928, when he won four regional races and finished 17th in Milan-San Remo as an independent. Wearing the grey Maino jersey, Guerra won three races in 1929 while riding as a *gregario*. It was the following year that Guerra's prodigious talent emerged in the Giro d'Italia and the Tour de France, as well as the World Championship road race.

In 1930, the Tour de France director, Henri Desgrange, convinced that the race based on trade teams had regressed into a shambles, introduced a new competition involving national and regional squads. It would be another three decades before trade teams returned to the Tour. Bereft of the financial support from the teams – who still paid their riders – Desgrange found another means of revenue, sponsors who would pay for the privilege of having their advertising cars follow the race. The well-known tour caravan was created!

The 1930 race should have been the clash of the century with the best riders from each nation competing together in their respective teams. The French line-up comprised some of the nation's best-ever riders: Charles Pélissier, André Leducq, Antonin and Pierre Aagne, Victor Fontan and Marcel Bidot. Pitted against them was a formidable Italian squad including Alfredo Binda and Learco Guerra. Not only did Binda extract a promise from the Giro organizers to not race their event, he also obtained a fee from Desgrange to ride the Tour. No wonder he finished his professional career as a relatively wealthy man!

Although Guerra was to finish second to André Leducq, his performance made him a national hero in Italy. Following Binda's abandonment, Guerra was virtually alone amongst the might of the French. This became apparent on the 16th stage, when Leducq crashed twice, lost consciousness and sustained a bloody gash on his leg, but was coaxed back into the race by his team-mates, who after a gruelling two-hour chase caught the Italian breakaway close to the finish line at Evian. It was a magnificent effort from a champion team, which won 12 of the 21 stages, Charles Pélissier taking eight of them, a record in one Tour only equaled by Eddy Merckx (twice) and Freddie Maertens in the 1970s.

Guerra returned to Italy a hero, having won three stages and having held the lead for seven days. Binda, whose reputation was damaged by his abandonment, went on to defeat Guerra in the World Championship, but a true rival had emerged. Guerra claimed the Italian National Championship that year, the first of five consecutive titles, demonstrating his power in one-day races. The great sporting contest, so loved by the Italian populace, had begun. As Girardengo had faded and Bottechia had mostly raced in France, Binda had been unrivalled. That now changed. The great rivalry between Binda and Guerra was fueled by the press and championed by their supporters.

In 1931, Guerra became the first rider to wear the *maglia rosa* – the now familiar pink jersey of the race leader. In 1919 – perhaps earlier – Henri Desgrange had chosen a yellow jersey – *maillot jeune* – in response to a request by journalists for some recognizable identification of the leader of the Tour de France each day. Yellow was significant; it was the colour of the paper upon which *L'Auto* was printed. Over a decade passed before the organizers of the Giro decided to replicate the French practice.

As *La Gazzetta dello Sport* was printed on pink paper, *rosa* was the obvious colour for the leader's jersey. Having announced the decision, the organizers ran into the might of the fascist regime. Mussolini proclaimed the colour effeminate. How could the leader of the nation's – the world's – toughest race wear such a colour? Ultimately a compromise was reached; the leader would wear a pink jersey, but it would also have emblazoned on it the *fasces* – the symbol of an axe in the middle of a bundle of rods – of the regime.

Binda graciously returned to the 1931 Giro, anticipating his sixth victory against a crack field. With the emergence of Guerra, the organizers hoped that it would not be another procession. Binda's dominance had become so total that he was jeered for winning the 1928

Giro, leading Emilio Colombo to write in *La Gazzetta*:
> This athlete, who has elevated Italian cycling to a different level, who has delivered us our first World Championship, deserves better. By all means offer him less of your applause but don't ever, ever whistle at a great champion again.

The *tifosi* wanted to see their champions struggle in a seesawing contest of physical strength and mental will. This was to be the year: the *campionissimo*, Binda, pitted against the people's favourite, Guerra. Binda had out-sprinted Guerra in the traditional opening event for the season, Milan-San Remo, so the scene was set for a major battle in May. The peloton was probably the best ever assembled in the two decade history of the Giro. It included the reigning titleholder, Luigi Marchisio, who at just over 21-years of age had become the youngest winner to date; Michele Mara, a great sprinter of the era; and Luigi Giacobbe, the runner-up in 1930. Antonin Magne, a future Tour de France winner and World Champion, made the journey from France, while Jean Aerts the inaugural amateur – and later professional – World Champion came from Belgium. The first Spaniards to contest the Giro, Mariano Cañardo and Ricardo Montero were also at the start. Cañardo was the reigning Spanish Champion who was to win his country's then-greatest race, the Volta a Catalunya, seven times between 1928 and 1939.

With the added incentive of the first stage finishing in his home area of Mantova, Guerra delighted his fans and the regime by being the first wearer of the *maglia rosa* which he held for another stage until Binda claimed it in the hilly third leg. It appeared that Binda would prevail again, even though his lead over the next few riders was tight, until a crash brought down the leading group in the sprint into Rome. Binda injured his back, and despite starting the next stage two days later, he abandoned, leaving Guerra to win and move back to seventh placing, just over 2 minutes behind the new leader, Luigi Marchisio. In the following stage, Guerra soloed away from the field to reclaim the *maglia rosa*. It looked like 'the human locomotive' which Guerra had been named, would claim a popular victory. But fate intervened in the form of an over-excited fan, which brought down the leader, causing a deep gash to his back. Guerra was taken to hospital, his Giro over. Neither of the two favourites completed the race. In the end,

Francesco Camusso, who had abandoned his first Giro the year before, defeated Luigi Giacobbe and Luigi Marchisio in a stirring three-way fight to the finish.

If the *tifosi* were crestfallen by the loss of Guerra from the Giro, he redeemed himself in the World Championship. The organizers of the world title race at Copenhagen decided on a novel format, a 172-kilometre time trial. The race suited Guerra's smooth, powerful pedaling style. Riding a single geared bike, he defeated his adversaries by almost nine minutes. Binda could only manage sixth placing. Guerra returned to Italy a 'Fascist Superman', according to Mussolini's administration. There is no evidence that Guerra was an active supporter of the fascists, but his role as the popular, working class, anti-Binda hero was used by the regime as part of the ongoing propaganda for Mussolini's totalitarian state. The regime understood the benefits of association with the popular event and *Il Duce* offered prizes to Giro contestants. His sons, Bruno and Vittorio, enthused about the sport, and adored Guerra as a national hero.

The great rivalry continued. Binda won the Giro di Lombardia to bookend his season, although Guerra took the *maglia tricolore* from his shoulders in the national championship. Binda won the Giro again in 1933 before Guerra finally triumphed in the 1934 grand tour by just 51 seconds after a monumental battle with Francesco Camusso.

By the mid-1930s, sport, including cycling, had become entangled in the overarching canopy of the fascist regime. Mussolini's Italy was all encompassing. As early as 1927, *Il Comitato Olimpico Nazionale Italiano* (the Italian Olympic Committee) was controlled by the Fascist Party. When Italy scored a goal in extra time to defeat Czechoslovakia in the second World Cup at the Stadium of the National Fascist Party in Rome in 1934, the regime hailed the result as a symbol and evidence of political and ideological supremacy. Politics and sport had become intermixed in the national narrative. Although cycling remained partially an individual pursuit, tensions between the riders and the regime would emerge over the next decade. At the centre of this tension would be a rider destined to become one of Italy's greatest cyclists, Gino Bartali.

Giovanni Brunero, first three-time winner of the Giro d'Italia (1921, 1922 and 1926).

5

The Changing Order

If the nineteenth century was the century of individualism . . . it may be expected that this will be the century of collectivism, and hence the century of the State
-- Benito Mussolini.

The cyclist's career and life is like human evolution, a continul development
-- Gino Bartali.

Three weeks after the heir to the Austro-Hungrarian throne, Archduke Franz Ferdinand, was assassinated at Sarajevo, Bosnia, and ten days before the Empire declared war on Serbia, Gino Giovanni Bartali was born at Ponte a Ema, a small village six kilometres south of the bustling city of Florence in central Italy. The new bambino was the third child of Torello and Giulia Bartali, struggling labourers in the surrounding farmlands of the Tuscan countryside.

The Bartalis were a typical family of the era. Although manufacturing had expanded over the previous two decades, especially in the North, agriculture remained the staple industry. Italy had experienced remarkable economic progress during the Giolittian period – essentially the first decade of the new century – with GDP growth, overall and per capita, outstripping many other European nations, but the advances largely excluded agriculture. Sixty per cent of the workforce depended on farming, but there was much under-employment. Torello Bartali was a typical example. He laboured on the nearby farms when work was available. When it wasn't, he worked in a local quarry, as a bricklayer, making cement, or doing other odd jobs. In order for the family to survive, Giulia also worked, often in the vineyards of the nearby Chianti region.

Not that the Bartalis complained about their situation. Ponte a Ema, named after the bridge across the small tributary of the Greve and Arno rivers, had more opportunities for work than many other parts of Italy. Laundry businesses, set up along the river, employed many women in the cleaning of clothes and linen for wealthy and middle class Florentines. The Giolitti period saw reforms of the labour laws as many workers joined unions. Compared to their parents' generation, Torello and Giulia enjoyed some basic protections. The working day for women was limited to 11 hours; children could not be employed under the age of 12; a compulsory day of rest was instituted; and early forms of maternity, sickness and old-age benefits were introduced for some employees. The average industrial worker earned 435-lire a year, but labourers like Torello received less. Life was tough, but not impossible.

It was this world that Gino, his older sisters, Anita and Natalina, and his younger brother, Giulio, grew up. Like most apartments, the Bartali home comprised a single room and a kitchen in a three story building on the main street, Via Chiantigiana. Crude toilet facilities were shared with the other tenants. While the development of hydro-electricity from the late 1880s spurred the industrial expansion over the following two decades, houses like the Bartalis had neither power nor running water.

When not at school, the children spent their time with other youngsters, playing on the streets. This is where they entertained themselves until their parents returned from work and the family crowded into their small room for an evening meal and sleep. Sunlight regulated the rhythms of daily life.

Ponte a Ema had the basics of a small village. Amongst the bank, the barbershop, the grain mill and the wine store were two buildings that were influential in the life of the young Gino: the shop of the local bicycle mechanic and the parish church.

The bicycle was the most popular form of transport at the time, and every paese and village required a mechanic to fix the usual problems:

punctured tubes, worn tyres, broken forks and disintegrating chains, amongst them. The bike mechanic's shop was the modern-day garage.

A young boy of Gino's era was attracted to the bicycle shop as the automobile garage fascinated a youngster of later times. Each represented a new horizon, a freedom to explore the world beyond the known boundaries. Torello owned a bicycle. It was his means of transport, a vehicle to carry him from home to work and back again. The bicycle was not just a means of transport for labourers and workers: the local doctor, the parish priest, and the delivery boys for the local traders all used the machines. For the young Gino, it was an exciting contraption, a challenge beyond his experience, and a pathway to an exotic world beyond the confines of Ponte a Ema.

Unknown to his father, the young Gino started to ride Torello's bike, at first hesitantly, but before long with confidence. He was a poor school student, distracted in the classroom, and more interested in the outdoors. The bicycle was his great reward. But Torello was determined that his son would complete year six before being required to join the workforce. That involved a journey from Ponte a Ema into Florence, a journey that young Gino undertook by bicycle. In order to obtain the necessary machine, Gino was required to work to afford the bicycle, as he was then 12. This came in the form of unravelling raffia strands from palm leaves for use as ties in vineyards and nurseries.

Soon Gino was exploring Florence, not just the familiar roads between home and the Arno. The climb to Fiesole, the summer residence of the Medici overlooking Florence from the north, soon became a favourite route. From the crest, the young brothers, Gino and Giulio could gaze across the magical city, like the Italian princes before them, pointing to the Duomo and the Palazzo Vecchio in the distance, before plunging headlong onto the descent to the river below and the ride home.

Gino's newfound transport also allowed him to visit a busy bikeshop in Florence where his cousin, Armando Sizzi, worked. There he soaked up the atmosphere amongst the aspiring professional cyclists, amateurs and regular commuters wanting their bicycles repaired, or inspecting the latest frames and gleaming new machines.

The other building of significance for the young Gino was the local church. The Italian state may have rejected the Church, but the local parish remained the most significant claim on the sentiments and activity of the majority of people. The Bartalis were no exception. There were a dozen parish churches within a few kilometres of their home on Via Chiantigiana, a reflection of both the piety of the people and the parameters of their worldly experience, but it was the local church on the street that Torello and Giulia and their children attended. On Sundays, dressed in their finest clothing, the Bartali family, along with many of their neighbours would process along the street to the parish church for Mass. It was the centre of their lives, a spiritual and social hub in the small community of Ponte a Ema. The Bartalis were orthodox Catholics, a good working class family who laboured hard, trusted in God and sought the best for their children. The simple piety of Gino's youthful experiences remained with him throughout his life, and provided a pivot to the fame that would envelop him shortly. It was the counterpoint to celebrity and fortune that anchored his life in the most troubling of times.

Church and State

Although the vast majority of Italians were Catholics, and Rome had been the throne of the Papacy for centuries, relations between church and state were strained following the defeat of the Papal States in 1870. A secularist and anti-clerical thread was a strong component of the quest for reunification. These tensions continued to play out for decades. The capture of Rome resulted in an uneasy tension between the Kingdom of Italy and the Catholic Church, the Pope retreating inside the walls of the Vatican, and refusing to recognise the new state. The church had become a 'state within a state', separate but still holding considerable sway over the populace. Catholics were discouraged from participating in the political process, leaving the state largely in secular hands. In the 1870 elections, less than half the electorate participated, with even lower numbers in much of the North. The hopes of reunification ran up against a schism between church and state. For the next four decades, one of the most significant historical Italian institutions, and most of its adherents, was divorced from government. It would be another half a century before the balance was corrected.

By the 1890s, the changes wrought by industrialisation, especially the challenges of capital and labour, increasingly become the focus of political, economic and social discussion. This resulted in a renewed involvement by the Church in social issues and the publication in 1891 of the encyclical, *Rerum Novarum*, on the Rights and Duties of Capital and Labor, as well as government and citizens. The first two words of the title 'of revolutionary change,' captured the mood of the era. In the document that formed the basis of Catholic social doctrine for the next century, Pope Leo XIII supported the right of workers to form unions, rejected socialism and unrestricted capitalism, and affirmed the ownership of private property. Based on notions of dignity, the common good, civil society and subsidiarity, the Pope endeavoured to address, from a Christian perspective, the emerging social, economic and political conflicts that had arisen in the developed world. A decade later, the slow re-engagement of Catholics and the Church with the state commenced with the formation of the Italian Catholic Electoral Union in 1905 following the partial relaxation the previous year of the Papal ban on Catholics participating in the electoral process. Its impact at first was slight. In 1909, the prohibition was further relaxed, as the Church under Pope Pius X preferred participation in the democratic state over the continuing rise of socialism. The voter turn out increased significantly in many places and some Catholics were elected deputies. The historic tensions remained on both sides of the aisle: many were wary of the re-engagement by Catholics, while the Church insisted that Catholic Deputies were not representatives of it.

The issue demonstrated the Roman ability to proclaim a principal but work around it pragmatically. Unless the so-called 'Roman question' – the issue of the relationship between the Kingdom and the Church – was solved, arrangements would remain pragmatic and fluid. Prime Minister Giovanni Giolitti's decision to invade Libya in 1911 was the backdrop to the beginnings of a denouement between the institutional church and state. Although the invasion was militarily successful, the increasingly powerful socialists denounced it, leaving Giolitti politically exposed.

Giolitti walked a tightrope: on one hand his traditional Liberal supporters would baulk at any concessions to the Church; on the other hand, he needed the support of Catholics to retain his political ascendency. While proclaiming that Church and State were 'two parallel lines, which should never meet,' Giolitti was negotiating in secret to secure the Catholic vote. Pressing his political decision to court the Church was the passage of new electoral laws in 1912 to extend suffrage to most adult males. The result was an almost three-fold increase in eligible voters, from 3 million to 8.5 million. The changes had been part of an attempt to attract the Socialists into government, but had failed, leaving Giolitti increasingly exposed.

Giolitti turned to the *Unione Elettorale Cattlolica Italiana* – the Catholic Electoral Union – led by Count Vincenzo Ottorino Gentiloni, to secure his government in the 1913 elections. In return for promises to fund Catholic schools and oppose divorce laws, the Union encouraged its followers to support Liberal candidates. The strategy worked for Giolitti. Some 200 Deputies were elected through the arrangement, keeping the Socialists, who had increased votes, from forming government. The victory however proved phyricc for the crafty Giolitti. When knowledge of the so-called Gentiloni Pact became public, Giolitti, who relied on a coalition of Deputies, lost Parliamentary support, and his government collapsed, paving the way for the prime ministership of the conservative Antonio Salandra, who was to take the nation into the Great War.

The revelations ended the Giolittian era, and increased the political power of the Vatican in Italy, although a formal rapprochement was still more than a decade away. Throughout the Giolittian era, Pope Pius X, who was troubled by the march of modernism and the support for radical socialism across Europe, led the church. A pacifist, Pius, who had been unwell, was deeply shocked by the outbreak of the Great War, dying on the day the German forces invaded Brussels. His replacement, Benedict XV, was no less concerned, describing the conflict as "the suicide of civilized Europe." Twice, in 1916 and 1917, Benedict initiated peace efforts. While Britain and Austria were receptive, France, which had broken relations with the Church, and Germany, stymied the efforts. His warnings about the triumph of the primitive human urges of vengeance and violence were ignored both during the war and at its end. Sensing that the Versailles conference was motivated by similar urges, he counselled against imposing impossibly large restitution payments on Germany, a warning that was ignored.

His concern about the weakness of the various states that succeeded the Austro-Hungrarian Empire reverberated for the rest of the century. And his worry about the League of Nations being ineffective proved true. Tragically, the seeds of another Great War had already been planted as Europe entered the 1920s.

An unlikely party, Benito Mussolini, resolved the 'Roman question'. Following his 1925 declaration of authority, Mussolini progressively created his totalitarian state. By the end of the following year, he had prohibited all non-fascist political activity. Parliament was effectively replaced by the Fascist Grand Council, which compiled the list of Deputies. The media was tightly controlled as Mussolini increasingly assumed all ultimate power to himself. Why then, did Mussolini agree to resolve the 60-year standoff with the Catholic Church?

In his earlier life, Mussolini expressed anti-clerical sentiments, calling the Vatican "a nest of robbers" and priests "black germs", but on becoming Prime Minister commenced an accommodation with the church. Although married to his second wife, Rachele Guidi, in a civil ceremony in 1915, the couple renewed their vows in a religious ceremony a decade later. He also had his children baptised. Whatever residual antipathies Mussolini had towards the church, he commenced negotiations to settle the 'Roman question.'

Mussolini realised that a reproachmont with the Church could serve the cause of building his ideal state. Although he modelled his aspiration on the Roman Empire, he understood that the twin claims of loyalty to the state and the church created tensions that would counter his desired outcome. Better the two great institutions worked together. Writing on behalf of Mussolini in *La Doctrina del Fascism*, Giovanni Gentile proclaimed:

> The Fascist state does not attempt, as did Robespierre at the height of the Revolution, to efface God from the soul of man.

Faced with the march of atheistic communism elsewhere in Europe, some in the Church, including Pope Pius XI himself, viewed fascism as a less evil alternative.

The seeds of a more democratic Italy briefly flowered after the Great War. Mussolini's rise to power was not inevitable in the early 1920s, but the inability of the various forces opposed to the fascists to co-operate and the resulting splintering of the opposition rendered the final totalitarian victory. No party could command a majority in the Parliament, and the diverse interests and intense rivalries prevented any long-lasting coalition emerging.

Two new parties – Don Luigi Sturzo's *Partito Popolare* (Popular Party) and Benito Mussolini's Fascists, were to play a central role in the unfolding drama. The Popular Party, led by the Sicilian priest, Don Luigi Sturzo, emerged after the Great War when the half century ban on Catholics engaging in political life was lifted by the Vatican. The Party gained widespread support, but ultimately encountered insurmountable forces. Even though it was independent of the church, the fear of spreading Marxism remained potent at the highest levels of the Vatican, undermining any possible cooperation with the socialists, even after the socialists and communists split into separate parties. But the rock on which the new party founded was the 'Roman Question'. Sturzo believed the relationship between the Vatican and the Kingdom would emerge in the right circumstances, but the Vatican, embroiled in financial difficulties, and embued with decades of worry about the issue, remained eager to resolve the dispute. When Mussolini guaranteed the Vatican finances, retreated from higher taxes on the church, restored church buildings and returned religious instruction to the schools, accomodation with him became more and more attractive. Widespread strikes and mounting fascist violence led many to look for a strong leader as an andedote to the continuing unrest and threat of civil war. Mussolini exploited the situation with a combination of blandishments, intimidation and violence, eventually forcing a vote in the Parliament to end proportional representation and guarantee the party with the relative majority of the vote two-thirds of the seats. For the next two decades, Italy would be under the grip of the fascists. Like the socialists and other parties, the Popular Party would be outlawed. Sturzo had been forced to resign, and eventually sought exile in the United Kingdom. His replacement in the last year of the Party, Alcide De Gasperi, was to emerge 20 years later as the leader of the newly formed Christian Democrats and Prime Minister of Italy. Sturzo was more fortunate than others. Many opponents of the fascist regime were arrested and imprisoned, including Antonio Gramsci, the head of the Communist Party, who died in custody in 1937. His successor, Palmiro

Togliatti, escaped to Moscow, where he remained in exile until the death of Mussolini.

The historian, John Molony, concluded:

> The men of the *Risorgimento* had bequeathed to Italy all the outward forms of a modern democracy but the one basic thing they were unable to impart was its spirit. Thus in a land weakened by war, ravaged by ideological armours, embittered by poverty and rendered aimless in its search for national identity, democracy went to the wall.

Mussolini offered security and stability, a brake on the excesses of capitalism, and – despite his earlier associations – a counter to communism. This was an attractive proposition for many, including some in the Catholic hierarchy.

The final catalyst for the subsequent agreement with the Vatican was the education system, where Mussolini's desire for a virile, patriotic and disciplined youth, found accord with the church's interest in religious instruction in the school system. *Il Duce* believed he had recruited the church to his cause, while the Vatican grasped the opportunity to spread its message. Despite some ongoing tensions, the negotiations ultimately concluded in the 1929 Lateran Treaty and the associated concordat, so-named as Mussolini and Pietro Gasparri, the Cardinal Secretary of State, signed them at the Lateran Palace. The Vatican State was created and compensation paid for the loss of the Papal States. Mussolini marked the event by commissioning the *Via della Conciliazone* (the Road of Conciliation) running from the Vatican to the Castel Sant'Angelo. It is easy with hindsight to argue that the Church had paid a high price for the sovereignty over 109 acres of land on Vatican Hill and the declaration that Catholicism was the state religion. Amongst the concessions was that the state could control the appointment of bishops, anathema to the earlier and later church.

The historian, Christopher Duggan writes:

> The resolution of the Roman question was a great political coup for Mussolini, it increased his personal prestige, internationally as well as at home; and more importantly, it allowed fascism to realise the dream long harboured by the liberal state of using the Church as an instrument for securing mass political consent.

The latter occurred within weeks of the Treaty, when Italians voted overwhelmingly to accept the single list of Deputies proposed for the Parliament.

> The regime had a new degree of moral legitimacy; and Mussolini — 'the man sent by providence', as the pope called him — appeared impregnable. In turn, Mussolini declared in Parliament that the Fascist state is Catholic.

Yet within two years, the concordat was faltering. In 1931, Mussolini shut down Catholic newspapers, and attempted to suppress the Church's main lay body, Catholic Action, including its youth groups, which had been permitted to continue to operate autonomously, provided it remained apolitical. It was on this issue that the relationship between the fascists and the Church soured. Pius XI published a strongly worded encyclical letter, *Non Abbiamo Bisogno*, defending the movement from Mussolini's attacks and condemning the pagan worship of the state. He made it clear that fascism was not Catholic:

> Fascism declares itself to be Catholic. Well, there is one way and one way only to be truly Catholic — Catholics in fact and not sham Catholics... Is to obey the Church and its head.

In the face of the Pope's onslaught, Mussolini retreated. The Church consolidated its position and would over time break further from the regime. But this took many years. Many Italian bishops and priests shared the sense of national pride that Mussolini cultivated. In the aftermath of the clash with the fascists, Catholic Action continued to grow, providing a counter to totalitarianism, and a training ground for many of the post-war Christian Democrat leaders of Italy. For a young Gino Bartali, it was to become a source of strength, and the connection to his wartime activities.

Fascism takes hold

The rise of fascism impacted on individuals and families throughout Italy. The Bartalis were no exception. As a labourer, Gino's father, Torello, had sympathies for the socialist promise of better conditions and a fairer outcome for workers like himself. The Giolitti reforms had improved conditions for the working class, but the divide between rich and poor remained wide. Life remained precarious; employment could be spasmodic. Hard work was a reality for the overwhelming majority of Italians as they eked out an existence.

The terror that the fascists cultivated became a reality for the Bartalis in 1925 when one of Torello's employers, Gaetano Pilati, was murdered. Pilati, a World War I veteran and a supporter of the anti-fascist *Italia Libera* movement, was shot and killed by fascist thugs. Gino was just eleven, but he quickly learned that the totalitarians would use brutal means to achieve their objectives.

Torello abandoned his public support for the socialists, knowing that the fate of Pilati, or the socialist Deputy, Giacomo Matteotti, who was killed after speaking out against Mussolini, could be the fate of anyone. Totalitarianism didn't have to kidnap and kill many people; it simply created a frightening climate of suspicion that shut down public debate and opposition. Torello and Giulia instead concentrated their attention on raising a growing family in a changing world. At least there was continuing work in Ponte a Ema as the world reeled from the Great Depression.

Mussolini's desire to remake Italy as the 'new Rome' drove both the cult of personality that he encouraged, and his economic policies. Initially, he benefitted from the upturn in the world economy in the first half of the 1920s. He was able to balance the budget, reduce the taxes on war profits and bring down public expenditure.

Over the 1920s, Mussolini launched a series of grandiose schemes – designated as 'battles' in the fascist lexicon – that achieved some gains, but mostly failed. These were the Battle for Births, the Battle for Land, the Battle for Grain, and the Battle for the Lira. The Battle for Births, launched in 1927, reflected Mussolini's dream for a great Italian nation. Noting that a declining birthrate had been a significant factor in the downfall of the Roman Empire, he proposed a population of 60 million by 1950, an increase of some 20 million people. With the south of the country already overcrowded and relatively poor, and the onset of the Great Depression, the adventurous objectives were unattainable, despite widespread propaganda lauding large families, special taxation benefits, and other incentives to have more children. The birth rate fell between 1927 and 1934. Italy's population reached 47 million by 1950, due largely to declining mortality rates.

Mussolini planned 5,000 new farms as part of his ambitious Battle for Wheat. In order to make Italy self-sufficient, he proposed to increase grain production. The first project, involving farms and a town named Mussolinia, was commenced on Sardinia. It was followed by similar projects on the peninsula. The scheme had serious unintended consequences, especially the decline in cheaper fruit and vegetable production, increases in bread prices, falling domestic consumption, high tariffs and subsidies that increased national debt.

The Battle for Land involved the clearing of vast areas of swamps and marshland for agriculture and housing. These included the low-lying areas surrounding Rome and the Tuscan Maremma, the region in the southwest of the province bordering on the Tyrrhenian Sea. The most ambitious project saw the clearing of the Pontine Marshes, the extensive low-lying area between the Tyrrhenian Sea and the Antiappenni Mountains, southeast of Rome. A fertile area during the Roman Empire, it had become infected by malaria. This massive project employed 124,000 workers at the peak of construction that extended from 1929 until completion in 1935, when the workers were dismissed.

The battle was successful in providing employment in the years following the Great Depression. But the development of small plots of land undermined the Battle for Wheat, which required larger holdings to be successful. The Pontine Marsh works were largely destroyed during World War II. The project was finally recommenced and completed during the post-war reconstruction of Italy.

Mussolini's final scheme was the Battle for the Lira, and his Gold for the Fatherland project. In pursuing his dream for the great new Italian nation, Mussolini inflated the value of the Lira in 1926-27. The initiative drove up the price of exports, which increased the number of people unemployed as Italian businesses struggled to sell their products internationally.

Although there were positive features of all of the schemes, they suffered from inconsistent objectives, contrary political forces, and the narrowly based agricultural economy. The latter benefitted the country, compared to more industrialised nations, in recovering from the Great Depression, but the reliance on small-scale agriculture remained a long term weakness for the Italian economy.

Cycling and the Story of Italy

Inconsistent political and economic objectives significantly undermined possible success. In particular, Mussolini's declaration of a political monopoly in 1925 unleashed other forces that weakened economic progress. Widespread strikes by the fascist unions pressing for the radical restructure of the state on syndicalist principles broke out across the country in 1925 alarming Mussolini. Contrary to the syndicalists who wanted to see industries owned and managed by workers, Mussolini's fascist dream was a totalitarian state. His Minister for Justice delivered legislation that gave the fascist unions sole representation for industrial negotiations and established compulsory arbitration, but outlawed strikes and left the employers free of state supervision. A grand Charter of Labour was honoured in its breach and the syndicalist movement effectively abolished. Together with the revaluation of the Lira, the state corporatisation of key industries, and the introduction of costly welfare schemes designed to support families, these measures undermined the economic growth the nation required.

It was into this uncertain era and a world of hard work and subsistence life that Gino Bartali was destined, had it not been for his remarkable ability on a bicycle. It was to lift him – and his family – out of the daily grind of low paid toil to fame and fortune. Yet, it almost did not happen.

Gino's father, Torello, was firmly opposed to his son's growing interest in racing. Once Gino had his own bike, he, his younger brother, Giulio, and their friends regularly rode along the roads surrounding their home, and further afield into the Tuscan hills. It was an exhilarating adventure for the group of teenagers. Like all young men, they would test their speed and endurance against each other. It soon became clear that Gino possessed a rare ability, although Giullio, two years younger, was also fast and strong.

The occasional encounter with local amateurs training on the nearby roads enabled Gino and his friends to test their ability. Riding heavy bikes, Gino in particular, would often keep pace, and sometimes best, the amateurs on the Tuscan hills. His talent was soon noticed and remarked upon.

It was a training ride with Oscar Casamonti, an amateur racer who operated the cycling shop at Ponte a Ema where Gino had part-time work, that established his reputation. Of the group that went on the 90 kilometre route, only Gino stayed with Casamonti, as he charged back home ahead of his training partners. It was an impressive performance from the youngster on a heavy, single-speed bike.

Despite Casamonti's urgings, and subsequently others, including the local parish priest, Torello and Giulia were opposed to Gino entering competitive events. He was a slight boy, prone to sickness. His parents steadfastly refused the admonitions to allow him to race, worried that he would be injured or killed in an accident. Gino kept training, building his strength, hoping against hope that one-day his parents would relent.

That day came in 1931 when his father unexpectedly allowed him to compete in a race, rather than allow the younger Giulio to participate. The next day Gino entered the race for 14- to 16-year-olds and won – but was later disqualified as he had turned 17 the previous day! It was the beginning of a prodigious career as a cyclist.

6

Changing of the Guard

Life means riding a bike
-- Gino Bartali.

Once Gino had received his father's approval to race, there was no stopping him. It was like he had found his purpose in life, away from the drudgery of work. No matter how many hours he spent on the bicycle, it was always an exhilarating experience, a challenge of mind and body against the elements. There is no more gruelling sport than road cycling. It requires long hours of training each day, building the strength, suppleness and endurance to race vast distances, day after day. Slowly the body adjusts, gaining in strength little by little, until high speeds can be maintained for hours at a time over all types of terrain.

There were no carbon frames, multiple gearing or power meters to monitor the body's output when young Gino started racing. Instead he had a steel framed bike with fixed gearing. The typical professional racing bike of the era weighed 11-12 kilograms, compared to the legal minimum weight today of just 6.8 kilograms.

The fixed gearing had advantages for the cyclists like Gino. From the outset, they learnt to ride a high cadence with the ability to both sprint on the flat and climb in the hills and mountains. This ability to turn the pedals fast builds the endurance that road cyclists require for success. From an early age, Gino developed a unique style on the bike that remained a feature throughout his cycling career. Unlike other riders, who tended to climb either in or out of the saddle, Gino

Alfonsina Strada, the only female ever to ride in the Giro d'Italia (1924).

appeared to haphazardly alternate, sometimes in the seat before jumping off the saddle for a burst of frantic climbing. This unpredictability mesmerised his opponents, which the talented young rider employed to his advantage.

The design of the bicycle changed very little for three decades. By the 1880s, cyclists had discarded the unwieldy and dangerous Penny Farthing for the new 'safety' bike. The new bicycles had rudimentary suspension, brakes, a chain drive, and although a fixed wheel, foot rests for the rider when rolling downhill. A free hub eventually replaced the fixed rear wheel but single gearing remained a feature of early bikes. The basic diamond frame that still features today was at the centre of the design. In the early 1900s, the famous American track rider, Marshall Taylor added a head stem to his bike, moving the handlebars forward and allowing the rider to bend lower over the bike and have more control over his front wheel direction. But little else changed for years.

Later a second larger cog was added to the other side of the rear wheel. This allowed the rider to stop and reverse the wheel to use the larger rear cog for climbing the steeper mountains. Gino's strength allowed him to ride further up steep ascents than many other riders before having to stop and quickly turn over the rear wheel. By the time Bartali had turned professional, two other significant mechanical devices had been invented. The pioneer of this work was the Italian, Tullio Campagnolo, who first invented the quick release wheel system that is used to this day on most bicycles. But it was his second invention, the Cambio Corsa gearing system that revolutionised competitive cycling. Primitive by today's standards, the new invention allowed the rider to select one of four different sized cogs on the rear hub by the use of two levers that released the wheel and moved the chain sideways onto another gear. It saved the cyclist the time of stopping, climbing off the bike, switching the rear wheel over, and then starting off again, often on a steep slope. The subsequent invention of the Osgear refined the process, with the device first allowed in the 1937 Tour de France, won by Roger Lapébie using it. Tullio Campagnolo continued to experiment with gearing, inventing the modern derailleur which Gino Bartali used to his advantage in the post-war races.

Although he had been an unenthusiastic student at school, Gino threw himself into cycling. Not only did he start training early in the morning before working as a bike mechanic in the shop of Oscar Casamonti, he sought out any advice he could find about how to improve his fitness and strength. Long before the computers and power meters that are an essential part of the modern cyclist's training package, the star riders looked to any means to improve their performance. Gino was obsessive in his quest. In addition to his long training rides, he began a rigorous exercise program. Gino was fastidious about his new fitness regime, soon earning the nickname 'the accountant' for the manner is which he recorded his program and activities.

Although possessed of considerable talent, the young Bartali's early years as a cyclist were a struggle. Torello and Guilia were not wealthy, so affording a racing bike and equipment, along with the food to sustain him for many kilometres of training was a challenge. His job at the bike shop paid little, although he could make the necessary repairs and adjustments to his bicycle himself or with the assistance of Oscar Casamonti.

Gino joined the L'Aquila amateur cycling club, and was soon winning races, even doing deals with other competitors to share in the prize money. His raw talent impressed the organisers, and Gino was soon paid a small amount to race. It provided a level of financial security for both Gino and his family. He could concentrate on rising through the amateur ranks and the dream of a professional contract.

That rise came relatively quickly. Although he was riding for an amateur team, there was not the same discipline of the professional squads. Riders like Gino could take their chances in a race, which he often did, being one of the strongest youngsters of the era. By 1933, the then 19-year-old Bartali completed the year by winning the third edition of the Bologna – Raticosa. The Tuscan race was an early opportunity for the young rider to display his climbing prowess on the Passo della Raticosa.

Bartali followed up that victory with three significant wins in 1934. He won the Coppa Bologna in Emilia Romagna, defeating older riders, Callisto Fabiani and Augusta Ciapelli. Gino also claimed the Giro del Casentino in Abruzzi, before displaying his climbing skills on Monte

Grappa. In the race from Bassano del Grappa to the top of the nearby mountain, Gino was victorious, defeating Enrico Bolis and Randolpo Gervasini. Bolis was later to finish 7th in the 1940 Milan-San Remo.

The victories attracted the attention of the professional teams that were always on the lookout for young *gregari* to assist their star riders. In 1935, aged just 21, Gino's youthful dream came true when he was signed to ride for the Frejus team. It was a talented squad, comprising 10 Italians and the gifted German stage winner, Karl Altenburgen.

Antonio Giuseppe Negrini was a star of the team, having finished second in the Giro di Lombardia in his first year as a professional in 1926. The following year, he finished third in both the Giro d'Italia and the Giro di Lombardia. He finally won the 'Race of the Falling Leaves' in 1932. Also in the team was Giuseppe Mariano, who had won the amateur Italian and World Championships in 1930. In 1933, he finished third in the Tour de France, beaten by a time bonus. Rinaldo Gerini, who finished 8th in 1935 Milan-San Remo, was a new teammate to Gino. Another neo-professional, Enrico Mollo, won the Giro di Lombardia in his first year for his new team. This was the capable group that Gino joined for his initial year in the professional ranks.

Like many young riders, Gino was impatient for success and often railed against team discipline. As an amateur, he could ride mostly as he pleased. Being the strongest young rider on the L'Aquila team, he had greater latitude to race as he liked. But that freedom had been traded for a salary and opportunities in the professional peloton.

Despite his impatience, Bartali's first year as a professional was impressive. His first win came in the Coppa Bernocchi, a race at Legnano that had first been run after the Great War, and was one of the minor classics of the era. He was also victorious in the Giro delle Due Province Messina in Sicily. But it was in two other events that Gino made his mark. First, he became only the fourth cyclist since 1913 to claim the Italian National Road Race Championship. Costante Girardengo wore the national tricolour from 1913 until 1925. This included seven consecutive victories between 1919, when the race resumed after the war, and 1925. The *campionisssimo* was dislodged from the top of the podium in 1926 by Alfredo Binda, who went on to win the following three national championships. By the time Gino lined up for the 1935 title, Learco Guerra had made the race his own, claiming the national title for five years running. The new professional joined some of the nation's greatest cyclists when he defeated Aldo Bini and Vasco Bergamaschi for the title. It was the first of four national championship jerseys he would own, the last in 1952 when he was in his late 30s.

Bartali had started the season with a fourth to the Bianchi rider, Giuseppe Olmo, in Milan-San Remo. A small group comprising Olmo, Bartali, Learco Guerra and Mario Cipriani sprinted for victory in San Remo in the second fastest edition of *La Classicissima di Primavera* to date. Gino concluded his season in October on the third step of the Lombardia podium. The 'race of the falling leaves' was easily won by Enrico Mollo, with Mario Cipriani out sprinting Gino for the second placing. The bookend events to the Italian season demonstrated Gino's ability as both a sprinter and a climber.

It was in two other tours that Gino's prowess as a climber was noticed. One was the Vuelta Ciclista al Pais Vasco – the Tour of the Basque Country – which had been founded in 1924 but had not been raced since 1930 due to conflict in Spain. Little known outside his native Italy, the young rider made his international mark in the Tour that would not be run again until 1969 when the great French rider, Jacques Anquetil would win it. Gino won stages two, three and five of the climber's race before taking overall victory in the August tour. The Basque tour predates the Vuelta a España by a decade, and was the major Spanish race in the early years.

It was in the Giro d'Italia that the young Gino impressed the *tifosi*. By the early 1930s, the Giro had become a truly European contest, with cyclists from France and elsewhere regularly crossing the Alps for a chance against the locals. For the first two decades of the Italian tour, only two foreigners had made the podium, Marcel Buysse's third to Girardengo in the resumption of hostilities after the Great War, and Jean Alavoine's third to Gaetano Bellini in 1920. As much as the Italian fans basked in the attention of the foreign competitors, they remained fiercely loyal to their local champions. When the great German rider, Herman Buse, a winner of the oldest monument, the arduous Liege-Bastogne-Liege, gained an 11 minute lead over his rivals after six stages of the 1932 Giro, the *tifosi* turned on their compatriots, accusing them of not trying. Whether it was the wrath of the masses, or the tactics of the locals, the Wolsit and Legnano teams combined their resources to deliver victory to Antonio Pesenti.

The Italians were on notice that they could not take their tour for granted. Apart from Buse, the 1932 peloton included the talented French rider, Antonio Magne, who withstood attacks by Pesenti and the Belgian, Joseph Demuysere, to claim the 1931 Tour de France. The taciturn Magne, nicknamed 'The Monk' for his shyness around journalists, did not fire in Italy, but went on to win the 1934 Tour and the 1936 World Championship. Kurt Stopel, the first German to wear the yellow jersey in the Tour, and who finished second to Andre Leducq because of the time bonuses for stage wins, eventually finished fifth to Pesenti in the Giro. The talented field also included Julian Vervaecke, winner of Paris-Roubaix, and Raymond Louviot, who would win the Grand Prix des Nations in 1933, and be crowned French National Champion in 1934.

The format of the Giro was also changing in the early 1930s, coming to resemble the modern Grand Tour. Instead of stages of several hundred kilometres, separated by rest days, more regular, shorter stages of an average of 180-200 kilometres became a feature. The critical ability to climb was formally recognised with the first award of the *Gran Premio della Montagna* – the King of the Mountains – that Alfredo Binda claimed as well as the overall General Classification victory in the 1933 Giro. In crowning a King of the Mountains and adding an individual time trial to the race format, the Giro was ahead of its great rival, the Tour de France.

Individual time trials against the clock had been a feature of competitive cycling from the earliest days. Team time trials had also been introduced in the early years of the Tour and the Giro, but it was not until 1933 that an individual time trial was incorporated into the Giro d'Italia. After the 1931 world Championship Road Race at Copenhagen had been conducted as a 170-kilometre time trial, there was little enthusiam for repeating the format. But the idea gained new currency when Gaston Benac, the enterprising Sports Editor of the *Paris-Soir* newspaper, a rival for *L'Auto*, decided to take a leaf from the page of his competitor by also establishing a cycling race. In order to cultivate a difference, Benac resolved upon an individual time trial, which he named the Grand Prix des Nations. The first event in 1932 was a gruelling 142-kilometre race against the clock, starting near the Palace of Versailles and traversing hills, cobbles and a forest before finishing on the Buffalo Velodrome in Paris. Maurice Archambaud, a short man with huge thighs like a modern track sprinter, won the event before setting the world one-hour record of 45.767 kilometres on the Vigorelli velodrome at Milan in 1937, a record that stood for five years until bettered by Fausto Coppi.

Noting the success of the Grand Prix des Nations, Armando Cougnet immediately included an individual time trial in the following year's Giro – a shorter 62-kilometre dash from Bologna to Ferrara. If the addition of the race against the clock was designed to even the balance that favoured climbers in the three week event, it had little effect in 1933, when Alfredo Binda demonstrated his superiority, clocking almost 40 kilometres an hour to defeat the Flandrian, Joseph Demuysere, by just over a minute. Binda's dominance of the race was complete: not only did he win a record fifth Giro, he claimed the Time Trial and the Climber's Classification. In all, the 'trumpeter of Cittiglio' wore the *maglia rosa* for 13 of the 17 stages. It was the culmination of an illustrious cycling career. Although he started the Giro twice more, Binda never stepped on the podium again, conceding two minutes in the 1934 Time Trial to Learco Guerra, the eventual winner, before crashing and abandoning the race. A broken femur in the 1936 Milan-San Remo brought to a conclusion the career of the second *campionissimo*.

As Binda's career was fading, Italy's next great champion was emerging. The 1935 Giro was to be the last for Binda – but the first for a young Gino Bartali. The discerning *tifosi* may have perceived that they were witnessing the end of one brilliant career – and the beginning of another, as the prodigious young climber demonstrated that he would be a force in the changing peloton. Winning the Tour of the Basque Country was an important milestone for the young Tuscan, but for Italians, only one Tour counted: the Giro d'Italia. In his first start in the Grand Tour, the young Gino demonstrated the awesome talent that would make him a new national hero within a year.

It was a strong field featuring not only Binda, but the ageing Girardengo, then 42-years-old, the previous year's winner, Guerra, Maurice Archambaud, winner of the first Grand Prix des Nations, and the two-time Tour de France victor, Andre Leducq. But it was the newer riders who blossomed. Guerra won a number of stages, but it was his *gregario*, Vasco Bergamasci, who would lead the peloton back to Milan. Over three mountain stages, the young Bartali smashed open the field, dropping many of the favoured riders in the process. In the seventh stage, the 21-year-old demonstrated his sheer power, riding off the front of the field over the Capannelle pass in Abruzzi, and finishing almost two minutes ahead of Ambrogio Morello and Bergamasci at L'Aquila. Bartali attacked again in the hilly 12th stage, going solo on the climb to Radicofani, before being caught by a small group, including Bergamasci, who prevailed in the finish at Florence and retained the *maglia rosa*. His daring climbing, now the talk of the *tifosi*, had burnt off the Giro favourites, including Leducq, who abandoned the race.

If Gino had not already established his credentials as a rising star of the peloton, he did so on the climb over the Sestriere Pass, the brutal ascent on the second last stage of the 1935 Giro. The young Tuscan crested the climb ahead of the field, cementing his claim on the *Gran Premio della Montagna* – the King of the Mountains title. It was a prestigious beginning to his Grand Tour career.

The dance of war

By the mid-1930's Mussolini's popularity had started to wane despite his national development plans. Although the Great Depression had less impact on the peninsula than elsewhere in Europe, Mussolini's economic plans were often conflicted and had mixed outcomes, partially because *Il Duce's* vision was for a nation established on ideological, rather than material foundations. His ideology, which took ancient Rome as its inspiration, was increasingly reflected in the overtly militaristic features of the totalitarian state. As popularity at home waned, Mussolini turned his attention to foreign interests, especially in Africa.

European designs on the African continent trace back centuries, but it wasn't until the 1800s with the abolition of the slave trade, the growing independence of other colonies and the expansion of commerce, including the construction of the Suez Canal, that colonisation of the continent intensified. Africa was the last of the continents that European nations colonised. The Spanish and Portuguese had swept through South America in the previous centuries; the British East India Company was founded in 1757; and Australia had been settled later that century as the Americans won their independence from Britain. The process of African colonisation, which began in fits and starts, resulted in claims to vast areas by Britain, Portugal and France. In 1884, the German Chancellor, Otto von Bismarck, created an orderly process of further colonisation at the Berlin Conference, but this ended in a hectic scramble for huge tracts of the continent after Bismarck's departure from office. Resistance to settlement and conflict increasingly ignited towards the end of the 19th century as other nations, including Italy and Germany, sought to realise their designs on parts of Africa.

Italy's initial foray into Africa in the 1890s ended in disaster. In 1893, Prime Minister, Francesco Crispi, sent a force of nearly 18,000 troops into Ethiopia to unite the country with the existing Italian colonies in Eritrea and Somalia, only to have more than 5,000 of his soldiers killed in the 1896 Battle of Adwa after being outnumbered by the larger forces of Emperor Menlik. Riots broke out across Italy when the news of the rout reached the nation, and Crispi was forced from office.

A decade later, the Italian invasion of Libya was militarily more successful, but it came at a high economic cost and continuing Arab resistance for the following three decades. The conflict was ongoing when Mussolini grasped the Prime Ministership in the 1920s.

Imperial expansion and the creation of empire was a theme of the fascist ideology. Mussolini's stress on the need for colonial expansion was partially a response to his drive for a larger population, and partly a manifestation of fascism's militaristic bent. He supported terrorist groups in the Balkans in the mid 1920s, and later turned his attention to Africa in his quest to create a new Roman empire.

The ongoing local resistance to Italian colonisation of Libya erupted in the early 1930s, leading to harsh retaliation by Mussolini against the rebellious tribes. The fascists' use of deadly gas and the imprisonment of captured tribesmen in concentration camps evoked widespread condemnation. Driven by his belief in a glorious new Italy, Mussolini was unperturbed. He was already planning a return to Ethiopia, which he did in 1935, avenging the inglorious defeat the Italians had suffered four decades earlier. The invasion was popular at home, but it outraged the international community. The League of Nations imposed sanctions on Italy that placed more pressure on the nation's economy. Worse, countries were taking sides in a dance of war that would end in another terrible global conflict.

Despite his antagonism towards the Nazis after they assassinated the Austrian Chancellor, Englebert Dollfuss, a friend of Mussolini, in 1934, the reaction to the events in Africa increasingly drove *Il Duce* away from Britain, France and the allied powers. Antagonism towards France was not a new phenomenon in Italy: Crispi had endeavoured unsuccessfully to involve Bismarck in war against their common neighbour decades earlier. Mussolini increasingly referred to a 'Rome-Berlin axis'.

By the mid-1930s, many of the tensions that had been brewing across Europe morphed into civil conflict, especially in Spain. The 1920s and 30s witnessed increasing political turmoil on the Iberian peninsula as anarchists, monarchists, and republicans battled for national supremacy. Separatist movements, especially in the Basque – or *Euskaldunak* – north sought independence.

The origins of the deadly conflict trace back over a century to the growing tensions between adherents to the old monarchical order and the supporters of a new republican regime; between the Carlists who maintained the primacy of the Kingdom and the radicals of different persuasions who longed for change; between the Church and the new class of intellectuals who rejected it. A first republic had been created in 1873, only to be replaced by the monarchy the next year. Following the Great War, Spain found itself in the political and ideological turmoil that spread across Europe. A combination of the economic slowdown after the war, the influenza epidemic, an uprising in Morocco and domestic strikes added to the instability of the early 1920s.

A period of order and stability seemed to have returned to the country in the mid 1920s after General Miguel Primo de Rivera was appointed Prime Minister. This order rapidly descended into instability as the increasingly erratic de Rivera lost the confidence of even the military, and eventually, the king. When Alfonso XIII deserted the throne and fled the country after the Republicans won a landslide in the municipal elections of 1931, the second republic was proclaimed. But it would become engulfed in a terrible civil war that pitted Spaniard against Spaniard and ripped apart the country.

By 1935, wildcat strikes, open gang warfare between forces of the right and left, and riots broke out across the country. A military coup the following year morphed into an open civil war that would last three years and cost hundreds of thousands of lives. The historians, William and Carla Phillips, observed:

> All of the anger, frustration, class antagonism, and other corrosive forces that had eaten away at Spanish society for at least a century spilled over into the conflict, making the Spanish Civil War one of the worst internal confrontations in European history. Individuals defined their true loyalties based in religious adherence or rejection, political ideology, economic class, occupation, family history, or a combination of factors.

Many nations were so concerned about the conflation spreading beyond Spain that 27 countries signed an agreement not to take sides. Although Germany and Italy were signatories, they both entered the war on the side of the Nationalist forces of General Francisco Franco. In addition to planes, Mussolini sent about 120,000 Italian troops, almost half of whom were killed or injured in the bloody conflict.

About half a million people died during the war – in battle, air raids, disease and executions. The reprisals were brutal. Some 20,000 people, including nearly 7,000 Catholic priests and religious, were killed or executed by militants. While some Church officials and priests supported the Republicans, especially in the Basque areas, most favoured the Nationalists, especially when the Jesuits were banned and the new republican government sought to remove Church involvement from education. The experience of the Spanish Civil War had a chilling impact on the leaders of the Church throughout Europe and beyond.

Many leading figures on both sides were executed, including Jose Antonio and Fernandez, the sons of Primo de Rivera, and founders of the Falange fascist party. Another 200,000 republican prisoners were to die from disease, malnutrition and executions. The forces of Franco eventually prevailed in the terrible conflict, leading Britain, France and the United States to recognise the new government in 1939. As the world breathed a sigh of relief at the conclusion of the horrific conflict, another more deadly war was about to engulf Europe. Hitler, who had sent airforce squadrons to Spain, was on the march. And Mussolini was in lockstep with him.

Tensions increased across Europe as the Spanish war dragged on. Mussolini increasingly aligned with Germany where Hitler asserted his supremacy. The prospects of accommodation with France and Britain receded by the month. Mussolini was feted by the Nazis on a visit to Germany in early 1937, where he addressed huge crowds and pronounced his intention to march together with Hitler. Christopher Duggan writes:

> Hence forward Mussolini was to all intents and purposes in thrall to Germany; and under the influence of nazism, fascism underwent a final metamorphosis, reverting to its anti-bourgeois radicalism of 1919-20 and attempting, with an air of almost comic absurdity, to manufacture the 'new man' that it so signally failed to create in the previous decade and a half.

Everyday life was little changed for most Italians, but the seeds of division, conflict and war were already germinating. These divisions would split Italy, pitting institutions against each other, and reaching into the lives of ordinary people. Even sporting stars like Gino Bartali would be affected. But little did the young Tuscan realise the turmoil that lay ahead as he prepared for his second season as a professional cyclist.

Triumph and turmoil

As the winter of 1935-36 drew to an end, and the northern snow receded, Gino stretched his training for the *Primavera*, the early one-day classic of the European season and the first of the monuments of cycling. It was to be a disappointing start to the season, with Bartali only managing to finish 23rd, 16 minutes down on the winner, Angelo Varetto. Yet, within three months, the great promise that Gino had displayed the previous season was fulfilled in the Giro d'Italia.

Bartali had been hired for the new season by Eberardo Pavesi, the savvy director of the Legnano team. Pavesi had assembled a formidable squad over the years. It was the choice of champions, Alfredo Binda and Learco Guerra.

Although Binda had retired, and French riders did not enter the 1936 Giro because of the fallout from Italy's incursions into Africa, the Grand Tour featured a stellar field of cyclists, including the ageing Girardengo. The first seven stages over relatively flat terrain resulted in a series of bunch sprint finishes featuring the pre-race favourite, Giuseppe Olmo, who had broken the world hour record the previous year. But it was two young professionals who made their mark in one of the most exciting tours ever raced.

Olmo took the honours on the first stage sprint into Turin, but lost the *maglia rosa* to the 21-year-old Aldo Bini who prevailed in the sprint into Genoa. The young Tuscan was to hold the famed jersey for the next four stages (although sharing it with Olmo for stage seven when tied on both points and time). Bini went on to finish second in the World Road Race at Bern later in the year, and to win the Giro di Lombardia and three more stages of the Giro d'Italia in 1937. Like so many talented riders, World War II interrupted Bini's career, although he won the Giro di Lombardia in 1942 and a stage of the Giro d'Italia again in 1946.

It was another young Tuscan, Gino Bartali, who was to turn the established order in the peloton on its head with a daring win in stage nine. At the conclusion of the previous stage Olmo held the *maglia rosa*, but four other riders were on the same time, with Bartali just 30 seconds behind them. Then came Gino's daring 200-kilometre ride from Campobasso to L'Aquila. Taking off on the first of the climbs at Macerone, the young rider began to draw out the peloton. On each succeeding climb at Rionero Sannitico, Roccaraso and Svolte di Popoli, he extended his effort, leading the experts following the race to predict he would crack on the last difficult climb to L'Aquila. But Bartali rode with eagle's wings, distancing the struggling field by more than 6 minutes on the final tough ascent to the mountainous town. It was probably the greatest stage win in the first quarter century of the Giro and one of the best of all time. The rookie Gino Bartali was about to become the new hero of Italian cycling.

Despite the loss of time, Olmo was not about to hand up the nation's greatest sporting trophy to the 22-year-old Tuscan. Three years older than Bartali, Olmo had displayed brilliance as an amateur, winning the national championship and finishing second in the World Road Race in 1931 before partnering with Guglielmo Segato and Attila Pavesi to claim the gold medal in the Team's Road Race at the Los Angeles Olympics. Olmo had won two stages of the Giro in his first attempt, and four in 1935 to stand on the lower step of the podium. The rider from Celle Ligure was also acclaimed on the track, finishing second in the Paris Six Days race in 1933 and breaking the World hour record on the Vigorelli velodrome in Milan. Coming into the 1936 Giro as the favourite, Olmo eventually won 10 stages in his attempt to wrestle the leader's mantle back from Bartali. After pulling back over four minutes, much of it in a 39-kilometre time trial from Padua to Venice, Olmo exploited Bartali's tendency to inattention to his competitors and his weakness in the race against the clock. His younger compatriot responded to the danger he faced, winning two more stages and eventually securing the overall laurels by 2 minutes 36 seconds. Olmo was to claim the National Road Race Championship that year, and win Milan-San Remo in 1938.

Gino Bartali had become a household name in Italy. Success brought its rewards, and its challenges. He was now earning a base salary of 22,000-lire a year, plus the considerable prize money from the team's many victories and places. Gino had to employ an assistant to help him with the flood of letters, many of them seeking an autographed postcard. Not all the mail was positive. Cycling attracted fierce loyalties, intense rivalries and excitable fans. Amongst the adoring messages in the mail were the spiteful notes and hateful remarks.

Best of all, Gino was able to support his family, purchasing a new, larger two-story home for his parents closer to Florence. His father's reluctance about his son pursuing his ambitions as a cyclist was now replaced by an intense pride in Gino's achievements. But that celebratory world was about to come crashing down.

Gino's younger brother, Giulio was excelling in the amateur ranks, winning and placing in many races. Nothing pleased the older sibling more than to go riding with his younger brother, whom he believed was the more talented of the two. He looked forward to when they could ride together in the professional ranks, and for Giulio to reach the same dizzying heights on the national sporting stage.

A week after his stunning success in the Giro, the new cycling hero went to Turin to race, but widespread storms across the north of the country forced the cancellation of the event. Back in Tuscany, Giulio, by then the best amateur in the province, started another race, also in wet conditions. On a muddy descent, a car veered towards the three leading riders. Giulio's breakaway companions narrowly avoided a collision, but the younger Baratali was badly hit, breaking bones and suffering internal injuries. Taken to hospital, he was operated on and received blood transfusions, but died holding Gino's hand.

The Bartali world came crashing down. Torello's worst fears had come to pass. Giulia was heart-broken at the loss her younger son. And Gino was grief-striken, believing that his stubborn insistence on being a cyclist had led to the death of Giulio. It was a shattering event that turned his world upside down. An introspective Gino immersed himself in his Catholic faith with profound consequences in the coming years.

7

Triumphs and Tensions

We do not argue with those who disagree with us, we destroy them
-- Benito Mussolini.

The tour chooses its champions where the mountains bear the snows of winter
-- Phil Liggett.

A mood of deep melancholy engulfed the 22-year-old Gino Bartali. In 1936, people didn't speak of depression as we do today; but it is likely that Gino was seriously depressed. It was his determined insistence to become a cyclist that ultimately led Torello to allow his sons to race. Yes, there had been considerable pressure. Even the parish priest had championed Gino's cause. For a devout, Italian Catholic family, this was influential. But Gino was grief-stricken and guilt-ridden about Giulio's death.

Every generation aspires to a better future for their children. It is every parent's worst nightmare to bury a child. Torello and Giulia had just consigned Giulio to his grave. Part of their life and its purpose had been taken from them. Any discussion of cycling was forbidden in the house. Heartbroken, Gino quit cycling, just a week after he had attained the one of the highest accolades of his sport, the victory laurels of the Giro d'Italia.

Instead of venturing out onto the familiar roads and hills of Tuscany, Gino retreated to the anominity of a beachside house. There he churned over the events of the previous few days, along with the

Alfredo Binda, the first World Road Race Champion (1927) and the second *campionissimo*.

now bitter-sweet memories of joyous times with the brother he would no longer see. Death has finality about it; and grief has many stages. What to make of this tragedy became Gino's consuming passion. "It's destiny," he told his grieving father, but he knew that was an inadequate response.

Already a devout Catholic, Gino turned increasingly to his faith to explain the tragedy, and, more importantly, to shape his response. Reflecting on his life, he recognised his own indulgent existence, fixated on performance and success. Slowly he came to believe that his cycling, his natural ability, his hard work, and the fame it brought had to be in aid of something more, in service of a cause greater than himself and his own desires. The Gino Bartali who returned to Florence eight weeks later was a changed person; a young man whose talent on the bicycle was not an end in itself, but part of a greater design.

This new certainty didn't occur overnight; there were still many regrets and doubts, but assisted by friends and supporters, Gino gradually returned to the world of cycling. What else could he do? Like many young people of his era, not a good student, and only partially educated, his prospects were limited. Success at cycling was not assured, and could come crashing down in an instant, as Giulio's death had revealed, but it was what Gino knew best and was very good at. Slowly he concluded that his future prospects were in the world of racing, but his life involved more than life on the bike. This realisation would shape his life, both on and off the bike, for years to come.

With the encouragement of friends, fans and teammates, Gino Bartali returned to training. Five months after his victory in the Giro, Gino capped off his topsy turvy year by winning the Giro di Lombardia, traditionally the last major race on the European calendar. His victory over Diego Marabelli, who subsequently won three stages of the Giro, and the Italian born, French-based climber, Luigi Barral, marked the return of the young champion to the national sporting spotlight.

Rising tensions

By 1937, tensions deepened throughout Europe with the rise of Hitler in Germany, Mussolini's campaign in Africa, and the civil war across Spain. Two years earlier, Hitler had violated the Treaty of

Versailles, introducing conscription and rebuilding the German armed forces, while reassuring worried neighbours that his intentions were benign. Increasingly, the tentacles of the fascist regimes in Germany and Italy reached into everyday life, including the world of sport. The incursion of the political into the sporting reached a zenith with the 1936 Berlin Olympics.

Although the Games of the XI Olympiad had been awarded to Germany before Hitler came to power, and he was ambivalent about them, his propaganda chief, Joseph Goebbels, was excited about the opportunity to project the superiority of the Aryan race. Hitler had banned Jews from the German team, including some of the best athletes in the world, as part of his master plan, while persuading other concerned nations to participate. The Games were a massive public relations exercise for the Nazi regime. Goebbels commissioned the renowned movie director Leni Riefenstahl, who had produced the Nazi propaganda documentary, *Triumph of Will*, to film the events. Her cinematic masterpiece, shown in two parts as *Olympia* in 1938, depicted voiceless athletes in almost machine-like motion. Afro-American athletes competing at the Games were referred to as 'American Black Auxiliaries' by German broadcasters, and the great sprinter, Jesse Owens, as 'the Negro Owens'. His two world records and four gold medals agitated the *Führer*, but he was overjoyed that Germany triumphed over the United States winning 33 gold and a total of 89 medals to 24 and 56. The Nazis had commandeered sport to their cause: "Like the bludgeon of Thor's hammer on white-hot steel, the feet of our cyclists pushed our opponents into the dust. Our young, Aryan warriors triumphed and the medals were ours." Sport had become another tool of the fascist regime. Gino Bartali would experience it in the coming years.

Turning point

Giulio's death remained with Gino for the rest of his life. It was a defining moment that cemented his determination and focussed his attention. His religious faith became the bedrock of his life. Like many Catholic children of the era, the young Bartali joined the Catholic Action youth wing while still at school. The *Azione Cattolica Italiana* – Catholic Action – had been established in 1905 by Pope Pius X in response to what the Church perceived as the growing threats of modernism, many adherents of which rejected religious belief. Established as a non-political lay organization and favoured by Pope Pius XI over the short-lived *Partito Popolare*, Catholic Action quickly grew within the structure of parishes and dioceses across the nation. By the end of the 1920s, it had more than half a million youth members. Counting parents and supporters, the organisation had enormous influence throughout Italy. Although Mussolini abolished political parties, including the Catholic *Partito Popolare Italiano*, Catholic Action, as a non-political movement, remained a vibrant and countervailing force to fascism.

The Bartali family built a small chapel in the new family home, which was blessed by the Archbishop of Florence, Cardinal Elia Dalla Costa. While it was common for Catholic families to display a religious symbol, such as the cross or a small shrine to the Madonna, outside their home, and some had a prayer space, a blessing by the Cardinal Archbishop was a rare event for an ordinary family. But the Bartali's were no longer ordinary. Winning the Giro d'Italia had thrust Gino into the national sporting spotlight. He attracted not only the fierce interest of the *tifosi*, but the attention of the powerful in both Church and State. As a national sporting hero, the 22-year-old Bartali was the ideal model for Catholic youth. Increasingly he engaged in the activities of the movement, often speaking to youth groups about his life and faith. The Cardinal Archbishop became a family friend, officiating at his wedding in 1940. It was to become a critical friendship in Gino's life.

Bartali had regained all his enthusiasm for life and cycling as the grey days of the 1937 winter gradually lengthened and abundant sunlight returned to the skies of northern Italy. He didn't feature in the traditional opening foray of the season, the 280-kilometre slug from Milan to San Remo. It was claimed by another Tuscan, Cesare Del Cancia, who had won Milan-Turin the previous year and would take stages of the Giro in the future. Del Cancia skipped away from Pierino Favalla, the former national amateur champion, who would go on the win Milan-Turin three times, and finally claim *La Classicissima* in 1941. Marco Cimalli, who had teamed with Paolo Pedretti, Alberto Ghirardelli and Nino Borsari to win the team's pursuit at the 1932 LA Olympics, outkicked the bunch for the third position. Borsari later immigrated to Australia, establishing a well-known bicycle shop in the

Melbourne suburb of Carlton and becoming a leading business and sporting figure in the city.

Gino had a far more ambitious plan for the year, to do what no other rider had ever accomplished: to win the Giro and the Tour in the same year. He had an interrupted preparation for the great stage race, contracting bronchial pneumonia after being caught in the snow and rain during a training ride from Milan to Florence. When the peloton assembled in Milan for the 23-stage, 3,835-kilometres epic, the defending champion was still recovering from the infection that had interrupted his training schedule. Although favourite to repeat his dominance of the race, the early stages were claimed by independent and largely unknown riders before the powerful Frejus team of Giovanni Valetti and Olimpio Bizzi secured the next two finishes.

On the fifth day of competition, the cyclists faced a 20-kilometre team's time trial at Viareggio, the first-ever in the Giro, followed by a 114-kilometre race to Livorno. Bartali's powerful Legnano team won the time trial, putting the Tuscan favourite into the pink jersey. Bizzi spreadeagled the field in the afternoon, while Bartali lost time, handling the *maglia rosa* back to Valetti. With the reigning national champion, Giuseppe Olmo, struggling, the Giro was turning into a duel between Valetti and Bartali.

In the 20-kilometre uphill time trial at Monte Terminillo, Bartali gained almost a minute over Valetti on the snow covered slopes, to claim a narrow 20-second lead on General Classification. The two had drawn five minutes clear of Severino Canavesi as the Giro edged towards the half way point. Although out of contention for overall victory, the 35-year-old Learco Guerra out-sprinted the peloton into Naples. It was to be a bitter-sweet victory: his last stage win in his last Giro. The next day, the 'human locomotive' quit the race altogether.

Bartali's strengths and flaws were on display in the following stages. He soloed away from the peloton over the Apennines and led an escape in the following hilly stage, only to to miss a breakaway including his rival Valetti as the race returned to the north of the peninsula. With a 2 minute 40 second advantage, the 1937 Giro d'Italia would be decided in the Dolomites, which had been included in the national tour for the first time.

Cycling and the Story of Italy

In the first ascent of what have become regular stages of the Giro d'Italia, the Passo Rolle and the Passo Costalunga, Gino Bartali stamped his authority on the race, cresting both summits ahead of the peloton and taking almost 6 minutes from Enrico Mollo and Giovanni Valetti on the finish line at Merano. He had secured back-to-back victories in Italy's greatest sporting event. At just 23, he had secured his place in the pantheon of cycling greats.

Although Bartali had triumphed in the Giro, the effort in addition to his incomplete preparation took its toll. As July approached, he gradually realised that he had not recovered sufficiently from the punishing impact of the Italian race, and would have to abandon his dream of the Giro-Tour double. A clash with the fascists was about to occur.

Shattered dreams

For a professional cyclist like Gino Bartali, a niggling infection can be the difference between success and failure, between racing and having to rest from competition. Cycling hundreds of kilometres each week is a massive strain on the body, even for well-trained athletes who spend years developing their strength and speed. Driven champions are loathe to surrender to illness and miss an important race, especially one they had been aspiring to win, but they also learn that ongoing success requires a full recovery from injury and illness. Such was the position that Gino Bartali found himself in as the Tour de France inched closer in 1937. Reluctantly, he concluded that he could not compete in France.

Bartali's physical condition was a trifling excuse for the fascist regime. Believing that Italy's international standing had to be regained, and victory by their greatest sportsman in the Tour would garnish prestige, the fascists were furious. Notably the Party Secretary, Achille Starace. A decorated officer in the Great War, Starace was a fanatical supporter of Mussolini, becoming Party Secretary in 1931. He took leave of absence from his position to participate in the invasion of Ethiopia. He was an accomplished horseman and sports fanatic who also served as president of the fascist controlled Italian Olympic Committee. For Starace, sport was an obsession, and its propaganda value to the regime enormous. Although once described as "an obedient cretin" by Mussolini, who would end his days strung upside down next to *Il Duce*, in 1937 he was all-powerful.

The young Gino Bartali felt the full force of the fascist regime. Its paper, *Il Popolo d'Italia*, led the assault in the media, insisting that the country's national honour was at stake, suggesting – falsely – that Gino was demanding a fee of 200,000 lire, mocking his faith, and threatening his future. The naked power of fascism was on full display in the public square. Whether he liked it or not, whether he was fit enough to compete, Bartali was being ordered, like a soldier, to defend the national pride of fascist Italy. For a young man in Bartali's position, the threats were real. It was believed by many that the great cyclist, Ottavio Bottecchia, had been killed by the fascists for expressing his socialist sympathies. Mussolini himself was implicated in the assassination of the Deputy, Giacomo Matteotti, and the world heavyweight boxing champion, Primo Carnera, had his passport revoked once he failed to win international bouts. Athletes were not just sportsmen and women; they were ambassadors for the fascist regime abroad. International sport was a propaganda arm of fascism and its participants were puppets for the regime. Such was the control of the nation and the pervasive influence of the regime, that Bartali lined up with the 95 other starters in Paris on June 30.

Apart from Bartali, who started the favourite after his Giro victory, the Tour promised a re-run of the duel between the French and the powerful Belgians from the previous year. The Belgium team included Romain Maes, who had defeated the Italian *isolato*, Ambrogio Morello, and his compatriot, Félicien Vervaecke, the previous year; Sylvère Maes, who had also ridden as an individual in 1936, Marcel Kint, and Vervaecke. It was an impressive team of hard riders from the northern stronghold of European cycling. Pitted against them was an exciting group of locals, including the 1931 and 1934 winner, Antonin Magne, the 1933 victor, Georges Speicher, Maurice Archambaud and Rene Le Greves. Overseeing the Italian squad as the *Directeur-Sportif* was the original *campionissimo*, Costante Girardengo.

Individual riders, such as Maes and Vervaecke the previous year, were still an integral part of the Tour. The gruelling challenge of the great endurance races attracted a hardy band of adventurers, who, without any support, could challenge the best professional teams in the world. Henri Desgrange encouraged them, not just to make up the numbers, but because they represented his enduring vision for the *Grand Boucle*, a contest of man and machine, alone against the elements, in which only the strongest and fastest would emerge victorious. One of them, Mario Vicini, would eventually stand on the podium as the runner-up in the 1937 Tour. Vicini later rode for a number of teams, including Bianchi, and won the Italian Road Championship in 1939.

Henri Desgrange was a stickler for tradition. Very little would change in the three decades in which he directed the Tour, often leading to heated arguments with riders who had transgressed one or other of his autocratic rules. By 1936, Desgrange, then 71, was ailing, and had to hand the directorship of the race to Jacques Goddet, the son of Victor Goddet, who had been the Chief Financial Officer of *L'Auto* when the race was created all those years ago. With the younger Goddet taking full control of the 1937 race, one of the most significant changes was made to the event. The newly invented derailleur gearing system, which had been used in the Giro since 1933, and was allowed for individuals, was finally permitted for the professional teams. Technology had forced eventual change, as occurred in subsequent decades with aerobars, new materials such as carbon fibre, and radio communications with team directors. Without the revolutionary gearing, professionals were being beaten by the best individuals, especially on mountainous climbs.

The strong *rouleurs* dominated the early flat stages before the 1937 Tour reached the alps. After two days in the mountains, Bartali charged to a 9 minute 18 second lead over the Belgium individual, Edward Vissers, and the German, Erich Bautz. For the totalitarians and the *tifosi* alike in Italy, it appeared that their great hope would achieve the unprecedented: the Giro-Tour double in the same year. Across Italy, people, were glued to their radios, and eagerly awaited their morning newspapers to learn of the fate of their national hero. But no sooner had Bartali inflated national pride then his achievements came crashing down. Crossing a bridge on the following stage, Gino found himself falling headlong into the Calais River after crashing over a teammate, Jules Rossi, who had lost his wheel on the narrow wooden structure. Another teammate, Francesco Camusso, dragged the bloody and bruised Bartali from the shallow stony river where he remounted his bike. Despite the pain from the fall, Bartali completed the stage to Briançon, finishing ten minutes down on the winner, Otto Weckerling, but still in the *maillot jeune*, with a two minute lead over Bautz.

Still suffering from the shock and pain of his fall, the Giro winner started the next arduous stage, which included climbs over three 2,000 metre cols, the Izoard, the Vars and the Allos. While Camusso served as a faithful *gregario* for his team leader, Bartali's customary strength in the mountains deserted him. Already weakened by his previous illness and the arduous Giro, he lost more than 22 minutes to the stage winner, Roger Lapébie. But Gino Bartali was not about to give up on his dream. Supported by his teammates, he fought on for the next three stages. Although he had an obvious interest in the Italian remaining in the race, Henri Desgrange observed that Bartali appeared to be regaining his health and strength as each day passed. Then came the blow. The Italian Cycling Federation withdrew their champion from the race.

Gino was devastated. When unwell, he was ordered to race; when injured, ordered to continue; and when recovering, ordered to withdraw! The resentment towards the fascists that he harboured was now manifest. Rather than have their sporting 'ambassador' beaten, they demanded he abandon. The indignity was profound. And his dream to be the first cyclist to win the two Grand Tours in the one year had been shattered. That honour awaited his future nemesis, Fausto Coppi.

The Tour finished amidst controversy. With the Belgian, Sylvère Maes, leading the local hope, Roger Lapébie, the French fans entered the fray, pushing their hero up steep hills. Lapébie was caught holding onto a team car on the steep ascents, and drafting behind them on the flat, only to receive a minor time penalty. The Belgian exasperation reached a crescendo when a railway signalman lowered crossing gates after Lapébie had passed and just before the chasing group including Maes. Although in the yellow jersey, the Belgians quit in protest, leaving the victory to the French, ahead of the talented individual, Mario Vicini. It was to be the last year that individuals rode the Tour, as Goddet replaced them with two new groups, Cadets and Bleuets, to make up the numbers in 1938.

In the meantime, Bartali had returned to Italy. He was left to find his own way home by the Italian Cycling Federation, having to borrow money for the train ticket. Unable to protest the unfairness of his treatment, except in the family home, Gino let his legs do the talking. In October, he won the Giro del Piemonte before finishing runner-up to his junior arch rival, Aldo Bini in the final outing for the season, the Giro di Lombardia. It had been another eventful year for the young star.

As the autumn leaves fell from the trees, and the hours of light contracted, Gino was able to take a break from cycling and enjoy the Christmas ceremonies in Florence. As the new year approached, he renewed his aspiration to become the first cyclist to win the Giro-Tour double. Little did he expect that the fascists would thwart his plans again, but they did.

Because the Tour primarily comprised national teams, the Italian Cycling Federation decided who rode in it – and who did not. And the Federation was directly controlled by the Fascist Party. Even if it could not directly decide who would ride, the fascist influence was all pervasive. By 1938, few aspects of national life were not directed by Mussolini's machine. This was especially the case when international prestige was at stake. Winning at international sport was a priority. Apart from the World Cup, of which the Italians were the reigning football champions, the Tour de France was the most prestigious event in the world. Believing that Gino's failure in the previous Tour was a consequence of the taxing effort of winning the Giro, they reasoned that he would claim international victory for the regime if he started only in the later event. Despite his protestations that he could win both grand tours, Gino was told he had no choice: it was the Tour or nothing. The decision was his to make, but the threatening tone was clear. If he cared for his cycling career – and his future – he would take their 'advice'. He knew he had little choice, but was unsettled and unnerved by the situation.

Shifting alliegences

By early 1938, the deadly Spanish Civil War was drawing towards its final conclusion, with the forces of General Franco succeeding against their rivals. Mussolini had attracted international ire for his foray into

Ethiopia, while Hitler was amassing his forces in Germany. Treated as a pariah, Mussolini looked to new alliances. In the shifting sands of international relations, he reached out to Hitler, despite his earlier condemnation of the Nazis over their activities in Austria.

The war in Abyssinia (Ethiopia), which broke out in late 1935, exposed shifting allegiances and opportunistic decisions in Europe. In December that year, the United Kingdom Foreign Minister, Samuel Hoare, and the French Prime Minister, Pierre Laval, proposed to partition Abyssinia to end the brutal conflict. There is little doubt that the Italian forces perpetrated atrocities against the Ethiopians. Under the command of Rodolfo Graziani, more than 20,000 Ethiopians were massacred at Addis Ababa alone.

When the proposed partition became public, it was met with widespread outrage and indignation. It also strengthened the bonds between Germany and Italy. "Between Germany and Italy there exists a community of destiny," said Mussolini, "which was bound to become stronger and stronger." While the Italian leader grasped the opportunity to strengthen his position vis-a-vis Britain and France, Hitler played a double game, supplying weapons and coal to Italy, but also providing arms to the Ethiopian Emperor, Haile Selassie. His actions prolonged the conflict, distracting other nations from his rearmament at home and his intentions for Austria.

Mussolini decided to woo Hitler by inviting him on a state visit to Italy in May. While Gino Bartali was ruing his exclusion from the Giro, which was won by Giovanni Valetti, *Il Duce* was hosting the *Feuhrer* on a whirlwind visit to Italy. No expense was spared to showcase the southern nation. Millions of lire were expended on renovating buildings and sprucing-up the three cities that Hitler visited: Milan, Rome and Florence. The German dictator was treated to grand parades, feted at the Opera and State dinners, and impressed by the apparent might of Italy's military forces. Swastika banners were unfurled alongside Italian flags on the major thoroughfares of the cities, and 'undesirables' removed from the streets in a massive effort to impress Hitler. From his first enthusiastic handshake with Hitler to his final declaration that "no force can ever separate us," Mussolini set out to impress the German Chancellor. And succeed he did: within two years, the two nations would be allies in another war even more deadly that the one that had occurred just two decades earlier.

In the meantime, sport had become the proxy contest in the battle of international rivalries. The intense feelings of football fans at the 1938 World Cup in France, at which the *Forza Italia* team was the defending champion, ignited national passions back in Italy. When the Italians turned out in black shirts, they were met with the loud derision of the French, much to the chagrin of the fascist controlled press. Not that the French were selective; they greeted the German team with even greater protests. These demonstrations heightened fascist paranoia on the peninsula. When the Italians eventually prevailed in the final, defeating Hungary 4-2, the win was more than a victory in international sport: it was a validation of the place, primacy and pride of fascism. The winning team was feted by the fascists and photographed with Mussolini in their military uniforms. It was against this backdrop that Gino Bartali, Mario Vicini, Giuseppe Mattano, Jukes Rossi, Aldo Bini and Vasco Bergamschi prepared to take the train to Paris for the 1938 Tour de France. It was no longer just a bike race: it had become a test of national pride, ideological superiority, and the iron will of the fascist regime. At the apex of this expectation was a 24-year-old cyclist, Gino Bartali. On his shoulders – more precisely on his legs – were the expectations of Mussolini's Italy.

In its century-long history, few editions have carried the acute interest as the 1938 Tour de France. The 4,694-kilometre event was run in a counter-clockwise direction, racing south from the French capital to the Pyrenees before turning eastward to the Alps and returning to Paris. The fascists had reason to presume that their countryman would prevail in the great enduro. Not only was Bartali the favourite, but the team also comprised a previous Giro winner, Bergamaschi, and Vicini, the runner-up in the 1937 Tour. Directing them was one of the greatest riders of all-time, Costante Girardengo.

The French team included the great champions, Antonio Magne and Georges Speicher, but both were probably past their prime. The greatest threat to Italian dominance was from the Belgiums, the hard men of European cycling. The team comprised Sylvère Maes, who won in 1936 – and probably should have won the following year, Félicien Vervaecke, who was hungry for victory after a second and 2 third placings, Marcel Kint, Eloi Meulenberg, Jukes Louie and Ward Vissers. Then there were the riders who comprised the Cadets and the Bleuts, the new categories devised by Jacques Goddet. Amongst them, André Leducq, the victor in 1930 and 1932, and René Vietto, who had sacrificed his chances in the 1934 Tour for his team leader, Antonin Magne. When told that Magne had crashed behind him, the 20-year-old Vietto rode back down the Col de Portet d'Aspet to give Magne his bike, losing his chances of victory in the process.

At 34-years of age, Leducq was considered by many as past his prime, but what the native of Saint-Ouen lacked in speed and power, he compensated with his guile and the ability to read an unfolding race. This talent was on display in the early, relatively flat stages as the peloton sped south towards the first great upwards encounters of the Tour. Leducq was in second placing after the first two stages, and then jumped into a breakaway towards the end of the first week, gaining almost two minutes on the peloton, and claiming the *maillot jeune* once again. The 1924 Olympic Gold Medallist and winner of both Paris-Roubaix and Paris-Tours demonstrated that he was not yet a spent force.

The 1938 Tour had not begun in earnest as the major contenders watched each other closely as they pedalled through the rolling farmlands of central France. It was at the start of the second week that the race came alive. Stage eight was a monstrous series of climbs through the Pyrenees, the great mountain range on the border of France and Spain. At first considered too imposing for the cyclists, the massive climbs of the south were only added to the Tour in 1910.

Facing the cyclists as they departed Pau were a succession of arduous climbs over four massive cols, the Aubisque, the Tourmalet, the Aspin and the Peyresourde. Their destination, Luchon on the Spanish border, involved more than 4,000 metres of climbing in the 190-kilometre stage. The race was suddenly going uphill, and the climbers would come to the fore. On the first climb of the Aubusque, the slight Italian emerged from the peloton, pushing ahead of his fellow cyclists on the punishing slopes. By the summit, the figure in green, white and red was alone. He was joined by two Belgians on the descent, only to drop them, one by one, on the Tourmalet. He repeated the effort on the Aspin, alone now amongst the throngs of people who crowded the remote mountain paths.

Television viewers of the contemporary Tour watch the tens of thousands of fans who crowd the climbs of the modern race, often camping out for days to catch a glimpse of their heroes struggling up the steep ascents. From the earliest days of the races, fans made their way, by car, bus and foot to the remote mountain passes to cheer on the cyclists. It was no different in 1938. Thousands lined the slopes of the famous cols, some coming from as far away as Paris by train. And they could be as boisterous and unmanageable as the cheering French, Italian, Dutch and Germans of later years. On the dangerous descent, one of the thousands of spectators ran in front of Bartali, causing a crash. Uninjured himself, Gino had to replace a broken wheel, allowing Vervaecke to catch him again. Bruised and battled, Bartali lost time on the final climb of the Peyresourde, finishing the stage 55 seconds behind the winner and 2 minutes and 18 seconds behind his Belgian rival on General Classification. For the tens of thousands of cheering fans who lined the narrow gravel tracks, the stage had surpassed Henri Desgrange's prediction that it would be "the most important of the Tour."

The brutal stage had smashed the peloton. Some of the best riders in Europe, including Vicini, Magne, Leducq and Maes, were up to half an hour behind the leading trio. Others were eliminated for missing the time limit. Georges Speicher's tour came to an inglorious end when he was disqualified for clinging to a car on the climbs. Félicien Vervaecke's lead see-sawed up and down over the next few stages, losing time on climbs but gaining against Bartali in an individual time trial, one of the Italian's weak links. By the time the peloton reached the Alps, the scene was set for a major showdown between the leading protagonists. It came on stage 14, the gruelling 219-kilometre climb over the Allos, the Vars and the Izoard from Digne to Briançon. It was to be the day that Gino Bartali exorcised the demons of 1937 and joined the pantheon of the greatest cyclists of all time. If he needed it, two events that day encouraged the young star: first his father visited before the start at Cannes, a year after the death of Giulio; and then massive crowds of the Italian *tifosi* lined the daunting climb of the Izoard to urge on their countryman.

"The mountain is there and you have to confront it alone," Gino was later to write. At first only one rider, the talented Belgian, Ward Vissers, was able to stay with Bartali as they ascended the 2,250-metre gravel strewn Col d'Allos. Vissers was a powerful criterium and *kermesse* rider in Belgium, but could also climb well on the steep slopes of France. Bartali sprinted over the crest of the first ascent, winning bonus points and dropping Vissers in the process. The Italian led again over the Col d'Vars, only to flat on the descent and loose the lead to his teammate, Mario Vicini. But it was on the unrelenting Izoard that he triumphed, defeating Vicini by over five minutes, and with the help of time bonuses, stamping a 17 minute 45 second lead over the Luxembourg cyclist, Mathias Clemens, on General Classification. It was the stage on which Gino Bartali won the Tour de France. He demonstrated his climbing prowess again on the final mountain stage over the Col de la Faucille, extending his lead over Vervaecke to more than 20 minutes. Feeling unwell, Bartali rode within himself on the following stage over the Galibier and Iseran, but still finished a few seconds behind the winner, Marcel Kint, while two of his main rivals, Mathias Clemens and Félicien Vervaecke struggled to the finish with the main peloton some 25 minutes later. The rest of the Tour was a procession for the yellow jersey wearer, even though he conceded almost two minutes to his nearest rival in the final 42-kilometre time trial. Unlike today, when the final stage is a procession to Paris that ends with a final sprint on the Champs-Élysées, the ultimate day was then contested like any other. Short of a disaster, the podium had already been decided, with Bartali over 18 minutes ahead of Vervaecke, and close to half an hour in advance of Victor Cosson. In the circumstances, the peloton honoured two previous dual winners of the *Grand Boucle*, Andre Leducq and Antonio Magne, who together entered the Parc de Princes velodrome some five minutes ahead for their final appearance in the Tour. Hand in hand, they crossed the finish line to the thunderous applause of the tens of thousands of Parisians, a fitting farewell for two champions of the sport.

But the Grand Tour belonged to Gino Bartali whose domination in the mountain stages earned him both the General Classification and the Climber's Classification As he stood on the podium, absorbing the plaudits of victory in the world's greatest race, little could he know that he would not return to defend the title the following year, or, in fact, that it would be a decade before he again started in the Tour. There would be only one more Tour before the world descended into a great global conflict – and no Italian team would participate. As Gino Bartali journeyed back to his homeland by train, grave changes were already occurring

Learco Guerra, the first cyclist to wear the *maglia rosa* in the 1931 Giro d'Italia.

8

The March to War

A great tragedy was to befall us all
-- Gino Bartali.

Gino Bartali's victory in the 1938 Tour de France was embroiled in political controversy well before he stepped onto the podium at the Parc des Princes velodrome in Paris on the first day of August. Although the Italian cyclist had been vigilant to maintain his commanding lead in the final stages of the Tour, the press concluded the event was all but over, and hunted around for other related stories. Bartali's personal life, including his religious orthodoxy, became their fodder. In largely Catholic France, the attention was understandable, but it annoyed Bartali. He wanted to be judged by his performance on the road. Perhaps he also sensed that media attention to his religious faith would be viewed with hostility by Mussolini's regime. While French nationalism was always a potent force, especially in international sporting competitions, Gino's faith served to differentiate him in France from the fascist regime in Italy. Negotiating the tensions between his faith and the expectations of the Italian regime was to become a constant in his life.

Gino's victory in the Tour was leapt upon by the regime as proof of the physical and moral superiority of fascism. He was "holding high the colours of Fascist sport" proclaimed *Il Popolo d'Italia*, the paper founded by Mussolini. *Il Duce* announced that the champion cyclist was to be awarded a silver medal. Bartali said as little as he could about the political claims of the regime, but let his actions speak loudly.

GREAT RIVALRIES

A regular mass-goer, even during stage races like the Tour, Gino set out for the Place des Petits Peres with the press in tow the morning after his triumph. In his hand was the bouquet of flowers with which he had been presented for winning the Tour de France. Reaching his destination, he found an important Marian shrine, the church of Our Lady of Victories, where he prayed and placed the flowers at the foot of the Statue of the Madonna. Was it naievity to believe that he could still be an ordinary private person – or was Gino Bartali, the Tour de France winner who failed to praise the fascist regime in his victory speech, expressing much more through his actions that morning in Paris?

If Bartali had expected a rapturous return to his native land, he was to be disappointed. There was no meeting with Mussolini; no reception by the Italian Cycling Federation. Under orders from the regime, the Italian media henceforth only reported on his cycling – and not his personal life or other activities. Many modern sports men and women would welcome less intrusion into their private lives, but in fascist Italy, the direction carried worrying portents. Worse still, every action, intended or otherwise, was judged as indicating support for or rejection of the regime. Such was the World Championship Road Race in which the Tour de France winner was regarded as the clear favourite. As befitting it's status, the World crown, which carries the honour of wearing the rainbow stripes around the victor's jersey for the following year – and on his collar and sleeves forever – is one of the most difficult races of the season. Moving from country to country, and location to location, the terrain varies from year to year. Sometimes it favours climbers, sometimes *rouleurs*, sometimes *puncheurs*, and sometimes sprinters. It is generally over a course that is only ever raced once, making preparation difficult and knowledge of the challenge imprecise. Being the right rider on the right course at the right time has been a factor in many world championship races over the decades.

The 1938 Worlds were raced at Limburg in the Netherlands. Conducted in the undulating countryside, the 272-kilometre race favoured the *puncheurs* from the Low Countries who had grown up on the flat, windy roads and short steep *murs* of Flanders and the Netherlands. Bartali had been in sparkling form, so a win was a distinct possibility, and certainly expected by the Italian *tifosi*. When the Tour de France champion failed, blaming poor team strategy and mechanical problems, they were unhappy. Rather than acknowledging that the victor, Marcel Kint – who was a criterium champion, a good six-day racer and a one day specialist on the road, and who had won three stages of the Tour – was a worthy champion, they turned on Bartali. On his return to Italy, he was booed by the large crowd at Milan's Vigorelli Velodrome and at other races. It wasn't the end of the season that he had contemplated. On his final outing of the season, the Giro di Lombardia, he was beaten into second placing by Cino Cinelli on the famous ascents around Lake Como.

The reaction from the regime – and some of the passionate fans of the sport – to Bartali's less than enthusiastic embrace of fascism should have been a warning about things to come for the young cyclist. Before long, faith and fascism would be in direct conflict.

The sinister embrace

Mussolini's embrace of Hitler had sinister consequences for Italy. While Gino Bartali was battling Félicien Vervaecke and the boisterous crowds in the French Alps on Bastille Day, a more worrying event occurred in Italy. A startling document, the *Manifesto of the Racial Scientists,* was published in the *Giornale d'Italia.* Signed by a group of scholars from some of the nation's prestigious universities, the *Manifesto* asserted that there existed a pure Italian race, Aryan in origin and civilisation. Ominously, the document claimed that "Jews do not belong to the Italian race," that they "represent the only population which has never assimilated in Italy" and "the purely European character of the Italians would be altered by breeding with any other non-European race bearing a civilisation different from the millennial civilisation of the Aryans."

Proclaiming that "it is time that the Italians declare themselves racist," the document noted that references to racial concepts had been found frequently in the speeches of the Leader. It was subsequently revealed that the document had been written in one of the regime's propaganda arms, the *Ministero della Culture Popolare* (the Ministry of Popular Culture), by a young scholar, Guido Landra, under the directions of Mussolini himself. While the authors sought to distance themselves from the theories of German racism, the publication represented a sharp swing towards a new virulent anti-Semitism on the peninsula.

Prior to 1938, the country's small Jewish population had lived in relative harmony, largely in the northern regions, especially in Trieste, Livorno, Milan, Turin, Florence, Genoa and Ferrara. Intermarriage and cultural similarities with the predominant Catholic population had improved interfaith relations over the previous century. The three founders of modern Italy, Cavour, Mazzini and Garibaldi, had a great interest in and appreciation for the Jewish people. Jews served in the national parliament, on municipal councils, and as generals in the Great War. Europe's first Jewish Prime Minister, Luigi Luzzatti, held office in 1910, decades before any other country. Well educated, compared to widespread illiteracy of the general population, Jews rose to prominence in business and academia, as well as public life. For a small population of just 47,000 in 1938, Italian Jews were probably the most integrated of all in Europe.

The claim in the *Manifesto* that racial concepts had been found in the speeches of the leader was partially true, but self-serving. Mussolini had said as early as 1921 that Italians were a "Mediterranean and Aryan" race, but had not displayed any particular animosity towards Jews. At the time of the Lateran Treaty with the Vatican in 1929, *Il Duce* proclaimed:

> The Jews have been in Rome ever since the time of the Kings; perhaps it was they who supplied clothes after the rape of the Sabine women. There were fifty thousand at the time of Augustus, and they asked to weep on the corpse of Julius Caesar. They will stay here undisturbed.

Within a decade, this assurance had been sundered. Despite his earlier reference to Italians being an Aryan race, relations with Germany were wary, if not hostile, in the mid 1930s. Hitler's designs on Austria, including the assassination of its chancellor, Englebert Dollfus, triggered animosity, as did the flood of anti-Italian racial propaganda from the Nazis. Italians were 'Latin and Mediterranean', Mussolini told the Florentine Blackshirts.

By the mid 1930's this was changing. In 1936, his newspaper, *Il Popolo d'Italia*, published an anonymous article, later attributed to Mussolini himself, which argued that "anti-Semitism is inevitable wherever there is exaggerated Semitic visibility, interference, and arrogance." The article was part of an attack on the left-wing coalition government of the Jewish Prime Minister of France, Léon Blum. The French government, known as the Popular Front, had remained neutral about the Spanish Civil War and was fearful of the rising militarism in Germany.

Mussolini was increaingly in the thrall of Hitler, visiting Germany in 1937. Angered by Hitler's invasion of Austria, *Il Duce* proposed a summit, held in Munich, which appeared to guarantee European peace. His widespread reputation as a international peacemaker was shortlived: the German invasion of Czechoslovakia, the Italian armed incursion into Albania, and the 1939 'Pact of Steel' with Germany cemented Italy's fate. The world would soon be at war.

Misfortune or interference?

By early 1939, the *tifosi* were baying for the clash of the century. Never before had two reigning Italian Tour and Giro champions gone head-to-head in the nation's great three week event. Two Italians, Ottavio Bottecchia and Giuseppe Enrici, had won the Tour and the Giro in 1924, but neither were on the starting line at Milan for the *Corsa Rosa* the following year. The traditional opening race of the year, *La Classicissima di Primavera*, was a cracker of a contest, with five riders breaking clear as the race neared the seaside destination at San Remo on March 19. As the tight group of Bartali, Mario Vicini, Aldo Bini, Pietro Chiappini and Osvaldo Bailo charged to the finish, the young Tuscan came through to claim a narrow victory, the first of two consecutive wins prior to the war. The scene was set for the Giro d'Italia a few weeks later.

The excitement was palpable as the 89 riders gathered in the Milanese lamplight early in the morning of April 28, 1939. In addition to the *maglia rosa* and *maillot jeune* winners of the previous year, Giovanni Valetti and Gino Bartali, there was Mario Vicini, the runner-up in the 1937 Tour; the 1935 Giro victor, Vasco Bergamaschi; Severino Canavesi, a former national cyclo-cross champion; and Cino Cinelli, best known now for his racing bikes, but then the reigning Giro di Lombardia winner. Ahead of them was a 19-stage, 3,000-kilometre trek that would take them only as far south as Rome before the return journey back to Milan.

After Bergamaschi claimed the first stage to Turin, Bartali sought to establish his superiority, driving clear of the peloton with Cinelli and Vicini in the race to Genoa. The trio gained more than five minutes on the main group which included the Frejus team's defending champion, Giovanni Valetti. Bartali's early ascendency was short-lived, as he missed the break on the following stage, and finished seven minutes down on a powerful group that included Valetti. It wasn't the first occasion in which Bartali's seeming inattention to the flow of the peloton left him languishing behind a successful break. The young champion found himself on the defensive.

The beneficiary of Bartali's inattention was Cino Cinelli, who was in fine form in the 1939 spring. Vicini was second, but the favourites, Valetti and Bartali, were five and seven minutes in arrears. Although the defending champion, Valetti, clawed back time on the race leader on an individual hill climb on Monte Terminillo in central Italy, the Lombardia champion continued to lead the favourites by over three minutes after the first week of racing. As the Giro turned north, along the Adriatic coast, through Tuscany and then to the Dolomites, interest in the contest reached fever pitch amongst the *tifosi*.

Luck may be what happens 'when preparation meets opportunity,' but misfortune can also be a significant factor in sport, as in life. Cino Cinelli experienced this truism in the tenth stage when an errant motorcycle struck him, resulting in a loss of time and the leader's jersey. As the race reached the half way mark, both Valetti and Bartali began to claw their way back into the contest. With the additional incentive of the eleventh stage finishing in his home town, Bartali led the charge over the Passo del Muraglione to take the stage on the familiar roads of Florence. As the Dolomites beckoned, less than two minutes separated the first six riders on General Classification: Valetti, Cinelli, Vicini, Adolfo Leoni, Severino Canavesi and Bartali.

Any doubts about Valetti fighting to secure back-to-back Giro laurels were put to rest in the 40-kilometre Time Trial at Trieste. The defending champion was victorious in the race against the clock, taking time from both Vicini and Bartali. Once again the individual time trial proved to be a chink in Gino's otherwise impressive cycling armoury.

Valetti held a 3 minute, 59 second lead as the race entered the great mountain range of northern Italy. Ahead of the peloton was a gruelling 591-kilometre trek through the Alps over three stages, an average of almost 200 kilometres a day.

The sporting stage was set for one of the great mountain duels of the Giro d'Italia. As the field assembled near the Boite River in the southern Alps town of Cortina d'Ampezzo for the start of the next stage, Bartali knew he had to attack to take vital minutes and seconds back from the Piedmontese wearer of the *maglia rosa*. But try as he might, Valetti was proving resilient in the defence of his title. Bartali had been unable to drop the race leader on the previous stage climb over the Passo della Mauria. The Tuscan hero had only three stages before the peloton raced into Milan in which to claim time from Valetti.

The Passo Rolle is not the highest pass in the Italian Alps, but it is a brutal climb. It was there on the 256-kilometre race to Trento that Bartali attacked, leading the peloton over the ascent before forming a small group with Mario Vicini to drive the pace. The attack finally found Valetti wanting, with the *maglia rosa* losing almost eight minutes, leaving him down 3 minutes 49 seconds when the stage finished at Trento. With excitement mounting, it looked like the race was now down to two chances, with Vicini just 58 seconds in arrears of the new leader.

The penultimate stage, a 167-kilometre race from Trento to Sondrio, the alpine town to the east of the northern reaches of Lake Como, became one of the most controversial in Giro history. It would turn the race on its head. Knowing that he had to be assertive in order to regain lost time, Valetti went on the offensive, but Bartali dragged himself back to the leader. Luckily, Valetti's Frejus teammate clung to the Tuscan's rear wheel, allowing him to swap wheels when his leader flatted. Bartali wasn't waiting, charging away on the ascent of the Tonale, only to have the two Frejus riders catch him, setting the scene for an exciting finish.

It was then Bartali's misfortune to suffer a flat tyre and crash on the rough alpine roads. What happened next is the stuff of intrigue and contention. The Frejus team car slid and stopped on the snow-covered road, delaying Bartali's Legnano team car from quickly providing mechanical assistance. By the time the car had been moved, Valetti had escaped. Then to compound Bartali's woes, the Frejus mechanics appeared deliberately to have wrecked their rider's wheel when he flatted, allowing them to quickly replace the entire wheel, rather than having to change a tyre in the wet, freezing weather. Valetti had turned the tables on his rival, leading by almost three minutes with just the final stage to race.

Bartali tried once more on the last stage to Milan, escaping on the famous climb to the Madonna del Ghisallo church high above Lake Como, but the peloton worked with Valetti's team to bring him back. The Tuscan won the final sprint into Milan, but Valetti had secured back-to-back tours, only the fifth rider to do so since 1909.

Subsequent research suggests that Valetti's victory may have involved more than good fortune for him and bad luck for his rival. The Piedmontese cyclist was a member of the Young Fascists, one of Mussolini's favoured groups. His success – and the defeat of the prominent member of Catholic Action, Bartali, who was distrusted by the regime – was an endorsement for fascism. Did the Frejus team driver accidentally slip in the snow, or was the disruption intentional? And did the race officials overlook the destruction of Valetti's wheel when he flatted with Bartali giving chase? Valetti had been in sparkling form in 1939, claiming five victories including his second Giro, but he never performed at the same level again, finishing second in just one stage of the 1940 event, and a third in the 1941 Giro della Toscana. He had no success after the war, and faded into obscurity, a forgotten champion of the Giro d'Italia.

Only one more Giro would be conducted before the war, but the portents for Gino Bartali were long clear. His prominence as a member of Catholic Action had generated considerable antagonism from Mussolini's fascist regime. As Europe lurched towards another terrible conflict, Gino Bartali's life was about to be challenged both on and off the bike.

9

A Star is Born

He rides like a great artist painting a watercolour
-- 1930 and 1932 Tour de France winner, André Leducq, describing Fausto Coppi.

To wear the yellow jersey is to mingle with the Gods of cycling
-- Phil Liggett.

The owners and managers of the major cycling teams were always on the lookout for talented young riders who could fill the role of the *gregari*, the team mates who helped the champions and team leaders during each race. Gino Bartali's Legnano team was no different. When a little known 19-year-old, Fausto Coppi, started to impress the commentators in 1939, both Costante Girardengo's Maino team and Eberardo Pavesi's Legnano squad were eager to sign him on.

Angelo Fausto Coppi was born to Domenico Coppi and Angiolina Boveri on September 15, 1919, less than three months after the Treaty of Versailles, which formally ended the Great War, was signed. Domenico had served in the war, a lucky one who had survived the bombardments and bloody slaughter in the north east of the country. The Coppis were peasant farmers in the small village of Castellania near the foothills of the Apennines in the Piedmontese Province of Alessandria. Although better-off than some of their neighbours in the tiny comune of about 400 people, with a larger than usual land holding, their few hectares were insufficient to sustain a family of five children. Fausto was the fourth child born into the family, following his sisters, Maria and Dina, and an older brother, Livio. Four years later, a younger brother, Serse,

A reflective Fausto Coppi, the third *campionissimo*.

was added to the family. Like many small farmers in Italy, Domenico had to sustain the family income by taking on whatever work he could find in the area. Poor, but not destitute, the Coppis had some valuable local connections. Domenico's brother was the mayor, his sister-in-law the school teacher, and Angiolina's uncle the local priest. Like most couples of the era, they were a hardworking, God-fearing family, eking out an existence while endeavouring to provide a better life for their children.

The suggestion that the young Coppi would become one of the world's greatest cyclists would have been met with disbelief: scrawny and diminutive, Fausto appeared anything but a future champion. When not at school, or helping on the farm, he and Serse played in the neighbourhood with the other children. Forever serious, even seeming distant, Fausto was a keen student, but like most of his generation left school at 12 to work on the farm. The farm, with a few cattle, and small crops, could not sustain the growing family. Encouraged by his parents, the young teenager found work in a butcher's shop at Novi Ligure, 20 kilometres away on the other side of the Scrivia River Valley. As a growing rail and road junction between Milan and Genoa, the town offered better employment prospects for the young Coppi. Within a year, Fausto had moved to another butcher's shop, boarding for the week in Novi and returning home by bike each weekend. Homesickness led the young Coppi to propose riding to and from work each day. Riding rough roads on a heavy old bike he had rebuilt, Fausto made the 40-kilometre round trip each day, gradually building his strength on the ascent to Castellania in the evening. Whether it was the hot summer days of July, or the cold and wet slosh through the mud of winter, Fausto cycled the round trip throughout the week. In addition to the ride to and from Castellania, Fausto used his bike for the delivery of meat to local households. Unbeknown to his employer, he would often ride a longer loop, adding many more kilometres to his daily score. Gradually the slight figure with skinny legs built his strength, covering the distance to and from home in ever decreasing time. Using money that his seafaring uncle had given to him, Fausto purchased a shining new Girardengo bike.

By the early 1930s, Binda as the reigning *campionissimo* had eclipsed

Girardengo, but the first great champion remained a hero in his hometown of Novi Ligure. More significantly, Novi Ligure was the home of Biagio Cavanna, the legendary trainer, coach and confidant of Girardengo. As fate had it, he was also a friend and customer of Domenico Merlano, the proprietor of the butcher shop where the young Fausto worked.

Having outpaced a number of the local amateurs – as well as a former Giro d'Italia participant – while riding in the countryside, Fausto decided to try his luck in the local cycling races. He was about 15 when Cavanna first encountered the slight young delivery boy in the butcher's shop. The older man, who would eventually lose his sight, had a keen eye for potential athletes. At first, he took little notice of Fausto, thinking him unlikely to make a good cyclist. His riding style was all wrong. Mostly, Cavanna worried that Coppi did not have the will to be a champion: only those who faced destitution had the drive to survive and thrive in the tough world of competitive racing, he believed. Despite his reservations, the older man agreed to train Fausto. It was to become a partnership that transformed the sport.

Great coaches create a symbiotic relationship with their athletes. They do more than map out a training regime. They motivate and inspire. Cavanna was this and more; a manager, mentor and masseur for his charges. Long before physiotherapy became a recognised health profession, the blind man could tell how his cyclists were performing as he massaged and manipulated their muscles. Kneading the legs, back and neck, he noted their fitness. Taking their pulse before and after training, feeling the sweat on their back, he sensed their preparedness for major races. He mapped out courses, ranging from a short seven-kilometre dash to nearby Serravalle, to two hundred kilometres through the Apennines. He advised them about life, and how to conduct themselves in public. His regime was tough and autocratic, but it produced some of the greatest cyclists ever to race in Italy.

In later years, when Coppi was at the height of his career, Cavanna's house and courtyard became known as the nursery for professional cyclists, but when the young delivery boy joined, there were only three pupils. Soon Coppi gave up his work in the shop to train full time. It was a regimented lifestyle, rattled out of bed early in the morning for a day in the saddle. Cavanna controlled his rider's lives: what they ate and drank; when they went to bed; even the side they slept on! Coppi couldn't afford to lodge in Novi Ligure, so his day was even longer, riding from Castellania to join the training squad each morning, then making the uphill journey home in the evening.

Coppi's first recorded win came as a 16-year-old in 1936, an amateur event at nearby Buffalora, which he won easily, claiming the 50 lire and a salami for first prize. Other races followed, with some placings and some in which he punctured. Gradually the master coach transformed Coppi's shabby appearance and awkward style on the bike into the epitome of elegance. Slowly, he made the transition from amateur to independent. In doing so, Fausto developed the physical and mental toughness required as a professional cyclist. At first, his progress was slow. In 1938, he claimed his first senior victory at Casteletta d'Orba, the best of a series of close results for the season. But Fausto was still learning how to race, often as not crashing out of events. Despite the repeated failings, and questioning from his family about continuing to pursue the sport, Fausto knew that he had strong legs and a stout heart, two central ingredients for success. In his first outings in open company, Coppi demonstrated hints of precocious talent, including second placing in the Coppa Bernocchi and third in the Giro del Piemonte and the Tre Valle Varesine. His performance in the Piedmont race was notable, having attacked and established a break on the field, before dropping a chain and having to stop to fix it.

With Cavanna's faith in his young charge, Coppi continued to improve, breaking through with a series of victories, including the 1939 Italian Independant's Championship in which he smashed the field at Varese. Another in the Circuito di Susa, the first race in which the 20-year-old was paid appearance money, followed that victory. By then, the skinny young rider, just out of his teens, was attracting the attention of the cycling press. Soon, the Maino and Legnano teams sought him out. Maino secured agreement from Fausto's family to sign the young rider, but Cavanna would have none of it, having separately agreed with Legnano to sign his charge. The old man won out, and Coppi joined the famous green team, managed by the legendary rider, then manager, Eberardo Pavesi. He was to be a *gregario* for the country's best rider, Gino Bartali.

The outbreak of war

By the time Gino Bartali wrapped up the 1939 season with a victory in the 'race of the falling leaves,' the world was lurching into war. The Commonwealth nations joined the United Kingdom in declaring war on Germany following the Nazi invasion of Poland in September. As the long nights set in during the winter months of 1939-40, darkness was descending on Europe. Few would expect it to last another six years. Hitler and his generals spent January preparing plans for further invasions. By the time the peloton assembled in Milan for what would be the last Giro before the conflict, German forces had marched into Denmark, Norway, Belgium, the Netherlands, Luxembourg and France. Before the riders had concluded their tour of Italy, Paris had fallen to the invaders and the crestfallen French leadership had signed an Armistice. Within weeks, *Luftwaffe* bombs would reign down on London.

Despite signing a 'Pact of Steel' with Germany in 1939, Mussolini remained diffident about relations with Hitler, not immediately siding with the Nazis. Hitler was equally ambivalent about the Italian, withholding military information. Drained of resources from the Abyssinian conquest, the Spanish Civil War and the Albanian excursion, Mussolini had little to offer his aggressive northern ally, apart from rhetorical support, for which Hitler, at least publically, was appreciative. Italy became increasingly reliant on Germany for critical resources as the economy weakened.

Despite Mussolini's embrace of Hitler, Italy was ill prepared for war. When the Nazis invaded Poland, Mussolini declared Italy to be 'non-belligerent' and sought to avoid engagement by requesting an impossible supply of munitions from Germany. As the German advance continued through Western Europe and into France, Mussolini was eventually drawn into the conflict, believing that it would be short-lived.

The day after Fausto Coppi claimed victory in the Giro d'Italia, Mussolini ordered his forces into France, supporting the German assault from the north. But Italian military resources were badly depleted. It would be another two years before Italy would join the war effort in substance. Mussolini continued to proclaim his aspirations to break "the chains that suffocate us" but was largely subservient to Hitler and hampered by his own lack of resources. When he did enter the conflict, it would prove disastrous.

The heir emerges

As the winter of 1939-40 receded on the Italian peninsula, Mussolini was eager for life to continue as normal, encouraging all the usual activities, including sport. Hence the road season started with *La Classicissima di Primavera*, the great one-day race from Milan to San Remo.

The early races of the 1940 season suggested that the established order in the peloton would hold for another year. Gino Bartali prevailed in the *La Classicissima*, defeating Puerto Rimoldi and Aldo Bini. Coppi, the young neo-professional, was hardly disgraced, finishing seventeenth. Bartali followed up his opening success with a win in the Giro della Toscana, establishing himself as the favourite for May's Giro d'Italia.

The worsening political situation in Europe robbed the Giro of most internationals, apart from the Luxembourg cyclist, Christophe Didier and the Swiss rider, Walter Diggelmann, who joined the Olympia team assault on the tour. Nonetheless, two powerful local teams lined up at the start, Legnano with Bartali at the helm, and the *squadra celeste* carrying the famous Bianchi colours for Valetti.

The crowds that cheered off the peloton from Milan on May 17, 1940 mostly expected that Bartali would wear the *maglia rosa* back into the Lombardian capital a few weeks later, despite the competition from Valetti's erstwhile team. After the first uneventful stage to Turin, in which the Bianchi rider, Olimpio Bizzi edged out the favourite, general expectations of a Bartali procession were upended. As many cyclists have experienced, including the Tuscan favourite for the tour that day, bikes and dogs don't mix well. As the peloton raced down the descent of the Passo della Scoffera, a stray canine dashed into the path of the Tuscan, bringing him down heavily on the rough surface.

Bruised, bloodied and battered, Bartali eventually got back on his bike, struggling the remaining 30 kilometres into the seaside city of Genoa in the company of two Bianchi adversaries, Mario Vicini and Olimpio Bizzi more than five minutes behind the stage winner, Pierino Favalli, and his young *gregario*, Fausto Coppi. The race doctors were horrified by Bartali's injuries, suggesting that he was in no condition to continue the gruelling 3,600-kilometre race. A proud, defiant Bartali was having none of it. He had come to win the Giro and intended to go on, injured or otherwise. The next day, still nursing his injuries, a stoic Gino lined-up at the start line for the third stage along the Mediterranean coast from Genoa to Pisa.

Like a pride of lions circling a wounded wildebeest, Bartali was targeted by a relentless series of attacks from the peloton in the 188-kilometre leg. The powerful Bianchi team knew that Bartali's injuries exposed Legnano. Driven on by their team leader, Valetti, the Bianchi *gregario*, Adolfo Leoni – a former World Amateur Road Race champion, who would go on to win Milan-San Remo two years later – and Mario Vicini, led the attacks on the coastal run towards Pisa. With the focus on Bartali, others, including the young Coppi, and the Olympia team rider, Enrico Mollo, were able to maintain forward positions in the stage rankings.

With third placings in each of the first two stages, the Bianchi rider, Osvaldo Bailo, wore the *maglia rosa* after three stages, from Pierino Favalli, the winner of the second stage, and Coppi. Bailo missed a break in the run to Grosseto, leaving his Legnano rival, Favalli in pink, with Coppi now just over a minute behind. Bartali had not given up, hoping as the days went by that he would recover sufficiently to make his mark. But significant injuries can knock the stuffing out of a cyclist, even the world's best. Even a small niggling condition can disrupt the rhythm on the bike; create doubts about attacking when necessary, resulting in a cautious, defensive attitude. Bartali's will was as tough and stubborn as ever, but his body was trying to recover from the crash as the peloton pressed its advantage against him on the subsequent stages to Rome and Naples before turning north via Fiuggi, Terni and Arezzo before racing to Florence.

Olimpio Bizzi, who had joined Bianchi from Frejus for the 1940 Giro, was the most consistent placegetter for much of the race, winning four stages, claiming second placing in four more, and a third. Bartali had been slowly improving, albeit with an inflamed knee, finishing fourth in the 183-kilometre stage from Fuigi to Terni before being outsprinted by his fellow Tuscan, Bizzi, into his hometown of Florence. In his career, Bizzi won 13 stages of the Giro, as well as the Italian Championship, the Giro della Toscana, and the Tre Valli Varesine twice.

As the 1940 Giro d'Italia raced into its second half, the established order was about to be turned on its head. Believing that Bartali couldn't recover sufficiently to win, and knowing that Coppi was riding exceptionally well, Eberardo Pavesi decided to allow his young charge to test his ability. Coppi was best placed of the Legnano riders, but had crashed twice during the event. As the peloton departed Florence on the 11th stage over the Apennines to Modena, Coppi was placed just 2 minutes and 42 seconds behind the race leader, Enrico Mollo, riding for the Olympia team that included the internationals, Christophe Didier and Walter Diggelmann. Although not favoured to win the Giro, the team had prospects for a high finish after a good first week.

Not only did the peloton have three major climbs, including the tough Abetone Pass, the riders were confronted with fog, rain and snow as they ascended the Apennines. A small group, including the *maglia rosa,* Enrico Mollo, Coppi, Bizzi and Diggelmann, were chasing the Gloria team cyclist, Ezio Cecchi, who had forged a break early in the stage. Given his freedom on the Abetone, the young Fausto launched a series of attacks on the group, breaking away and cresting the Pass well ahead of the others. Coppi had shocked the *tifosi* and commentators alike, as he rode with eagle's wings through the mud and rain. Who was this skinny kid, they asked. By the time he rode into Modena, Fausto led the chase group, including Bartali, who had mechanical problems during the stage, by 3 minutes and 45 seconds. He was the new wearer of the *maglia rosa.* In 181 kilometres, a new star of Italian cycling was born.

Unlike most cyclists in the professional peloton, for whom white socks were *de rigeur,* Fausto wore black ones. Asked why, he explained that white socks got dirty more quickly, and he couldn't afford to wash and replace them as often. His roommate, Mario Ricci, insisted that with the famed pink jersey on his back, he could now afford white socks!

At 20-years of age, Fausto Coppi, the poor farmer's son from the obscure village of Castellania, was the new darling of the excitable Italian sports fans. But he was young, still inexperienced and facing nine more stages, including three gruelling days in the Alps. Few begrudged his win, and his presence in the limelight, but many doubted he had the mental and physical experience to wear the jersey into Milan. Even with a strong team around him, the race leader is the focus of every other team and rider in the peloton wanting to win the race. As the Australian, Cadel Evans, recounted his experiences of becoming the first Australian to wear the *maglia rosa* in his initial Giro as a 25-year-old, he had to "empty himself beyond empty" and even then he lost time – and the pink jersey – in the relentless climbs in the Italian Alps. Six decades earlier, an even younger neo-pro faced a similar challenge.

From Modena, the 1940 tour ventured north to Ferrara then headed west through the Veneto to Trevisio, Abbazio and Trieste, before turning to the mountainous north. Coppi's 63 second lead was precarious, easily consumed by a mechanical problem, let alone a bad day in the saddle. With Bartali still suffering from his injuries, and in a bad mood, having seen his leadership of the team pass to his young *gregario*, the expectations of Legnano rested with Coppi. Pavesi encouraged Bartali to continue, although he had lost much time, believing that the youngster would need the guidance and assistance of more experienced riders if he was to survive the ordeal ahead. His approach proved prescient as the peloton headed into the Alps.

The relatively flat stages to Trieste were uneventful for Coppi, with Bizzi and Leoni vying for stage wins. Although Coppi finished 2 minutes down on Vicini on the run into the Adriatic seaside city, he had covered his nearest rival, Mollo, while not allowing other competitors within striking range of his lead to get away in a break. Baring accidents, the next three stages would determine the Giro d'Italia victor.

As Pavesi expected, the young Coppi would be challenged in the Dolomites. The first of the three mountain stages, a 202-kilometre trek from the Adriatic to the medieval fortress town of Pieve di Cadore nestled in the Alps near the Swiss border, was to test the perseverance and commitment of Coppi. Vicini attacked the peloton at a feed station when Coppi stopped, feeling nauseous from a meal of chicken he had eaten. Caught out by the attack, Coppi had to claw his way back through the caravan on the gravel roads, finally catching the breakaway leader at the foot of the Col de Mauria. In the meantime, Bartali had flatted, leaving his young teammate to fare alone. As the leaders began the climb, the nauseous Coppi climbed off his bike, seemingly unable to continue as the peloton raced by. Fortunately, the experienced Bartali came by in pursuit of the group. Stopping, he convinced Fausto to resume the race, insisting that it was far from over. Paced by the Tuscan, Coppi struggled through the stage, finishing a few seconds behind Bizzi and Mollo, and just three minutes down on Vicini. With Bartali's assistance, he retained the pink jersey.

Of the remaining stages, the next, the 17th, was the most brutal. Although a relatively short 110 kilometres to Ortisei, it involved three massive climbs over the Falzarego, Pordoi and Sella passes. Both Coppi and Bartali had recovered significantly to decimate the peloton, leaving Mollo over two minutes behind as they descended the final hill into the Val Gardena valley. The two riders had crested the Falzarego together. Legend has it that Pavesi instructed the owner of the cafe at the top of the pass to hand bidons of coffee to the first two riders over the hill. "How do you know that they will be your riders," the perplexed proprietor asked." One will be wearing the *tricolore* and the other the *maglia rosa*," was the reply. Pavesi's confidence was rewarded as Bartali in the green, white and red national champion's colours, and Coppi, the raceleader in pink, crested the ascent ahead of the peloton.

Despite riding together, the tensions of teammates and rivals were revealed in the rest of the stage. When Coppi flatted, Bartali waited for him, but on the final climb of the Sella Pass when the older rider suffered a blown tyre, Coppi accelerated, until reminded by Pavesi that a 'pact is a pact' on the road. Once Bartali's tyre was repaired, the two raced into Ortesei, with the chastened Coppi allowing Bartali to take the stage win. They were over two minutes ahead of Mollo, the Giro all but guaranteed for Coppi. Bartali had recovered much of his strength, winning the penultimate stage into Verona, and being pipped by Leoni in the final dash into Milan.

But the Giro belonged to Coppi, who, three months short of 21, became the youngest ever winner of the grand tour. He could not have done it without Bartali, who recounted later that "I was the one who saved him from disaster" in the Dolomites, adding, "If I had been from another team, he wouldn't have won . . . I didn't do it for him, but for Legnano who paid my wages." Italy's greatest sporting rivalry had begun in earnest. Coppi was thrust into the limelight. The 27,000 lire first prize was beyond the dreams of his family who made the trek from

Castellania to Milan to witness Fausto's crowning glory. As Coppi was receiving the accolades of the media, Bartali was already planning his revenge. Next year, he would turn the tables on his younger rival.

So began the great rivalry – and the national divide between the *Bartaliani* and the *Coppiani* – those for Gino and those for Fausto. Unknown to either of them, war would consume Europe for the next five years, and the Giro would not be conducted again until 1946. Had both not been relatively young – 24 and 20 – for such champion cyclists, it is unlikely that their great tour rivalry would have continued years later. While racing continued in a modified form for the next few years, their lives, like so many others, would take a different turn.

10

A Shifting World

Three cheers for the war. Three cheers for Italy's war in general. Peace is hence absurd or rather a pause in war
-- Benito Mussolini.

As Florentines ventured outdoors on the morning of Thursday, November 14, 1940, they braced the crisp air of mid-Autumn. The overnight temperature was steadily falling as winter beckoned, but the cooler conditions couldn't subdue the excitement of the small group gathered in the private chapel of the Archbishop of Florence, Cardinal Elia Dalla Costa. Italy's champion cyclist, Gino Bartali, was about to marry his sweetheart, Adriana Bani.

Gino had first noticed the dark-haired, sparkling eyed Adriana when she was a 15-year-old working in a clothing fabric store in Florence. It was 1935 and the somewhat awkward young man was already becoming a household name across the peninsula. While attracted to Bartali, Adriana – and her mother – was hesitant about the ability of even a famous cyclist to provide for a comfortable life together. Although separated by Gino's frequent races, the couple continued to see each other, forming a close friendship during his rise to fame in an increasingly turbulent world.

The young cyclist had become a role model for the Catholic Church as it sought to counter the totalitarian evils of fascism and communism that swept across Europe. As a devout Christian, Gino was attracted to the work of Catholic Action, especially the youth groups which

Gino Bartali leads the Giro d'Italia.

countered the regime's sway on popular thought. This in turn, brought the young cyclist into contact with the hierarchy of the church. The connection would have profound consequences for Gino in the years ahead.

The outbreak of war was the catalyst for Gino and Adriana's marriage. Four months after Mussolini entered the war at the side of Hitler, Gino Bartali received a call-up notice. Like most young men across Italy he was being conscripted into military service. If his fame could have provided protection against service, his disliking for the fascist regime negated any personal advantage. Paradoxically, it was the heart of the great endurance cyclist that saved him from action on the frontline and possible death, injury or imprisonment.

The routine military medical examination revealed Gino's irregular heartbeat, a condition that would usually preclude him from service. Unwilling to exempt Bartali entirely, he was assigned to the messenger corps and sent to a factory manufacturing warplanes at Lake Trasimeno near Perugia in Umbria. The region also hosted a major aviation school for Italian pilots, a key factor in the nation's war efforts.

Gino's fame won him concessions from his commanders: the use of a bicycle rather than a motorbike for delivering messages, opportunities to train, and time to compete in the few events still being conducted, during which he would also endeavour to visit Adriana 120 kilometres away in Florence. Gino Bartali was not cut out for the life of a soldier. He disliked fighting and warfare, kept to himself in barracks, and preferred to study the life of the saints than engage in soldierly commararderie. It was during these solitary nights at Trasimeno that Gino decided to marry Adriana, a proposal that she readily accepted.

The small gathering in Cardinal Dalla Costa's chapel reflected the austerity of the times. Food was rationed and even staples hard to come by. Instead of the large public gathering for a famous sports star, the wedding was a simple event with just a few people present. A modest reception followed at Adriana's sister's home before the happy couple departed for Rome by train. As they journeyed south, the war in Europe was in full flight. That evening, the German *Luftwaffe* bombed Coventry, destroying the famous Cathedral and killing more than 500 people. Arriving in Rome, the newly married couple toured the sights of the ancient city – and ventured over the Tiber to meet Pope Pius XII. Photographs depict Adriana in a lovely autumn dress holding the arm of the stylishly dressed Gino, surrounded by smiling Swiss Guards.

A dangerous new world

Eugenio Maria Giuseppe Giovanni Pacelli had been elected to the seat of Peter in March 1939. The Roman born pontiff took the name Pius XII, following his predecessor, Achille Ratti, who had assumed the title, Pius XI. Together with their two predecessors, Pius X and Benedict XV, the four men led the church through the most tumultuous era of modern European history, from the turn of the 20th century, the rise of communism, the Great War and the expansion of fascism, culminating in the most extensive conflict in global history, the Second World War, and the subsequent Cold War.

It was an era in which the Church struggled with significant change: the loss of most of its sovereign territory – the Papal States – and the self-imposed exile of Popes in the Vatican; and the challenges of modernism and the rise of communism and fascism. It was a period in which the influence of the Pope had to transition from the temporal and spiritual leader of a nation-state to a moral voice in the world.

The Church's response to the new era of industrialisation that swept the world from the late 1880s, and the competing claims of socialism, authoritarianism and democracy, would dominate much of its thinking in the 20th century. The old order had been sundered in the previous decades. The Church struggled to be heard in the seething contest of ideologies that spilled onto the streets of Europe. Its immediate attention was directed to the rise of Marxism which attracted increasing support in intellectual circles in the last decade of the 19th century and which would be played out through revolution and bloody terror in the next.

The industrialisation that brought rapid economic progress across Europe and this new world was also fertile ground for conceptions of a novel political order. As workers organised into trade unions, to win better conditions in the expanding factories, the earlier Enlightenment notions about the rights of the individual were challenged by new political theories.

Cycling and the Story of Italy

In 1891, Pope Leo XIII responded to these developments with the social encyclical, *Rerum Novarum*, which sought to apply the Church's belief in the inherent liberty and dignity of the individual, having been made in the image and likeness of God, to the emerging social and industrial order. The enormity of the change was acknowledged in the opening paragraph:

> That the spirit of revolutionary change, which has long been disturbing the nations of the world, should have passed beyond the sphere of politics and made its influence felt in the cognate sphere of practical economics is not surprising. The elements of the conflict now raging are unmistakable, in the vast expansion of industrial pursuits and the marvellous discoveries of science; in the changed relations between masters and workmen; in the enormous fortunes of some few individuals, and the utter poverty of the masses; the increased self-reliance and closer mutual combination of the working classes; as also, finally, in the prevailing moral degeneracy. The momentous gravity of the state of things now obtaining fills every mind with painful apprehension; wise men are discussing it; practical men are proposing schemes; popular meetings, legislatures, and rulers of nations are all busied with it — actually there is no question which has taken deeper hold on the public mind.

In the encyclical, Leo posited an alternative to the militant atheism and radical proposals of Karl Marx, Friedrich Engels and others, who condemned religion as 'the opiate of the masses' and envisaged a new order in which the workers would join together to own and direct the instruments of production for their own ends, sharing in both the work and the rewards.

"The history of all hitherto existing society is the history of class struggles," wrote Marx in his 1848 *Communist Manifesto*. A socialist society, in which private property and the means of production would be replaced by common ownership, was his solution to conflicts throughout history. His political philosophy underpinned the twin strains of totalitarianism that wrought a reign of terror in the following century, communism and National Socialism.

The Pope recognised the plight of workers, but rejected the Marxist solution:

> By degrees it has come to pass that working men have been surrendered, isolated and helpless, to the hardheartedness of employers and the

greed of unchecked competition. The mischief has been increased by rapacious usury, which, although more than once condemned by the Church, is nevertheless, under a different guise, but with like injustice, still practiced by covetous and grasping men. To this must be added that the hiring of labor and the conduct of trade are concentrated in the hands of comparatively few; so that a small number of very rich men have been able to lay upon the teeming masses of the laboring poor a yoke little better than that of slavery itself.

With prescience, he observed:

To remedy these wrongs the socialists, working on the poor man's envy of the rich, are striving to do away with private property, and contend that individual possessions should become the common property of all, to be administered by the State or by municipal bodies. They hold that by thus transferring property from private individuals to the community, the present mischievous state of things will be set to rights, inasmuch as each citizen will then get his fair share of whatever there is to enjoy. But their contentions are so clearly powerless to end the controversy that were they carried into effect the working man himself would be among the first to suffer. They are, moreover, emphatically unjust, for they would rob the lawful possessor, distort the functions of the State, and create utter confusion in the community.

Responding to the increasingly volatile clash between workers and the owners of capital, the Church sought to reconcile the rights and duties of each in a manner that enhanced the individual while countering the emerging new authoritarianism. Hence it supported both the ownership of private property and the rights of workers to form unions. A century later, Leo's successor, John Paul II, who had endured the 'everyday reality' of Marxism in his native Poland, rejected the 'fascinating abstraction' of communisim in favoutr of individual economic initiative and regulated markets based on a moral order that promoted human dignity and flourishing.

The events of the late 1800s and early 1900s led to increasing conflict across Europe from the beginning of the 20th century, including riots in Italy in June 1914. It was in Russia that the Marxists were most successful, where the confluence of peasant poverty, ethnic tensions, government restrictions on employees, economic stagnation and discontent amongst students and workers provided a fertile foundation for the emerging socialist ideology. Workers' strikes in the early years of the century morphed into open revolution in 1905 that resulted in the creation of a consultative Duma and a Manifesto granting rights to the people and expanded powers for the parliament. These changes – and an improvement in the economy – curtailed revolutionary zeal for another decade, but the seeds of bitter conflict had already been sown.

The major protagonist for the violent revolutions that would sweep the country in 1917 was Vladimir Ilyich Ulyanov, known since by his pseudonym, Vladimir Lenin. The child of a wealthy, middle-class family, Lenin was radicalised at university and came to advocate the violent overthrow of the Tsarist regime. Breaking with Marx' belief that a middle class revolution had to proceed the ultimate socialist revolution, Lenin agitated for the proletariat overthrow of the Tsar, and the creation of a new socialist state. His Bolsheviks, so-named as they represented the majority – the *bol'sheviki* – in the Socialist Revolutionary Party, increasingly turned to violence and terror in their quest.

Following significant losses in the Great War, riots in Petrograd (now St Petersburg) in February 1917, the then capital of the country, led to the abdication of Nicolas II, and the installation of a provisional government. But this did little to end the conflict, with ongoing conflict and strikes, leading to a further revolution in October when the Bolsheviks seized control.

The bloody revolution in Russia, the execution of the Tsar and his family, and the resulting civil war between the Bolshevik Red Army and the coalition White brigades, and the final ascendency of the Leninist regime paved the way for the collectivism of agriculture, including the nationalisation of lands formerly belonging to both the aristocracy and the Orthodox Church, restrictions on press freedoms, and the replacement of the legal system with Revolutionary Tribunals and People's Courts.

Widespread famine and the hoarding of food by peasants resulted in more violence and terror at the behest of Lenin, mass executions and the establishment of concentration camps under the administration of a new agency, the Gulag. Tens of thousands of Russians, including many priests and pastors were eliminated during the Red Terror. Predating

Stalin's murderous regime, Lenin's totalitarian state established a pattern of terror and oppression that was to be copied by other dictators throughout that century and the next.

Stalin expanded Lenin's bloody regime, sovietising most of Eastern Europe, along with the states to the south of Russia. Some four million people were starved to death during the 'Red Famine' in the Ukraine in 1932 and 1933 alone.

Long before the rise of fascism in Italy and Nazism in Germany, communist totalitarianism had wrought destruction and misery across Russia, with its attraction spreading to neighbouring countries and influencing political movements across Europe.

The Church responds to Bolshevism

These events had a profound impact on the Church, especially Achille Ratti, who was elected Pope Pius XI in 1922 upon the unexpected death of Benedict XV from pneumonia. Ratti had been the Apostolic Visitor to Poland before being appointed Apostolic Nuncio (Papal Envoy) in 1919. When the Red Army advanced on Poland, Ratti was the only diplomat to stay in the country, lending moral support to the locals, who routed the advancing Bolsheviks in the Battle of Warsaw. It was a decisive victory – which Stalin avenged 20 years later when he massacred the military leadership of the Polish nation in the Katyn Forest – halting the spread of communism to Europe. The stories of the persecution of religion under the atheistic Lenin had a profound impact on the future Pope and the leadership of the Catholic Church. A British diplomat to the Vatican later wrote: "Everything in the Vatican is dominated by the Pope's fear of Russian communism, that the soviets may reach Western Europe."

While Ratti was in Poland, his future Secretary of State and successor, Eugenio Pacelli, was the Apostolic Nuncio to neighbouring Bavaria, and then Germany. They shared a similar distaste for communism, and denounced it regularly.

Eugenio Pacelli's Roman father served as a lawyer in the Vatican. The family's fidelity to the Church, especially in the decades of papal exile, and his father's profession influenced his subsequent vocation as a priest and canon lawyer. The bookish young man with a love of classical music entered the seminary in 1894 when Leo XIII was leading the Church to address the emerging economic, social and political movements of the 19th century. Eugenio left the college the following year, suffering from the ill health that would afflict him throughout his life. His nervous disposition, hypochondria, and highly strung character surfaced regularly throughout his life, resulting in periods of mental and physical rehabilitation away from the stresses of life.

Through his parent's Vatican connections, Pacelli was allowed to live at home while he continued his studies. In fact, he lived the next 23 years in his mother's home as he undertook his studies and subsequent duties as a canon lawyer. Subsequently, he was cared for by Sister Pasqualina Lehnert, who became his housekeeper and confident for more than four decades. The usual pastoral duties of a parish priest were remote from the reserved Pacelli. His world was of books, concordats and laws after being recruited by Monsignor Pietro Gasparri to the Vatican's Foreign Office, then known as the Congregation for Extraordinary Ecclesiastical Affairs.

Gerard Noel writes of the future Pope:

> In later years, Eugenio Pacelli as Pope Pius XII, was viewed as ascetic and dispassionate, a man almost incapable of earthly emotions and desires. The truth was very different. He was a man filled with such an enormity of emotion that he feared to express it particularly to himself. His mother and Pasqualina gave him an abundance of love.

Prior to the 19th century, the Church was a loose Federation, in which the local hierarchy – and Royal Houses – in various nations and states exercised power and control of their own dioceses while in communion with and ultimately subject to the Pope. Aided by rapidly developing communications and new, faster means of transport, a more rigid hierarchy centred on the Roman Curia began to emerge. The outcome of the First Vatican Council lent support to these developments. Having debated the role of the Pope, it never considered the complementary role of the bishops and the broader church when it was suspended as a consequence of the Piedmontese occupaton of Rome. Following the loss of the Papal States, a belief developed amongst leading figures in the Vatican that the Church's position in the world would be enhanced by concordats with various nations in which adherence to the Code of Canon Law would protect and enhance the role of the Church.

While Eugenio Pacelli didn't invent this approach, he became its most enthusiastic advocate as he rose through the hierarchy, first as a young Foreign Affairs official, where he worked on the new Code of Canon Law that reinforced the central role of the Pope and the Roman Curia in the Church, then as Nuncio (Ambassador) to Germany, and subsequently, as Secretary of State – in effect the Pope's Prime Minister.

Having written his doctorate on the nature and uses of concordats, Pacelli was to pursue them relentlessly until his death in 1958 – concluding some 25 of these international agreements. Despite the mixed outcomes of these agreements, including the disastrous consequences of the first such agreement with Serbia in 1914, Pacelli believed that they gave Catholics a platform to resist persecution. His role, especially during the Second World War, has remained controversial and will be subject to more scrutiny when the Vatican archives of the era are opened.

Germany was a nation of divisions and bitter rivalries when Pacelli was posted there in 1917. Old divisions between Catholic Bavaria and Protestant Prussia were still potent. Bismark's *Kulturkampf*, with its savage persecution of Catholics, continued to divide Germans long after the 'Iron Chancellor' had died. Undaunted by their treatment, Catholics organized a grassroots movement that spawned the Centre Party, which after the Great War would exercise considerable power in Germany. Their numbers grew in the 1920s, such that by the end of the decade, Catholics were a third of the population with considerable influence. Still, the tensions between Bavaria and Prussia remained – which Pacelli would exploit as he pursued a concordat with Germany.

Pacelli had been appointed to Munich as Nuncio in 1917, in the last terrible year of the Great War, and remained there until 1925 when a concordat with Bavaria was finalized. Of medium height, slim and with a typical Roman nose, the bespectacled Pacelli often appeared the austere prelate, but in smaller groups could be a lively host and conversationalist. In the absence of a Nuncio for Prussia (or all Germany), Pacelli in effect fulfilled the role, as well as being a representative to Russia with which he conducted secret peace negotiations until ended by the Vatican in 1927.

Germany after the Great War was in a state of disarray. Kaiser Wilhelm was dismissed, and civil order maintained in the face of a campaign to blame the war defeat on the nation's leadership and elements of the military, especially the German navy. German communists began organizing demonstrations throughout the country, but were crushed by units of *Freikorps*, demobilized veterans who were encouraged in a bloody campaign by the government. Clashes between the *Freikorps* and communists became a feature of the nascent Weimar Republic, with bloody assassinations of key political figures commonplace.

It was during these heady confrontations that a previously unknown figure – who would dominate global relations for more than a decade and drag the world back into another great war – emerged in Munich. He was Adolf Hitler, a 30-year-old, Austrian-born, decorated veteran of the Great War, who had developed a hatred of religion – Jews in particular – and blamed them for the ills of the world and Germany's defeat in the war.

At first attracted to the right-wing *Freikorps*, Hitler investigated a German Workers Party meeting, only to join them. Within two years, the fiery speaker had become leader of the group, after wresting the role from the founder, Anton Drexler, and changing the name to the National Socialist German Workers' Party. Drexler and Hitler had written a 25 points *Manifesto* for the Party, which, they stated, constituted the "unalterable and eternal objectives of National Socialism." Bringing together nationalism and socialism, the two added a specific anti-Semitic character to their other objectives: the government expropriation of land without compensation, nationalization of basic sectors of national industry, the abolition of market-based lending, and the confiscation of all income unearned by work. Hitler would later proclaim "we are all socialists" and that "National Socialism and Marxism are the same." A decade later, as *Feuhrer*, he proclaimed;

> That the individual should come to realise that his own ego is of no importance in comparison with the existence of his nation: the position of the individual ego is conditioned solely by the interests of the nation as a whole . . . that above all the unity of the nation's spirit and will are worth far more than the freedom of the spirit and will of the individual. . . . We understand only the individual's capacity to make sacrifices for the community, for his fellow man.

The German historian, Gotz Aly observed:

> The National Socialist German Workers' Party was propagating two

age-old dreams of the German people: national and class unity. That was the key to Nazi popularity, from which they derived the power they needed to pursue their criminal aims. The idea of the *Voltstaat* – a state of and for the people – was what we would call a welfare state for Germans with the proper racial pedigree.

The later involved Hitler's fanatical anti-Semitism. In an interview in 1922, he said: "If I am ever really in power, the destruction of the Jews will be my first and most important job," describing how he would publicly hang every Jew in the country. But little of this was noticed in the early 1920s as the country struggled to cope with the cost of defeat in the Great War and the seething contest for the heart and soul of the German people.

Despite his ability to generate huge propaganda, and attract thousands to his rallies, Hitler's chances of success appeared dim in the mid-1920s, when an attempted coup was defeated and he was jailed. This was to change in the late-1920s when the combination of the burden of war reparations and the onset of the Great Depression enabled him to manipulate national fears to win government.

While Germans wrestled with their future in the early-1920s, Eugenio Pacelli continued to concentrate on negotiating a concordat. Having signed an agreement with Bavaria, in 1925, the Nuncio turned to his ultimate prize: an agreement with Germany itself. This was to be fulfilled in 1933 – a concordant between the Holy See and the Third Reich. Despite the fact that the treaty with Mussolini was already falling apart, Pacelli pressed on. The concerns of local Catholics seemed less important than his grand plan. If the Lateran Treaty had been a political triumph for Mussolini, the concordat with Germany was a masterpiece for Hitler, who had seen the Vatican agreement with Italy as a blueprint for abolishing the Centre Party and removing any remaining vestiges of democracy in the nation. For Pacelli, who thought and reasoned on a different plane, the series of concordats he was intent on establishing would elevate Canon Law and the place of the Vatican to new heights in global affairs. His motives were honourable, but his understanding of politics possibly naïve. His fear of one strain of Marxism, the revolutionary communism that had taken hold of Russia and threatened to spread throughout Europe, possibly lessened for him another strain, the national socialism that commenced as an expression of democratic will but soon morphed into sinister totalitarianism. In the hands of dishonourable men, Pacelli's concordats were of limited value in promoting an international moral order. But they ultimately had one significant benefit: they aided the Church in many places to aid the escape of thousands of Jews fleeing Hitler's deadly holocaust. Pacelli's role throughout the conflicts, especially the later Nazi perseculation of Jews, has been the subject of considerable controversy ever since.

By the end of the decade, the Third Reich had invaded most of Europe and a war even greater than the previous one was exacting its bloody revenge across the world. It was this terrible conflict that ensnarled the lives of Gino Bartali and Fausto Coppi like millions of others across the globe.

Fausto Coppi's war

While Gino Bartali was wiling away his time as a military messenger when not training, racing or visiting Adriana, his younger rival was experiencing a similar existence. Fausto was first deployed to the Alpine Front in Mussolini's tilt against France, but that soon came to an end and he returned to Tortona, just 20 kilometres from Novi Ligure, and even less distance to his parent's home at Castellania. He was able to continue training, visiting Cavanna in Novi, and participating in the races still being conducted. This was a much different to the experience of many conscripts into Mussolini's war, of whom nearly 300,000 would die or remain missing in action.

Despite his bellicose rhetoric, *Il Duce's* forces were ill prepared for military engagement. His tilt into France was an opportunistic engagement against his old rival when it seemed that Hitler was already close to conquering the country. Mussolini cynically told the Chief-of-Staff of the Italian Army, Marshal Badoglio, that "I only need a few thousand dead so that I can sit at the peace conference as a man who has fought."

The Italian leader's object was the Mediterranean Sea where he aspired to become a powerful presence. Often appearing to know better than his Generals, and itching to please the Germans, Mussolini launched campaigns in Eastern and Northern Africa, and Greece in 1940 and 1941. Initial successes were short-lived; as the British and other allied forces repelled the Italian armies before the arrival of the German might, to which Greece surrendered in April 1941. The Italians were under-equipped, inadequately trained, and dispersed to many fronts, including some 200,000 men to Russia in 1941-42.

Although the Italian forces were driven out of Ethiopia, they made gains in North Africa, especially after the German *Africa Korps* under the command of General Erwin Rommel joined the fight in Libya and Egypt. The allied forces desperately defended their hard won territory, especially in the two Battles of El Alamein in 1942, eventually turning the tide against the Axis powers.

Fausto's life, although far from idyllic, was a world away from the conflict that ravaged Europe. Food was rationed and life in barracks boring, but he was able to train and race as the months passed by. In August 1940, Coppi met Bruna Ciampolini, who was to become his wife. Younger than Fausto, the shy brown-eyed girl had been sent by her parents from Genoa to stay with relations in the village of Villalvernia, about mid-way between Tortona and Castellania. Their association slowly blossomed into a romance and engagement.

In December 1941, Coppi received news that his father, Domenico, had been crushed in an accident while yoking oxen, and died soon afterwards. Fausto was devastated, slipping into a mood of depression and isolation. Cajoled by his family and friends, he eventually returned to the bike and resumed racing. But the threat of being called-up to the war front remained a daily worry. Friends suggested that Coppi flee to Switzerland; and Cavanna offered to provide a cocktail that would require hospitalization. Coppi declined the offers, knowing he would be criticized for cowardice.

In early 1943, the inevitable occurred: Fausto was called-up for another Italian assault in North Africa. With Mussolini's dream of being the great power in the Mediterranean slipping from his grasp, he threw one more effort into the conflict in the spring, sending a new force to Tunisia. Among the troops who flew into the conflict from Sicily was Fausto Coppi, who was displaced from his routine for the war front by Mussolini's desperate need for more infantrymen. It was to be a short-lived campaign as the allied armies routed the Axis forces, forcing them into retreat and finally defeat. The campaign had been doomed from the outset. Hit by dysentery, low morale and a lack of supplies, the Italians had little will to fight. Out of ammunition and food, they were an easy target for their English opponents, who captured Coppi's unit at Cape Bon in April 1943. Unlike many of his compatriots, Fausto was lucky to have survived the suicidal campaign. He would spend the rest of the conflict as a prisoner-of-war, first in Tunisia, and later near Naples.

Mussolini's grandiose plan to create the new Roman Empire had ground to a whimpering halt in the deserts of Africa. His opponents would soon be assaulting the Italian peninsula itself. For many of his compatriots, this would be the most dangerous stage of the long war, as conflict reached their homes and cities. That danger intensified when the Allied forces began their final push against the Axis powers, invading Sicily in July 1943.

An unlikely cyclist.

11

The Descent into Darkness

Good is something you do, not something you talk about. Some medals are pinned on your soul, not your jacket

-- Gino Bartali.

Soon after the invasion of Sicily by American and British Commonwealth forces, Allied bombers began their assault on Mussolini's backyard, raining destruction upon Rome and other cities. Within a week, the Fascist Grand Council voted to return full constitutional powers to the king, who promptly dismissed *Il Duce* from office and imprisoned him. While the appetite for an ongoing fight was evaporating amongst Italians, German forces defended Sicily for weeks, ferrying equipment and troops to the mainland, before the island fell. The Italian government signed an Armistice with the Allies in early September, by which time the Germans had displaced the locals and reinforced their defence of the peninsula.

In September 1943, a small contingent of elite German paratroopers descended by gliders on the ski resort hotel high in the Apennine mountains where Mussolini was imprisoned, rescuing the dictator from his Italian captors. Mussolini was flown to Germany to meet Hitler in a propaganda exercise for the Axis powers, before being installed as the leader of a new fascist state at Salò in northern Italy. A few days before the rescue, King Victor Emmanuel III, his family, and senior military officers fled Rome, effectively abandoning the country to the German occupiers, who would fight a bitter war against the advancing Allied forces for the next 20 months. The country was engulfed by a civil conflict, as Italians loyal to the fascists and the Germans fought both Allied forces and the resistance movement.

The imprisonment of Mussolini and the collapse of his government was a more ominous portent for many Italians, especially the Jewish community. Although Mussolini had restricted the activities of Jews, locked them out of jobs, and forced many into confinement, he had not pursued Hitler's murderous campaign against them.

Jews had supported the fascist regime in its early days, with hundreds joining the Party and some 200 participating in the March on Rome which precipitated Mussolini's appointment as Prime Minister. In 1928, he had stated: "Fascism had to contend with too many problems to desire to create more. For us Fascists, there can be no antagonism to Jews." His then mistress, Margherita Sarfatti, was Jewish, as was a member of his Cabinet, Aldo Finzi. By 1933, almost 5,000 Jews – about one-in-ten of all the Jews in Italy – had joined the Party.

As Nazi antagonism towards Jews in Europe intensified, many sought refuge in other countries, including Italy. In 1939, the Union of Italian Jewish Communities formed the *Delegazione Assistenza Emigrati Ebrei* to assist Jewish refugees in Italy. Known as Delasem, the Genoa-based organisation was established with the concurrence of the regime. Over the following four years, Delasem assisted more than 15,000 Jewish people, many of whom were detained in internment camps. The organisation was supported by the government, which retained close supervision of the activities as thousands of Jews sought refuge on the peninsula.

Of the 57,000 Jews in Italy in 1939, 10,000 had sought refuge from other parts of Europe. The Racial Laws required non-Italians to leave the country, but by the due date in March 1939, only 3,720 had left – and 2,486 more had entered. Despite more stringent border controls, Jews fleeing the Nazi regime continued to make their way into Italy by their thousands. It was in these circumstances that Delasem was founded in December that year, with the clear understanding that the Regime was not intent in returning Jewish refugees to their country-of-origin. Delasem's purpose was to aid them while in Italy, and to assist their passage onwards, especially to the land that would become Israel.

While government policy about non-Italian Jews was at times confusing, the regime generally supported their emigration from the country, providing visas and other immigration documentation. Nonetheless, thousands of Jews were interned in numerous camps.

Mussolini's opportunistic entry into the European war when France was about to surrender and the might of the British army was cornered at Dunkirk had heightened the fears of Italy's Jewish community. Tens of thousands sought passage through the country to safer destinations. If entering Italy was becoming increasingly difficult, departing was just as problematic as the war engulfed the sea lanes of the Mediterranean. The escape route to Portugal via Spain was increasingly limited as the outwardly neutral Franco regime restricted passage to escaping Jews. By early 1942, some 8,000 people were interned in 170 camps across the nation. This had risen to some 10,000 foreign refugees by mid 1943.

Hitler's 'Final Solution'

Hitler's 'Final Solution' had not begun with the Jews. It was the disabled who were victims of a euthanasia programme that Hitler introduced in 1940, eliminating some 70,000 intellectually infirm people in gas chambers before widespread condemnation by Church leaders, including the Bishop of Munster, Clemens von Galen, and the great Lutheran theologian, Dietrich Bonhoeffer, and protests by ordinary Christians, halted – or at least severely constrained – the practice. Hitler wasn't alone in advocating euthanasia: eugenics societies flourished in the 1920s and 30s in the United Kingdom, the United States and elsewhere, of which prominent people such as John Maynard Keynes were members.

It was the Jews, however, for which Hitler had a lasting hatred. In his twisted mind, he connected his other targets, communists and Christians, with the Jewish people:

> The Jew is the ferment of decomposition in peoples... The heaviest blow to humanity was the coming of Christianity; Bolshevism is Christianity's illegitimate child. Both are inventions of Jews... Saul became Paul and Mordechai became Marx.

Although Pacelli had negotiated a concordat with Germany in 1933, the Church soon came to regret their trust in the honour of the

Germans. In 1937, Pius XI issued an encyclical which was smuggled into Germany and read in every Catholic Church on Palm Sunday. *"Mit brennender sorge..."* it began. "With burning concern and mounting consternation we have been observing for some time now the cross carried by the Church in Germany and the increasingly difficult situation of those men and women who have kept the faith..."

The encyclical especially urged Catholics to resist the idolatrous cults of state and race:

> Race, nation, state... all have an essential and honorable place within the secular order. To abstract them, however, from the earthly scale of values and make them the supreme norm of all values, including religious ones, and divinize them with an idolatrous cult, is to be guilty of perverting and falsifying the order of things created and commanded by God...

The latter was a reference to Hitler's directions to establish a new state religion – the National Reich Church – in which Christian symbols and artefacts were to be replaced on altars by a copy of *"Mein Kampf* (to the German nation and therefore to God the most sacred book) and to the left of the altar a sword." The instructions also demanded "the immediate cessation of the publishing and distribution of the Bible."

Hitler's hatred turned from thoughts and words to action on November 9, 1938. The assasination of the German diplomat, Ernst von Roth, in Paris by a 17-year-old Polish Jew, Herschel Grynszpan was exploited by the head of the Security Police, Reinhard Heydrich, with Hitler's concurrence, to organise 'spontaneous' riots and attacks on Jews throughout Germany. The pogrom of torching synagogues and vandalising Jewish homes and businesses left 91 Jews dead, scores more injured, and swarthes of property damaged. Reflecting the broken glass on the streets of Germany, the infamous event became known as *kristallnacht*.

Over the next three years, the Nazis unleashed a horrific assault on their opponents, enslaving populations in occupied lands such as Poland and Russia, starving prisoners-of-war to death, and executing *en masse* groups suspected of resistance. But it was the Jews who were singled out for special treatment.

Within three weeks of *kristallnacht*, Eugenio Pacelli had initiated a programme to save Jews from the Nazis. On November 30, he instructed archbishops around the world to apply for visas for "non-Aryan Catholics" – a coded reference to Jews that was designed to mislead the Nazis – pursuant to the concordat with Germany. Sixty years later, it was revealed that some 200,000 Jews had been secreted away from the Nazi regime under these arrangements. Their freedom was exceptional; the vast majority of Europe's Jews were killed in the holocaust.

As early as April 1941, Hitler informed Goering and Himmler of his intention to exterminate all Jews in Nazi controlled lands. Less than a year later, Heydrich proposed his plans for the 'final solution' – the systemic mass execution of (mostly) Jews in concentration camps to which they had been deported. By 1945, six million people had been gassed to death at Auschwitz, Dachau, Sobibor and Treblinka. At the subsequent Nuremberg trials of the leaders of Nazi Germany, a leading member of the party, Adolf Eichmann's deputy, Dieter Wisliceny, claimed that it had been Hajj Amin al-Husseini, the Grand Mufti of Jerusalem, who had repeatedly urged Eichmann and Himmler to exterminate the Jews, although the Nazis had already commenced their deadly program before the Mufti met Hitler and the Nazi official may have been seeking to deflect responsibility.

Less than a year after the infamous *kristallnacht*, Hitler invaded Poland. The next morning, Eugenio Pacelli and his Secretary of State, Cardinal Luigi Maglione, prepared coded messages for nuncios in many countries, instructing them to prepare thousands of baptismal certificates to give to Jews to allow them to escape to the Holy Land and elsewhere. The Pope also approved a request to allow the Pallottine religious order to establish a network to bring German Jews to the safety of Rome. Across German-occupied Europe, church leaders and officials implemented informal networks that enabled thousands of Jews to escape Nazi clutches, providing false papers and smuggling them across national borders to safer countries. Many were able to escape via Austria, Yugoslavia, and neighbouring nations. Dalesem provided relief for the thousands that found refuge in Italy.

Despite having a concordat with Germany, Pius XI condemned Hitler's anti-Semitism. In a widely disseminated 1938 speech the Pope reminded Christians that they were the spiritual seed of Abraham and that therefore antisemitism is intolerable: "No, no, I say to you it is impossible for a Christian to take part in anti-Semitism. It is inadmissible. Through Christ and in Christ we are the spiritual progeny of Abraham. Spiritually, we are all Semites."

Pacelli, as nuncio in Germany also recognised the evil of the Nazi regime. Gordon Thomas writes:

> Of the forty-four speeches he made as nuncio, forty denounced aspects of the emerging Nazi ideology. In 1935 he wrote an open letter to the bishop of Cologne describing "Hitler as a false prophet of Lucifer." Two years later at Notre Dame in Paris he said Germany was being led astray into "an ideology of race." Hitler ordered the Nazi press to brand him as "a Jew lover from the Vatican."

When Pacelli was elected as pope in 1939, the Nazi newspaper Berlin *Morgenpost* wrote:

> The election of Cardinal Pacelli is not accepted in favour in Germany because he was always opposed to Nazism and practically determined the policies of the Vatican under his predecessor.

The Nazi leader later authorised a plot to kidnap Pacelli after he had been installed as Pope, a venture that only abandoned when knowledge of it became public.

German occupation

Romans awoke from their weekend on July 19, 1943 to the sound, quiet at first, but then rising in a crescendo, as a mass of American B-24 Liberator bombers thundered towards the eternal city. Their beacon was the shining dome of St Peter's Basilica. There had been planes overhead in previous weeks, dropping propaganda leaflets on the city, but this was different. There were more aircraft – some 512 in total – and they were higher in the sky. As Church bells rang out at 8 am across the city, the roar of the engines was replaced by the sound of explosions as bombs rained down. Their target was the vast freight yards at San Lorenzo near the Termini station. As much as the planes targeted military and non-civilian installations like the railways and nearby steelworks, nearby structures including the Basilica di San Lorenzo and the 600-year-old Sapienza University were hit. Some 700 people were dead by the time the planes had emptied their lethal cargo, and twice that number injured.

Cycling and the Story of Italy

Rome's Ciampino military airport, from which Mussolini had flown to meet Hitler in the Veneto the previous day, was also in ruins. The war had reached Rome, and unknown to *Il Duce*, his days as leader of the country were numbered. King Victor Emmanuel had already approved a plot involving the British Intelligence Service, MI6, and the Chief of Staff of the Italian Defence Forces, General Vittorio Ambrosio, to remove him. When Ambrosio returned from the summit with the news that Mussolini had pledged to continue the war, the plan was executed.

The Fascist Grand Council overwhelmingly voted the following Saturday to remove Mussolini, who then sought an audience with the King, only to be stripped of office and arrested. Marshall Pietro Badoglio was sworn in as the replacement. Once the Allies landed on the mainland, he and Victor Emmanuel negotiated an unconditional surrender before fleeing the country.

On hearing the news, Hitler ordered his armies into Italy. Despite significant local resistance and Allied bombings, the Germans gradually won the battle in the Alban Hills south of Rome before advancing on the city. By September 10, the German forces of Field Marshall Albert Kesselring, the Supreme Commander of Italy, had occupied the city. It marked the beginning of a dangerous new period for two groups in particular: the thousands of allied soldiers who had fled to Rome when their Italian captors had abandoned prisoner-of-war camps; and the Jews, both original residents of the city, and the thousands that had been smuggled out of Germany and elsewhere in Europe by church and other groups.

Few Italians had the stomach for Hitler's ongoing war. Only 94,000 Italian soldiers accepted the offer to continue to fight for the Germans; over 700,000 refused, with many of them transported to Germany as slave labour. Many fled or hid, often in the rugged hills and fought a resistance campaign against the Third Reich. As invaders over the centuries have learnt, Italy, with its mountain ranges and disparate provinces, is a difficult country to easily conquer. It is designed to defend, as the Allies discovered in their slow, arduous advance against the Germans from the south. Eventually they would reach Naples, freeing prisoners-of-war along the way.

Rescue operation

Those unfamiliar with the Catholic Church often imagine it to be a great monolithic structure, ruled from Rome by the Pope, with the cardinals and bishops his commanders enforcing discipline around the world. The reality is different, akin to a loose federation or global franchise. While commmitted to a *magisterium* – a set of beliefs and doctrines – each bishop and priest has significant organisational independence in his diocese or parish. When Pacelli instructed nuncios to request bishops across Europe to assist Jews, the response and organisation was a matter for each diocese and parish.

Although the Germans had propped up Mussolini as leader of the Italian Socialist Republic at Salò on the western shores of Lake Garda after snatching him from his mountaintop prison, it was a puppet government. The Nazis were in control, and quickly moved to replicate their 'final solution' on the peninsula. Mussolini's more benign treatment of the Jews was replaced by Hitler's fanatical determination to eliminate them. No-one was safe, including the members of Dalesem and their collaborators, who had to quickly move their operations underground.

In the summer of 1943, hundreds of Jews had been secreted into Italy from Austria and Slovenia. Both Dalesem and the network established by the Pallottine Order also moved people into neutral Switzerland, but their activities became increasingly difficult after the German occupation in autumn. The first object of the German Gestapo was the removal of the entire Italian gold reserves, but it was the arrival in the country of *Hauptsturmfuhrer* (Captain) Theodor Dannecker that carried more sinister portents. Dannecker had already overseen the deportation of Jews from France, Belgium, Holland, Poland, Bulgaria, Greece and Yugoslavia to death camps. He was responsible for the deaths of hundreds of thousands of Jews before he arrived in Rome that fateful October day in 1943.

Within days of the German occupation of Rome, Pius XII activated a network of safe havens for both Jews and allied soldiers who had escaped prisoner-of-war camps. The myriad church buildings – colleges, convents, parish houses and schools – both inside the Vatican and throughout Rome, were organised to house the escapees. While the church was relying on the Lateran Treaty, experience elsewhere in

Europe revealed that the Nazis had not respected its property and had sent priests and nuns suspected of helping Jews or speaking against the regime to concentration camps. Working closely with Dalesem and the Pallottine religious order, thousands of Jews had been secreted away in church properties across the eternal city, including hospitals, colleges and schools.

Pius met with the German commander, Field Marshall Albert Kesselring, obtaining a series of concessions that would aid his secret mission. Gordon Thomas writes:

> All vehicles bearing the Vatican City license plate, S.C.V., would pass unchallenged through the streets of Rome; all extraterritorial property would have a placard placed on their doors bearing the words PROPERTY OF THE HOLY SEE both in Italian and German and would not be entered by any German authority; the Vatican Railway train from Castel Gandolfo would not be stopped or searched; the German army would not cross the white line which marked its boundary with the Vatican.

These concessions helped the Church to move and hide thousands of Jews throughout the city.

A dangerous mission

Elia Dalla Costa, the Cardinal Archbishop of Florence, was repulsed by the Nazi ideology and eager to assist his fellow human beings fleeing Hitler's purge. The highly respected prelate had departed Florence rather than meet Hitler during the *Feuhrer*'s visit to the city with Mussolini in 1938. Although Pacelli was widely regarded as *papabile* – the person favoured to succeed Pius XI – the Florentine is said to have received nine votes in the first ballot of Cardinals in 1939.

In 1943, Dalla Costa established a network of priests, religious and laypeople to assist Jews in his archdiocese. With the German occupation and the restoration of the fascist government, the activities of the local chapter of Delasem were problematic. It was also becoming more difficult for Jews to flee the country, as the German and Italians forces placed curfews on movement and strengthened their border controls. The focus of assistance increasingly turned to hiding Jews in Italy rather than assisting them flee.

In early autumn, Gino Bartali received a telephone call from the Cardinal, asking him to attend a meeting at the Archbishop's office in Florence. Bartali had known the Cardinal for many years: he had blessed his house and officiated at his wedding to Adriana, but the request was unusual.

Like his compatriots, Gino's life had become more problematic. Initially Mussolini's entry into the war on the side of the Axis powers had a minimal impact on everyday life. The 1941 Giro was abandoned, but other races continued as *Il Duce* sought to maintain the activities of everyday life. In part it reflected his belief that the conflict would be short.

A series of 8 one-day races constituted the replacement *Giro di Guerra* in 1942, which Bartali won. Racing was no longer financially beneficial for the riders who relied on the professional circuit for their income with any winnings directed to the war effort. Gino Bartali was better-off than many, having invested his winnings and sponsorship in properties. But with a new son, Andrea, in 1941 and a wider family to support, even he was affected by wartime deprivations.

Tens of thousands of Italian soldiers either filed for discharge from the military – or simply abandoned their posts – following the Italian capitulation to the Allied forces in 1943. Gino was one of them, but they remained in danger of being conscripted or interned by the German occupiers and their puppet Italian fascist government. At one stage, Gino moved his family to a farm near Nuvole in the Tuscan hills, but returned to Florence when his anonymity was breached. He had returned to the Tuscan capital when contacted by Cardinal Dalla Costa.

The meeting at the Cardinal's residence was fateful. The tall, lean 70-year-old was as warm as usual, but Gino detected this was something more than a friendly catch-up. The reason for the meeting soon became clear as the Cardinal moved the discussion from greetings and an inquiry about Adriana and the progress of young Andrea. The elderly prelate had a serious request of the champion cyclist: would he join the networks of trusted Catholics who were secretly working with Delasem to assist Jews escaping the Fascists? Specifically, would he become a courier, ferrying messages and forged identity documents to members of the network?

Cycling and the Story of Italy

Dalla Costa explained to Gino that identity documents were being forged at Assisi but had to be delivered to Florence, a 350-kilometre round trip through areas under the control of German and Italian forces, as well as various fascist groups. There were many checkpoints and army units. At any stage, Gino would be in danger of being stopped and searched. Even suspicion of helping the Jews would be enough to be detained, imprisoned or even shot.

Gino was close to a number of Jewish families who were hiding from the Nazis and their collaborators, so the pressure to assist the cause was enormous. But the dangers also played on his mind, especially the impact on his family should his mission be uncovered.

Dalla Costa's plan was simple in design, but dangerous to execute. Photos of Jewish refugees would be hidden in the bike frame and couriered to Assisi where they would be merged into counterfeit identity cards and returned to Florence. The superior of the San Damiano Monastery at Assisi, Fr Rufino Niccacci, had been enlisted by the Cardinal to oversee the operation in the famous hilltop town. Niccacci had already been protecting Jews, but was finding it increasingly difficult to move them to safe havens. Returning to Assisi, the priest had convinced a local printer, Luigi Brizi, to counterfeit the identity documents.

Within weeks of his conversation with Cardinal Dalla Costa, Gino Bartali began the first leg of his ride to Assisi, pedaling towards Perugia where he planned to stay the night at a local presbytery. He had informed Adriana that he was going training for a few days, a curious thing as the few events that had been conducted the previous year had ceased. Arriving at Assisi the next day, Gino removed his precious cargo of photographs and other documents from the seat post of his bike. It was the first of many such rides that expanded to journeys further south, including Rome, to convey messages to others who smuggled Jews into the Allied occupied south.

It was one of a number of such networks, operating clandestinely and often independently of each other in occupied Italy.

A dreadful choice

The situation for Jews in Italy worsened in October and November 1943. In Rome, the Nazis rounded up 1,259 Jews, 1,007 of whom were transported to Poland, where all but 196 were gassed to death. Similar round-ups occurred in other cities, including Florence. By the Spring of 1944, 6,500 Jews had been deported to Auschwitz alone. Thousands of others were saved by the network of secret hiding places across the country, including hundreds in the Vatican itself. Gino Bartali was one of the many people who helped hide a Jewish family from the Nazis in his own home.

Despite urging from senior figures in the Church and representatives of Allied governments, Pacelli remained firm in his conviction that public condemnation would expose many more people to Nazi retaliation. Pacelli's long-time housekeeper and confidant, Sr Pasqualina Lehnert, recalled Pius XII saying about the mounting criticism of his public silence:

> The Holy Father may go down in history as being anti-Semitic. The Holy See must aid the Jewish people, to the best of our ability. But everything we do must be done with much caution. Otherwise the Church and the Jews themselves will suffer great retaliation. Better the world think of Pius XII as being anti-Semitic than for the Holy See to wear its valor and virtue on its sleeve so that the Nazis can claim more victims.

His concerns were not unfounded. When the Dutch bishops publicly protested against the persecution of Jews in August 1942, Hitler had some 40,000 rounded up and executed overnight. Sr Pasqualina recalls the morning when the horrific events were reported in the newspapers. Returning to the open fire in the kitchen with two, large, closely-written sheets of paper in his hand, a graven Pacelli announced:

> I want to burn these papers. They are my protest against the gruesome persecution of the Jews, which was to appear in the *L'Osservatore Romano* this evening. But if the Dutch bishops letter cost 40,000 lives, my protest would perhaps cost 200,000. I must not and cannot be responsible for that. Hence it is better to remain silent in public and continue to do everything humanly possible for these poor people quietly.

Having burnt the papers, lest they be discovered by the Nazis should they invade the Vatican, and further retribution on Catholics and Jews result, Pius XII said ominously: "He is nailed fast and cannot free himself, can only endure and suffer. The Pope too is nailed to his post and must remain silent."

Hitler had been emboldened to authorise a plot to kidnap the Pope whom he described as a Jew lover, but the plan was subsequently abandoned when it became public. Sensing that the Allies were succeeding against Hitler, some of the leading Germans in Italy quietly worked against the *Feuhrer's* plans.

Arrest – and release

Gino Bartali's activities continued to place him in danger. In July 1944, the Fascist authorities in Florence intercepted letters to him, including one from the Vatican thanking the cyclist for his help. This aroused the suspicions of the head of the local fascists, Mario Carita, who likened himself to the chief of Hitler's feared Gestapo, Heinrich Himmler. The accounts vary, but Bartali was either arrested by the militia or summoned to Carita's headquarters. He was thrown into a dark basement cell where the instruments of Carita's gruesome torture adorned the walls. Accused in subsequent interrogations of supplying arms to the Vatican, Gino responded that the letters referred to the flour, sugar and coffee he had sent to people suffering the deprivations of wartime. Unconvinced, Carita detained Gino for another two days, but he was spared the torture meted out to many others. He was eventually freed after his former military superior at Trasimeno vouched for his honesty. It was a close call.

Luckily for the Bartalis and the Italian people, the Allied forces were advancing, taking Naples and Rome before moving to the north of the country. Adriana was pregnant with their second child. Despite moving to a quieter part of Florence, the stress of events took their toll. The child was stillborn and Adriana very ill. Thankfully, she recovered, but was worn down by the stress of war and the frequent absences of her husband.

The war in Italy eventually came to an end in 1945. Mussolini and his mistress, Claretta Petacci, were executed and strung up by their feet from the roof of a petrol station in Milan. A day later, Hitler and his wife, Eva Braun, committed suicide in their Berlin bunker as Allied forces advanced to the heart of the Third Reich. More than 50 million people were dead. Six million Jews had been sent to their death in concentration camps. In Italy, the Nazis had murdered 15 per cent of the Jewish population, which, along with Denmark, was the lowest proportion throughout Europe. Across the continent people struggled to rebuild their lives amidst the devastation wrought by the six year war.

12

The Resumption of Hostilities

The pedestal of fame is neither very comfortable, nor is it very secure
-- Gino Bartali.

Italy, like much of Europe, was devastated by the war. As the Germans retreated, they destroyed roads, bridges and other critical infrastructure. Allied bombing had consigned many other buildings to rubble. More than a million homes were destroyed in cities throughout the country. Homelessness was endemic, and food shortages widespread. Many people would struggle for the next few years to find adequate provisions to feed themselves and their families. Much of the already poor south in particular was decimated.

Two years after the European war had ended, the journal, *Foreign Affairs,* recorded:

> There is too little of everything — too few trains, trams, buses and automobiles to transport people to work on time, let alone take them on holidays; too little flour to make bread without adulterants, and even not enough bread to provide energies for hard labor; too little paper for newspapers to report more than a fraction of the world's news; too little seed for planting and too little fertiliser to nourish it; too few houses to live in and not enough glass to supply them with window panes; too little leather for shoes, wool for sweaters, gas for cooking, cotton for diapers, sugar for jam, fats for frying, milk for babies, soap for washing.

A wet winter followed by a dry summer in 1947-48 compounded

Gino Bartali using the new Campagnolo gearing system.

the food shortages across much of Europe. In 1946, the Italian painter, writer and poet, Luigi Bartolini, captured the continuing importance of the bicycle and the desperation of the era in his book, *Ladri di biciclette – Bicycle Thieves*. A young couple sells precious dowry items to buy a bike that will enable the husband and father of a young boy to ride to work, only to have it stolen on the first day. Turned into a film two years later by the director, Vittorio De Sica, the masterpiece captures the drama, pathos and hope of Italians struggling with postwar privations in Rome.

Almost a half of all workers were still employed in agriculture as Italians struggled to rebuild their country. Most factories were small, employing less than five people. The north was economically stronger than the impoverished south, but the outlook was pessimistic for many people. The travails of occupation and war had been replaced by the struggle for survival.

Starting over

Like millions of their fellow men and women, Italy's sporting competitors struggled to rebuild their lives, put food on the table, and assess their future prospects. The major cycling events had been abandoned during the German occupation. While some minor regional races were still conducted through the dark days of 1943 and 1944, local riders contested them.

Gino Bartali was both relieved and worried when the war ended: relieved that his secret mission was over and he was free of suspicion by the fascists and others; but concerned about how he would provide for his family and their future. The experiences of the war years seem to have aged him prematurely, his hair receding and his face lined from the worries of the war years. At 31, Gino, like many of the pre-war cycling generation, had lost years of training and racing. But what else could he do?

Fausto Coppi was transferred to Salerno near Naples in early 1945, having spent two years in a British prisoner-of-war camp in Africa. It was a lucky break for the champion cyclist, who had been recruited as a driver by his captors. An old bike was procured for him to return to training, which he continued in earnest after being released, having been treated as a co-operative prisoner after professing his support for the anti-fascist government. While the war still raged in the north, Coppi was able to contest some minor races in the liberated south, as well as returning to the velodrome in Rome, for which he finally received prize money. An enterprising Roman framebuilder, Edmondo Nulli, had sponsored the champion cyclist, allowing him to train and race again. Like Bartali, Coppi worried that he would not be able to reclaim his prewar form, having suffered the deprivations of captivity. His priority was to return home, a 600-kilometre journey that he eventually made mostly on his bike over war torn roads.

The Giro di Guerre

For the early years of the war, life in Italy had continued without great disruption for many people, including the cycling fraternity. The Giro d'Italia was abandoned after the 1940 edition, but other races continued. In 1942, the regime, wanting to project an atmosphere of normalcy across the nation, designated eight classic races as the Giro d'Italia di Guerra. Commencing with the traditional opening race for the season, the charge from Milan to San Remo, and concluding with the Autumnal 'Race of the Falling Leaves' – the Giro di Lombardia – the overall winner of the Giro was decided on a points system.

Although Gino Bartali had won the 1939 and 1940 editions of the *Primavera*, he had finished the 1941 in a large group 5 minutes 37 seconds behind his team-mate from Legnano, Pierino Favalli, who soloed away from Mario Ricci to win the classic. But another rider Adolfo Leoni, would claim the laurels in the traditional opening race for the season in 1942. He had out-sprinted a small group of eight that had escaped from the peloton, finishing 1 minute 45 seconds ahead of the Cino Cinelli and Bartali group, and over three minutes in advance of Coppi, Buni and Bizzi.

The peloton returned to the capital for the second event, the Giro del Lazio – now known as the Roma Maxima. Leaving Rome, the field made a loop to the south through the Alban hills, the scene of fierce fighting two years later, before returning to the eternal city where Osvaldo Bailo claimed victory.

The third race, the Giro di Toscana – first run in 1923 and won by the great Costante Girardengo – was claimed by Vito Ortelli, subsequently a National Pursuit champion, from Bartali and Glauco Servadei. After the first three races, Leoni, the winner of the opening charge to San Remo, held the *maglia rosa,* which he cemented with a win over Bini and Cinelli in the Giro dell'Emilia. The Giro del Veneto, first run in 1909, and one of the most prestigious races on the Italian calendar, kicked off the second half of the eight race series. It was a triumph for Pierino Favalli, riding for Legnano. The 27-year-old had been one of the best amateurs in the world, winning the 1934 National Championship, claiming the bronze in the 1936 World championship and just missing the podium at the Berlin Olympics. He had built on his amateur form upon turning professional, winning Milan-Turin from 1938-40 before claiming Milan-San Remo in 1941. He would subsequently win the penultimate race of the series, the Giro di Campania, the last win of his professional calling. Like many riders, the war would end his cycling career.

It was the sixth race in the Giro di Guerra that would produce a future star of the sport, Fiorenzo Magni, who claimed the laurels from Bartali and Favalli. After an indifferent start to the series, Bartali was finding form as the season progressed, but it was the young rider from Vaiano, a small comune to the north west of Florence, who won the Umbrian classic. With the series being decided on a points score, the overall victory was open leading into the final event, the famed Giro di Lombardia. Favalli had taken the *maglia rosa* from Adolfo Leoni by winning the second last race, but he was just ahead of Bartali.

The 47 cyclists who assembled for the start in Milan on October 17, 1942 included the stars of the Italian sport. Riding for Bianchi, Favalli wore the *maglia rosa*. Amongst the field was Quirino Toccaceli, an independent who wore the white jersey. Coppi was there, but the young rider was not having his best season. Bartali needed a podium result to win the tour. Aldo Bini, riding for Bianchi, prevailed in the Lombardian classic, but Bartali's second placing in the race around Lake Como was sufficient to gain him victory by just two points from Favalli and Leoni. He could add an unofficial Giro d'Italia to his *palmares*.

Two weeks later, Fausto Coppi attempted perhaps the toughest event in cycling, the world one-hour record on the Vigorelli velodrome at Milan. It was, he explained, an endeavour to lift himself "above the rest" at a time when there was little international competition. Cities in the north of Italy were already coming under bombing from the Allied forces and the velodrome was being used by the military for storage and as a air raid shelter. Coppi had not been able to train on the wooden track, and was underprepared for the challenge, a reality that became obvious in the early stages, when he trailed the record of 45.767 kilometres established by the Frenchman, Maurice Archambaud, on the same track five years earlier. Overcoming the exhaustion from pedaling at top speed for an hour, Coppi slowly gained on the record. At the end of the agonizing 60 minutes, he had surpassed the Frenchman by just 31 metres. This was the smallest increase in the distance from the time it was first established by James Moore at Wolverhampton at 23.331 kilometres in 1873, and Eddy Merckx's 49.431 kilometres at altitude in Mexico City in 1972, a time that would stand for 12 years until another Italian, Francesco Moser, using disk wheels and an aero skin suit rode 51.151 kilometres in 1984. Coppi's record time lasted some 14 years, until bettered by Jacques Anquetil in 1956.

Eight races, commencing with Milan-San Remo and concluding with the Giro di Lombardia were planned for the 1943 Giro di Guerre, but only the first four were raced. By the time the field assembled for the start of the *Primavera*, the Italian forces were being routed in Africa. Fausto Coppi was already missing from the peloton, having been called-up and posted to the Tunisia. Although enlisted, Bartali was still able to compete in the diminishing number of races on the peninsula. Despite the increasing privations of war, a crack field assembled for the traditional opener of the season in Milan.

Cino Cinelli

What was to be the last Milan-San Remo for three years belonged to Cino Cinelli, who won the bunch sprint into the Ligurian seaside resort. It was the most significant win of a short but brilliant cycling career that never resumed after the war.

Cinelli was one of a group of talented riders that grew up in Tuscany between the wars. Born two years after his future nemesis, Gino Bartali, the two shared a similar upbringing. The seventh of ten children, Cino was raised by his parents on a small farming allotment near Florence. Travel to school involved cycling kilometres from the farm each day.

Following his two older brothers, Giotto and Arrigo, the young Cino began racing in the local amateur events, outsprinting a young Gino Bartali for second placing in one of his first races. Economic hardship forced Cino to leave school and find work, eventually working with a publishing company where he was able to pursue his cycling ambitions while earning a living. At the age of 21, Cinelli gambled on joining the professional ranks after new management at the publishing company told him he would have to give away the sport if he wished to remain in their employment. His performances repaid the belief he had shown in his own ability, winning a number of races including the tough one-day Giro dell'Appennino in 1937.

By the end of the 1938 season, Cinelli had claimed the Giro di Lombardia from Bartali, having also won the Coppa Bernocchi and two stages of the Giro d'Italia while riding for the Frejus team. Cino was recruited by Bianchi for whom he would win a number of Italian classics over the next few years before his last major victory, the Milan-San Remo in 1943. By then he was enlisted, but was allowed to train and compete by the authorities that wished to project an atmosphere of normalcy in the increasingly troubled country. His last race win came in 1944 as the war reached the Italian peninsula. Post-war, Cinelli turned his attention to bicycle manufacturing, creating a world-renowned business building frames and accessories.

Cinelli eventually finished sixth in the shortened four-race 1943 Giro di Guerra. Olimpio Bizzi won the second and third races in the series, the Trifeo Moschini and the Giro di Toscana, but Glauco Servadei defended the *maglia rosa,* winning the event that turned out to be the last race, the GP Roma and taking the Giro di Guerra honours from Bizzi and Bartali. Both Servadei and Bizzi would resume racing after the war, but their cycling careers eventually ended in the late 1940s, their best days well behind them.

GREAT RIVALRIES

On the road again

The post-war priority for Italians was to rebuild their lives. Much of the vital infrastructure of the nation was destroyed or damaged. Bridges, housing and roads needed rebuilding or repair. Basic services were compromised. Everyday provisions, including food, were in short supply. The liberating Allied forces occupied much of the country. Italian families had to make do with what they had. This included the cyclists trying to start over again with few resources, little opportunity to race, and sparse prize money. Fausto Coppi returned from the war believing that he had the prize money from his Giro victory to rely on, but his parents had invested it in war bonds that proved valueless. Gino Bartali had property, but little income to support his wife and family. Like millions of Italians, they faced a bleak future, with high unemployment, and limited prospects.

Having few skills other than racing a bike, and few other prospects, a desperate group of cyclists led by Gino Bartali and Adolfo Leoni, one of the best sprinters of the era, formed a group to compete wherever they could. Moving from town to town like travelling circus performers, they raced at every opportunity. Leoni rigged an old car as their travelling van, carrying riders and bicycles throughout Italy. They hoped for prize money, but often had to settle for food or other goods, which they cold sell, barter or give to family and friends. The races were often the short circuit criteriums in local villages, or what the Dutch call the *Kermesse* – races on a longer circuit around and through local towns and villages. The riders would sprint for *primes* – prize money for the winner of a lap – in an attempt to increase their income. Although competitive, the mutual camaraderie of hardship usually meant some sharing of the paltry spoils available. Based in Rome, away from family and friends in the north, the group generated the rebirth of Italian cycling, competing on the roads and the available velodromes.

Within six months of the death of Mussolini and the end of the war in Italy, the cycling season was gradually returning to its decades-long pattern. Some of the more important national races resumed, including the Giro del Lazio, Milan-Turin and Tre Valli Varesine. The race that traditionally brings down the shutters on the annual cycling season, the Giro di Lombardia, marked the renewal of post-war racing. Conducted in late October 1945, 137 riders fronted for the start of the 222-kilometre classic near Lake Como, of which 41 completed the gruelling one-day monument. Mario Ricci, who had won the event in 1941, escaped from the field to claim victory for the Legnano team by over six minutes from Bini and Bartali. Ricci, who was the 1943 National Champion, also won the Trofeo Matteotti in Abruzzi and finished second to Leoni at Tre Valli Varesine. Gino Bartail could only manage third at Lombardia. Fausto Coppi had won the GP Lugano in Switzerland and the Ligurian Circuito di Ospedaletti, but it was his brother, Serse, who raced in the Giro di Lombardia, finishing 11th. Serse, who would be an important influence in the life of Fausto, also defeated his older brother in the Milan-Varzi one-day race. Fausto Coppi was gradually regaining his strength, showing a glimpse of the superb form that would be evident the following season, winning the Circuito degli Assi at Milan before a crowd of more than 50,000 people. A golden era of Italian cycling was about to dawn.

The post-war challenge

Italy suffered considerable turmoil following the cessation of hostilities. Up to 15,000 people were killed in reprisals and acts of retribution, especially in the provinces of Lombardy and Emilia-Romagna. The Resistance executed captured fascist leaders such as Roberto Farinacci and Achile Starace. The official response was more ambivalent, given the existence of the widely supported fascist government of Benito Mussolini until September 1943. Further, the Italians, having sided officially with the Allies after the German occupation, were free to try their own collaborators. The result was the derided *Scheda Personale* – a 'were you a fascist' questionnaire – that sought to distinguish those who participated in the post-occupation puppet government at Salò from the previous regime. Even then, sanctions were based on a vaguely worded Decree that censured 'acts of special gravity which, while not in the bounds of crime, [were] considered contrary to the norms of sobriety and political decency'.

The fact that public officials had been required to join the Fascist Party, and most of the judiciary hearing the cases had themselves been fascists, resulted in few dismissals from office and fewer prosecutions. The body administering the program was quietly terminated in 1946.

Of the 50,000 Italians jailed, most were released quickly. Only 50 were executed for collaboration. Leading business figures, which had gained from their involvement with the fascist regime, were unscathed. Most Italians were relieved to put the era behind them.

Ivanoe Bonomi's Labour/Democratic government had lasted just a year, to be replaced by Ferruccio Parri's Action Party administration. Tellingly, the administration of Prime Minister Ferruccio Parri, who hoped to lead a post-war resistance party, fell in six months, leaving the political field to the traditional groupings. Parri's Action Party was dissolved after gaining just seven seats in the 1947 elections. The Communist Party leader, Palmiro Togliatti, who had returned from exile in Moscow, and who had some 50,000 resistance members, followed the Soviet strategy, and supported the restoration of the parliament. Togliatti crafted the general amnesty that was proclaimed in 1946, officially ending the purge of the fascists. The consequence was that many of the public officials from the fascist era remained in office, including the prefects – the powerful centrally appointed heads of the provinces – and chiefs of police.

A new beginning

Uncertainty continued to abound across the nation as the winter of 1945-46 approached. Hundreds of thousands of Italians moved from the country in the first few years after the war, mostly to other parts of Europe in search of work. Some used informal networks of family and friends to emigrate further afield to countries like Australia. Unlike the earlier years of the century, when millions of Italians moved to America, immigration restrictions introduced in the United States in the 1920s meant that just a trickle could travel there after the war. Most had to make the best of their circumstances in a country struggling to rebuild from the war.

Once the war in the north had finished, Fausto Coppi returned in search of his family. Apart from his parents, his priority was to locate his fiancée, Bruna Campolini, to whom he had become engaged in 1943 before he was posted to Africa. Fausto had first met the brown-haired teenager after her parents, grocers from Genoa, sent their daughter to live with an aunt at Villalveria, a small commune on the Scrivia River just 8 kilometres from Castellania. They believed she would be safer in the countryside than in Genoa, which was heavily bombed during the war. In a turn of fate, the US Air Force bombed the village in December 1944, seeking to destroy the Italian Railway offices that had been moved from Genoa. Bruna was unscathed, but 114 people were killed and 235 injured.

In November 1945, Fausto and Bruna married. It was a festive occasion with family and friends. Gino Bartali had ensured that Coppi won a couple of races that would help with the costs and provide the winner's bouquet of flowers for the bride. The couple moved to Sestri Ponente, the suburb of Genoa where Bruna's parents had their shop, to live after the wedding.

Despite their hardships, Italians were determined to get on with their lives. Sporting competitions, whether in the local comune, or at a regional level, were embraced enthusiastically. The national football contest, which had ceased in 1944-45, was re-established, with Turin defeating Juventus for the honours. It would be two years before the summer Olympics resumed in London, at which Italy won two gold medal finals on the velodrome; and the winter games at St Moritz, Switzerland. It was another two years before the first post-war World Football Cup would be played in Uruguay.

As the winter of 1945-46 beckoned, cycling clubs and officials were already planning for the new season, with the *Primavera*, the great opening race from Milan to San Remo, slated for resumption in March.

It was an excited and anxious group of riders who assembled in the cool of the morning of March 19, 1946. The expectation of the large crowd was palpable as they watched the riders preparing for the resumption of the classic race. There was Vito Ortelli, who had won Milan-Turin; Adolfo Leoni, the Tre Valli victor, and Marco Ricci, the vanquisher at autumn's Giro di Lombardia. A few internationals had ventured south of the Alps, most significantly, Lucien Teisseire, the winner of Paris-Tours, and runner up in the famed Paris-Roubaix. Gino Bartali was there as the leader of the Legnano team. And there was Fausto Coppi, wearing the Bianchi colours for the first time, having been overlooked by team boss Eberardo Pavesi for the captaincy of Legnano.

There was no doubt about Coppi's brilliance, both on the track as a pursuit rider, and on the road, but Pavesi wondered about his endurance, and preferred Bartali to continue as team leader. It was a big call: Bartali was approaching 32, having won his first Giro when still 21. Coppi was 26. While a few precocious talents had won the Giro in their early twenties, including Coppi whilst still 20, and Binda at almost 23, professional cyclists seem to be at their best between their mid 20s and their early 30s. Ganna, Valetti and Bunero were all 25 when they first won the Giro; and the great Girardengo was 26. Few riders over 30 had claimed the laurels. Learco Guerra was almost 32 when he won in 1934, and Binda was still 30 when he took his last victory in 1933 but the records favoured riders in their 20s.

Rebuffed by Pavesi, Coppi signed a million-lire contract to don the celeste jersey of Bianchi. Coppi ensured that his brother, Serse, also a good rider, was also signed to the new team, as well as the mechanic from Legnano, Pinella di Grande, to care for his bikes, a key decision as broken or malfunctioning equipment could decide the difference between glory and despair.

Filled with inspiration by his mentor, Biagio Cavanna, Coppi was primed for an aggressive race, having ridden thousands of kilometres in training once the weather permitted it. Expecting the main protagonists such as Bartali to eagerly eye each other, looking for signs of strengths and weaknesses in the first great race for the season, Coppi chose boldness over caution, joining an early escape with the tracks riders. By the time the race he reached to top of the Turchino Pass, Coppi was alone, having dropped his competitors. *"Arriva Coppi,"* shouted the commentator from the race director's car – a descrition that would resound time and again throughout the young cyclist's dazzling career.

It was a brilliant beginning to the season. Coppi rode more than half the 290-kilometre race in the lead, cruising into San Remo a stunning 14 minutes in advance of Lucien Teisseire, and, significantly, 24 minutes ahead of Bartali who could only manage fourth placing. Bianchi was ecstatic; Bartali crestfallen; and the *tifosi* beside themselves. Amidst the post-war poverty and privations, Italians had a new hero to cheer-on. Coppi's tear-away style would feature again and again in the coming years.

Bartali was disappointed and frustrated. The war years seemed to have aged him, physically and mentally. And now his younger rival had thrashed him. Always methodical about his training and racing, to the point he acquired the nickname 'the accountant' for the manner in which he recorded his workouts, Gino became more withdrawn. Soon his opponents had dubbed him *Ginettaccio* – Gino the Terrible – as he faced the prospect of being displaced as the country's best cyclist.

The rivalry between Coppi and Bartali was riveting for the fans, but a more serious and significant issue faced the nation in 1946: the form of its post-war government. Two and a half weeks before Milan-San Remo, the government of Alcide De Gasperi, the Christian Democrat leader, who had become Prime Minister in December 1945, approved the holding of a referendum to determine if Italy would remain a monarchy or become a republic. The issue created great fervour across the peninsula. In May, King Vittorio Emanuelle III abdicated in favour of his son, Umberto, believing that the younger Monarch would be more likely to sway the populace. In the *Referendum Istituzionale*, held on June 2, the Italian people voted by a relatively small majority for a Republic, but the nation remained divided. The outcome was disputed and it was a week before the final result announced. Romans and southern Italians wanted to retain the Monarchy, but northerners preferred a new system of government. Four culturally distinct regions of the country were to be given greater autonomy, although this didn't occur for some time. Many of the fault lines of the Italian nation remained in place.

While political differences split the nation, the new rivalry in cycling was about to erupt. With many of the roads in Italy reduced to rough, pot-holed gravel beds, devoid of their pre-war bitumen, local cyclists were attracted to major events in Switzerland. Although not the cycling powerhouse that was Italy, France and Belgium, the Swiss had produced many champion riders, of which Ferdinand Kübler, simply known as 'Ferdi' was then the greatest.

Searching for form and victories, Gino Bartali ventured across the Alps for a series of races in 1946, winning four, including the Tour de Suisse, and placing in another two. But it was the Zurich Championships race in early May that is most remembered as the fuse that exploded the intense rivalry, already spluttering to light, between Bartali and his younger challenger, Fausto Coppi. Not feeling the best, as can happen to all cyclists from day to day, Bartali agreed not to contest the sprint if Coppi didn't drop him towards the end of the race. But Bartali reneged on the arrangement, out-sprinting his rival. For Coppi, who had been reminded as a young rider by Pavesi in the 1940 Giro that 'a deal is a deal' when he sought to take advantage of Bartali when he flatted, his opponent's actions were contemptible. Never again did he completely trust his older rival.

Giro della Rinascita

In January 1946, *La Gazzetta dello Sport* boldly proclaimed that the Giro d'Italia, absent from the peninsula for the past five years, would be conducted again in the European summer. It was an announcement almost as audacious as the proclamation in 1908 that there would be a grand tour of Italy. With daring confidence, Armando Cougnet, who had founded the Giro four decades earlier, would oversee the rejuvenation of the event. The paper, which he had joined in 1898 as a young sports writer, dubbed the event *Il Giro della Rinascita* – the Tour of Rebirth.

La Gazzetta had been reduced to a weekly edition, printed on white paper, during 1944 and 1945. Its editor, Bruno Roghi, had fled to Switzerland where he assisted Italians seeking refuge. Cougnet also recruited Vincenzo Torriani to assist him with the organization of the race. Torriani would succeed the Giro's founder in 1949, directing the event for the next 33 years.

The national referendum had left Italy divided, but the Giro organizers were determined that the tour would help unite the Italian people. Choosing a route was a major task. Roads had been reduced to rubble, bridges destroyed, and essential services including power and water severely interrupted. Food was in short supply and inflation rampant. Great swathes of the population were unemployed, desperate for food and even clothing. In many respects, the conditions were worse in 1946 than when the Giro commenced in 1909. Despite the challenges, the organizers pressed on. Eventually a figure eight route through northern and central Italy was chosen. Starting in Milan, the race would circle the north via Turin, Genoa, Prato, Bologna to Cesena before travelling down the east coast to Ancona and Chieti, then crossing the mountains to Naples before progressing north to Rome, Perugia, Florence, Rovigo and Trieste. The last stages would be through the Dolomites to Bassano del Grappa and Trent before the final charge to Verona, Mantova and back to Milan. The 29th Giro would be just over 3,000 kilometres.

The race would serve a purpose greater than the contest itself, proclaimed *La Gazzetta*:

> Neapolitans, Torinesi, Lombards and Laziali, Venetians and Emilians, all Italians, all regions with a single society and a single heart, all await the Giro as a mirror in which they can recognize each other and smile.

The peloton of 70 cyclists would be like "a rainbow of hope", added the paper. It would mark "the irrepressible optimism" of the Italian people.

Seven trade teams of seven riders each, and six club groups of four riders each lined up for the start on June 15, the date having been delayed for the national referendum. Only 40 riders would complete the race.

The choice of Trieste on the Adriatic coast was controversial and likely to be provocative to Yugoslavs, who had lost the disputed city to Italy in the postwar carve-up of the region.

Conducted over 23 days, with 6 rest days, the Giro comprised 20 stages or sub-stages, the longest being the 245 kilometres from Florence to Rovigo, and the shortest, the 30 kilometres from Montecatini to Prato, although it was followed by another 112 kilometres to Bologna the same day. *La Gazzetta's* promotion of the tour as a symbol of national hope, unity and reconstruction attracted prominent support. Pope Pius XII blessed the peloton before the stage start in Rome, and Prime Minister De Gasperi watched the mountain stage from Bassano del Grappa to Trent.

The expected fireworks between Bartali and Coppi didn't eventuate in the early stages of the race. A rider named Coppi did wear the mountains leader jersey after stage three, but it was Fausto's brother, Serse, not the more famous sibling. The Wilier Triestina rider, Giordano Cottur, a previous stage winner, claimed the *maglia rosa* after the first day's finish at Turin, but he would fade to finish 38 minutes down in eighth place by the end of the tour. Antonio Bevilacqua, who would subsequently win the World Pursuit Championship on the track, as well as Paris-Roubaix, won two stages and wore the pink jersey for the next three before relinquishing it to the French climber, Fermo Camellini. Fausto Coppi won the dash from Prato to Bologna, but never claimed the leader's jersey.

The decisive move of the tour came on the climb across the spine of the peninsula from Chieti to Naples when Bartali attacked and Coppi suffered both mechanical problems and a stomach upset, losing four minutes to the strong leading group also containing Mario Ricci, Vito Ortelli, Aldo Ronconi and Salvatore Crippa. Bartali's teammate, Mario Ricci, who had succeeded in the Giro di Lombardia in 1941 and the National Championship two years later, claimed the stage. However, it was the Benotto-Superga team rider, Vito Ortelli, who grabbed the *maglia rosa*, and appeared a significant threat to the favoured riders. Ortelli was in fine form, having won the Italian Pursuit Championship and Milan-Turin for two successive years. Aldo Ronconi was also having possibly his best year, winning the Giro della Toscana and National Road title.

The stage to Trieste proved as controversial as many expected: partisan Yugoslavs, protesting the loss of their city to Italy, blocked the route, leading to an all out conflict between them and the armed guards on the tour. Shots were fired and the stage finish abandoned; except for the Wilier Triestina team, which with the help of the American army were transported into the city for a finish, which the local champion, Giordano Cottur duly 'won'.

As described in the Prologue, the lead on the road soared in an intense battle between Bartali and Coppi in the subsequent mountain stages in the north of Italy, with Bartali recovering a significant deficit to Coppi on the charge into Bassano del Grappa. By the time the peloton reached the Arena in Milan, where tens of thousands assembled to witness the climax of the tour, Coppi had clawed back considerable time. In the end, Bartali won the Giro della Rinascita by just 47 seconds. They were 15 minutes ahead of the next riders, Vito Ortelli and Salvatore Crippa. The difference between Bartali and Coppi was just 0.01 seconds a kilometre.

Cycling and the Story of Italy

Both riders closed out their comeback season with more victories. Bartali won the Tour de Suisse and the Marchienne-au-Pont in Belgium, Coppi displayed superb form in the Grand Prix des Nations, a 140-kilometer individual time trial in France, winning by almost three minutes. He also closed out the season with victory in the Giro di Lombardia, although it has been reported that he paid the eventual third place-getter, Michele Motta 30,000 lire to allow him to escape from the break!

The 1946 Giro certainly marked the rebirth of cycling in Italy. It would be another year before the Tour de France would reappear, although there were a series of road races held throughout the country that season. The Giro was a massive undertaking that displayed both the devastation of the war and the optimism of the people. Amidst the struggles to rebuild lives and a nation, Italians found a cause to distract them, and a rivalry that excited passions.

Gino Bartali's 1948 Legnano bike with the Campagnolo Corsa gearing.

13

Great Rivalries

Sport, properly directed, develops character, makes a person courageous, a generous loser, and a gracious victor; it refines the senses, gives intellectual penetration, and steels the will to endurance

-- Pius XII

That's what you get when you suffer – you get results

-- Paul Sherwen, former professional cyclist and media commentator.

Widely held fears motivated behaviour of many nations following the war: Western Europeans were driven by a fear of a German revival; Eastern Europeans by the threat of Stalin's Soviet ambitions; and for many elsewhere, the concern of a collapse of the world economic order. The latter concern particularly motivated the American Administration as it responded to the physical and economic devastation of Europe and the pressures in the US to bring the troops home.

These fears had not suddenly arisen. More than a decade earlier in 1939-40, the Nazis and Stalin had made secret pacts dividing Europe. Subsequent meetings between the Allies and the Soviets underpinned the breakup of Germany and the Russian influence on Eastern Europe and the Balkans, arrangements which the famous conference between Churchill, Roosevelt and Stalin at Yalta in 1945 largely formalised.

In the first few months of 1947, the United States had loaned some $8 billion to European countries just to maintain essential supplies and services. While the bulk of $4.4 billion was directed to the United Kingdom, many other European nations benefitted, including $513 million to Italy. As the US Secretary of State, George C Marshall, later observed, the obvious destruction of cities and essential infrastructure "was probably less serious than the dislocation of the entire fabric of [the] European economy," adding "the breakdown of the business structure of Europe during the war was complete."

In a Commencement Speech at Harvard University in June 1947, Marshall summarised the economic failure:

> The town and city industries are not producing adequate goods to exchange with the food-producing farmer. Raw materials and fuel are in short supply. Machinery is lacking or worn out. The farmer or the peasant cannot find the goods for sale which he desires to purchase. So the sale of his farm produce for money which he cannot use seems to him an unprofitable transaction. He, therefore, has withdrawn many fields from crop cultivation and is using them for grazing. He feeds more grain to stock and finds for himself and his family an ample supply of food, however short he may be on clothing and the other ordinary gadgets of civilization. Meanwhile people in the cities are short of food and fuel. So the governments are forced to use their foreign money and credits to procure these necessities abroad. This process exhausts funds which are urgently needed for reconstruction. Thus a very serious situation is rapidly developing which bodes no good for the world.

By mid-1947, Marshall realised that the piecemeal response was failing to address the complete breakdown of the European economy and proposed a new approach.

> It is logical that the United States should do whatever it is able to do to assist in the return of normal economic health in the world, without which there can be no political stability and no assured peace. Our policy is directed not against any country or doctrine but against hunger, poverty, desperation and chaos. Its purpose should be the revival of a working economy in the world so as to permit the emergence of political and social conditions in which free institutions can exist . . . there must be some agreement among the countries of Europe as to the requirements of the situation and the part those countries themselves will take in order to give proper effect to whatever action might be undertaken by this Government. It would be neither fitting nor efficacious for this Government to undertake to draw up unilaterally a program designed to place Europe on its feet economically. This is the business of the Europeans. The initiative, I think, must come from Europe. The role of this country should consist of friendly aid in the drafting of a European program and of later support of such a program so far as it may be practical for us to

do so. The program should be a joint one, agreed to by a number, if not all European nations.

The Marshall Plan was central to the reconstruction of Europe. Over the next four years, some $12 billion (some $100 billion in today's dollars) was provided to the participating European nations. Originally, the Soviet Union and countries in the eastern block were involved, but Stalin withdrew, forcing other nations in the region to follow. The seeds of a new 'cold war' were being planted.

World leaders were also seeking to replace the structures that had failed prior to the war, significantly the League of Nations and the world financial system. The former resulted in the new United Nations Organisation and the latter, the Bretton Woods conference, championed by John Maynard Keynes and other leading economists. The International Monetary Fund, the World Bank and the General Agreement of Trade and Tariffs were born of these discussions.

In Moscow, Stalin presumed that his communist regime would control the affairs of the eastern bloc, expecting that the western alliances would eventually splinter. His confrontational approach ultimately produced a divided Germany, which, contrary to the desires of many European nations, regained its strength in the West. Continuing fears about the place of Germany in Europe gave birth eventually to the European Union as a device to develop trade and prevent further Continental wars.

Political, economic and strategic factors interacted with each other, producing both confluences and conflicts that played out differently across Europe. For Italians, the economic and political pressures were acute. The settlement of these issues would determine the directions of the nation for the following decades. At the forefront of Italian concerns were the reconstruction of the country and the alleviation of the widespread poverty that followed the war, and the maintenance of a united nation.

Reconstructing the State

The post-war Italian leadership was fixated on two political objectives: the continuing unity of the nation; and a constitutionalism that would avert any future lurch to the single party rule that occurred in 1922.

Despite the widespread appeal of the *Risorgimento*, parts of Italy strongly clung to their regional independence. This was particularly the case in Sicily which had resisted the 1860s reforms and voted in favour of retaining the monarchy. The resulting constitution was a compromise between a bicameral Parliament, universal suffrage and a Head of State with limited powers, and the establishment of regional Parliaments and governments in a number of culturally distinct regions, including Sicily, Sardinia, Val d'Aosta and Trentino Alto Adige.

The progress to peace and reconstruction was fraught. Two men in particular, Alcide De Gasperi and Palmiro Togliatti, one a Christian Democrat and the other a Communist, shaped the direction of the nascent republic. De Gasperi, a native of Tyrol in the Austrian Hungarian Empire before its accession to Italy, had served in the Austrian *Reichscrat* for six years before the Great War. He co-founded *Partito Popolare Italiano* – the Italian People's Party – in 1919 and served in the Parliament from 1921-1924. Arrested by the fascists, he spent a year and a half in jail before Vatican influence helped to free him. De Gasperi spent the next 14 years working in the Vatican library until the fall of the fascist regime in July 1943.

Palmiro Togliatti was born into a middle class family in Genoa. In 1921, he co-founded the Communist Party in Italy of which the General Secretary was the political theorist, Antonio Gramsci. With the imprisonment of Gramsci, Togliatti became the leader, a position he held until his death in 1964. He moved to the Soviet Union during the fascist era to avoid arrest, returning to Italy after the fall of Mussolini.

It was the interplay between these two men following the war, each sheltered during the fascist era, which would help to shape both Italy and modern Europe. De Gasperi's political ideals were founded in his social justice ideals; Togliatti's revolutionary spirit was shaped by Gramsci's belief, inspired partially by the spread of Catholicism, that successful change was based on a war of ideas.

With fascism as dead as Mussolini's lifeless body, the battle lines over the future of Italy were being redrawn. The split on the left between socialists and communists allowed De Gasperi to become Prime Minister although his party had only won 35 per cent of the vote in the first democratic elections for two decades. The new Prime Minister had not wasted his years in the Vatican library. In 1943, he published *Idee Ricostruttive* – Ideas for Reconstruction – that became the platform for the new Christian Democrat party. Although Catholic in values, De Gasperi was mindful of the demise of the People's Popular Party in the 1920s and maintained an arm's distance from the official church.

Considerable social unrest swept the nation in 1946-47. Mass lay-offs added to already high levels of unemployment. Those in work gained some concessions, including guaranteed national minimum wages and other entitlements, including an inflation pegging measure, but Italian workers remained some of the lowest paid in Europe. De Gasperi formed a new government in late January 1946 following the resignation of the previous administration after less than two months in the job. Further unrest broke out following the signing of the peace treaty that ceded the nation's colonies and transferred the navy to the victors.

Return to racing

Europe suffered a particularly harsh winter in early 1947. Across the continent, families shivered through harsh conditions, often bereft of fuel for heating, clothes for warmth and food to alleviate the pangs of hunger. Snow fell on the Ligurian plains in northwestern Italy, while to the east, the lagoons of Venice had frozen over.

The weather had warmed a little by March, but the temperature was still colder than usual as a field of 132 riders assembled in Milan on the 19th for the annual opening race of the season to San Remo. Of the 132 starters, 93 cyclists, including Fausto Coppi, would abandon the race. Gino Bartali emerged the victor, almost four minutes ahead of Ezio Cecchi, riding for the Welter team, and nine minutes in advance of a group of six including the brothers, Sergio and Luciano Maggini, and Fiorenzo Magni.

With Bartali and Coppi having won the the previous two Italian monuments, the Giro di Lombardia and Milan-San Remo, the scene was set for the 30th Giro d'Italia, which was returning to its traditional May running. The *tifosi* were beside themselves in anticipation. Sylvère Maes, the Swiss victor in the 1936 and 1939 Tour de France, joined the field, but the Italians were interested only in the contest between Bartali and Coppi. Their wild enthusiasm led the organisers to arrange guards to protect the cyclists throughout the 3,865 kilometre race which started in Milan and travelled to Bari in the south before returning north via the Dolomites.

Many great sporting events involve an heroic struggle between the contestants: England's 3-2 win over Germany in extra time in the 1966 World Cup; Bjorn Borg's epic five set win over John McEnroe in the 1980 Wimbledon final; and Greg LeMond's eight second victory over Laurent Fignon in the 1989 Tour de France.

Other contests can be determined in instant: a lapse of concentration, an accident or mechanical failure, or a commanding performance: Jesse Owen's domination on the track at the 1936 Olympics; Mohammed Ali's first round knockout of Sonny Liston in their second world title clash; and Bob Beamon's world record long jump at the 1968 Olympic Games.

The 1947 Giro d'Italia was the latter. It was the beginning of a new era, with the *isolato* – the independent riders – of the pre-war tours absent for the first time. Bianchi had not won the grand event since Gaetano Belloni's victory in 1920 – an extraordinary absence considering the company's longstanding commitment to the sport. Coppi was their great hope to break the victory drought, but Bartali was determined to repeat his previous year's performance.

It was Gino who got the first break in a see-sawing race after one of his *gregari*, Renzo Zanazzi, won the opening stage to Turin and donned the *maglia rosa*. Zanazzi held the jersey until the first climber's stage, which Coppi claimed. Bartali won the second stage, and took the leader's pink jersey on stage four. Many of the roads were still in a terrible condition, leading to a 'go-slow' by the peloton on the seventh stage to Rome. To the mounting excitement of his fans, Coppi won another stage, but Bartali clung to a lead of almost three minutes as the peloton raced south through Rome and Naples to Bari before turning northwards along the Adriatic coast.

Bartali retained his lead on the 15th stage, the first venture by the peloton into the Dolomites. He and Coppi finished together at Pieve di Cadore. The riders rested for two days in the small lakeside town near the Austrian border where the famous painter, Titian, had been born, before tackling the remaining four stages.

Cycling and the Story of Italy

Stage 16 was planned as a monster trek over three major passes – the Selle, the Falzarego and the Pordoi – to Trent. Heavy snow rendered the Selle impassable, reducing the stage to the two other ascents. Coppi and Bartali were evenly pitted as they departed Pieve di Cadore for the 194 kilometres trek through the Alps. In the days before the modern derailleur, riders had to use a lever fixed to the rear of the bike frame to move the chain from one cog to another. It was a major advance on having to dismount the bike to swap the rear wheel, but it was still an imprecise action that often resulted in the chain dislodging from the cogs. When Bartali dropped his chain on the Falzarego, Coppi seized the advantage peddling clear of his rival.

Six decades later, when the Spanish star, Alberto Contador, charged ahead of his Luxembourg rival, Andy Schlek, who dropped a chain three kilometres from the summit of the Port de Bales on stage 15 of the 2010 Tour de France, fierce polemics broke out amongst cycling fans. Contador should have waited, protested many, even though Schleck had initiated the attack, and was also fighting off two other rivals. But the Canadian star, Ryder Hesjedal, bluntly asserted the competitive reality in the peloton: "If you draw your sword and you drop it, you die."

Coppi must have subscribed to that view, cresting the Falzarego ahead of his nemesis. Bartali fought back on the descent, catching Coppi when the younger rider suffered his own chain problems. After crossing the valley below, the leading group came back together for the final climb of the day. Coppi sprouted wings on the rough switchbacks of the Pordoi, flying away from his rivals. In the space of half an hour, Coppi demolished the best cyclists in the world, rolling into Trent over four minutes ahead of the chasers. Barring misfortune, the Grand Tour was his. Coppi would retain the one minute 43 seconds lead that he established in that stage, winning his second Giro in Milan three days later. Unlike his previous win in 1940, the 27-year-old Fausto was able to celebrate his remarkable victory with Bruna and teammates.

Civil unrest grips Italy

As the three week Giro was beig raced around Italy, civil unrest fermented across the new republic. A new constitution had been adopted in March; and the Lateran Treaty with the Vatican reaffirmed.

High unemployment and low wages were the cause of increasing agitation. Secondary school teachers went on strike in April, causing the government to increase salaries for more than a million public sector workers by 15 per cent.

Elections for the first autonomous Parliament in Sicily, in which the Communist-Socialist-Actionist bloc won a third of the votes, compared to the Social Democrats one-fifth, stirred further unrest on the southern island. The surprising victory for the leftist bloc stirred speculation that the coalition of Palmiro Togliatti could win the national elections scheduled for October.

Togliatti, who had been exiled in Moscow during the fascist years, believed that the left could only succeed through Parliamentary support in a post-war, Allied-aligned Italy. Consequently, he supported the new constitution, including the incorporation of the Lateran Treaty, and was reluctant to capitalise on the widespread civil unrest.

On May 1, three weeks before the 1947 Giro was the start, eleven people, including four children, were killed and another 27 injured at Piano dei Greci, a small mountain valley village on the outskirts of Palermo. Machine guns had rained deadly fire on the parade in which they had been participating. A Sicilian separatist leader and bandit, Salvatore Giuliano, claimed responsibility for the massacre, although many suspected mafia involvement following proposals by the communists to redistribute any land holdings over 100 hectares. The tensions had been exacerbated by the decrees issued by the Minister for Agriculture, Fausto Gullo, between 1944 and 1946. A communist, Gullo, sought to breakup the large landholdings and encourage peasants to form farming cooperatives.

In response to a call by the Italian Labour Confederation, many workers went on strike, and as many as 6 million people attended mass rallies across the country. Talk of civil war swept the nation. When the Minister for the Interior told Parliament that the police considered the killings non-political, a brawl broke out between deputies in the chamber. Less than six months after its creation, the new republic was in danger of collapse.

Two weeks later the De Gasperi government resigned, but unable to find a successor who could form a viable administration, the Italian

President turned again to the Christian Democrat leader, who formed a new government. As the Giro d'Italia peloton cycled the country, the Prime Minister prepared a new program that narrowly passed the Assembly on the third last day of the grand tour. A week later, De Gasperi's government survived a vote of confidence after the majority elected to postpone the national elections to 1948.

Unrest continued throughout the latter months of the year. In September, widespread strikes, involving some two million farm and other workers, broke out across the Po valley. The release of prominent fascists from prison sparked further protests, with Togliatti threatening to unleash tens of thousands of armed partisans if the government did not "give us prompt proof of its democratic spirit." De Gasperi survived more votes of no-confidence in the Parliament as the country stumbled towards winter.

The great rivalry

Any thoughts that Fausto Coppi's victory in the Giro d'Italia was exceptional were forcefully dispelled by his performances over the season. He claimed the national championship in a series of eight one-day races, won the Tours of Veneto and Emilia, and rounded out the season by defeating Gino Bartali in the 'Race of the Falling Leaves' – the Giro di Lombardia. And for good measure, the Italian won the World Pursuit Championship on the track in Paris from his fellow countryman, Antonio Bevilacqua, and the champion Swiss rider, Hugo Koblet.

The 1947 season exposed the intense rivalry between Bartali and Coppi. Gino had started the season asserting that he would defeat his younger rival in the Giro, but ended claiming that Coppi had drafted off the convoy, and even that he had allowed him to win otherwise Bianchi would have withdrawn their sponsorship. Whatever his other qualities, Gino was a poor looser. His season was not without success: he won the Tour de Suisse and was runner-up in the Tour of Romandie, the two major races in Switzerland.

The *tifosi*, having endured another cold hungry winter, expectantly yearned for the resumption of the great rivalry with the opening race of the new season, the 290-kilometre chase from Milan to San Remo.

But their hopes of an exciting tussle over the Turchino Pass and along the Ligurian coast were unmet: Coppi simply rode away from the field, defeating Vittorio Rosello and Fermo Camellini by more than five minutes, with the others further behind. Bartali, along with Magni and the Swiss star, Hugo Koblet, was 30th, more than 11 minutes behind the winner. Coppi's victory was a portent of the year ahead. It was also an example of the attacking style that would mark him out as one of the greatest cyclists of all time.

Far from the clumsy teenager that Cavanna first encountered, Fausto had transformed into the complete cyclist. André Leducq, a dual winner of the Tour de France, marvelled:

> He seems to caress rather than grip the handlebars, while his torso appears fixed to the saddle. His long legs extend to the pedals with the joints of a gazelle. At the end of each pedal stroke his ankle flexes gracefully. It's as if all the moving parts turn in oil. His long face appears like the blade of a knife as he climbs without apparent effort. He rides like a great artist painting a watercolour.

In style and temperament, Coppi and Bartali could not be more apart. Gino was talkative, whether on a training ride or socialising with riders from the peloton. Fausto was more reserved than his older competitor. Gino often appeared impatient in a race, attacking repeatedly in an effort to gain a break on the field. Fausto waited patiently until the right moment, often a counter attack in which he simply put a few bike lengths on the peloton. But once away, he was always difficult to reel in. It was as if he preferred the solitude of the road to himself, his body and mind in unison with the bike – man and machine as one. Gino was a more powerful sprinter, but Fausto had the ability to ride a sustained pace for kilometre after kilometre. They were the yin and yang of the cycling world, acquaintances rather than close friends, fierce rivals on the road.

The political contest

An even greater rivalry gripped Italy in 1948. It would determine the future of the nation for decades to come. The immediate contest was the national election but it morphed into a proxy for the spawning conflict between the east and the west.

Cycling and the Story of Italy

The nascent conflict between the United States and the Soviet Union had gained momentum across Europe in 1947. The *Voice of America* commenced broadcasting into Eastern Europe until jammed by the Soviets in February the following year. The Soviets feared American domination of the continent, claiming that the United States was planning war. Stalin was also suspicious of the Marshall proposals, believing that US funding would draw the nations of Eastern Europe into the American sphere. In America, the concerns were different: the Republicans in particular feared that the Marshall Plan would become a bottomless pit of funding Europe. A Communist coup in Czechoslovakia in February/March crystallised the divide – the Cold War had started. American objections to the Marshall Plan evaporated, while the Soviet Union and the nations under its influence – Czechoslovakia, Bulgaria, Poland, Romania, Hungary and Albania – withdrew. Finland also declined to participate, fearing retaliation by the Soviet bear.

These events spilled over into the Italian national elections that had been postponed from 1947. Following the success of the socialists and communists in the Sicilian elections, the United States feared that the Left wing grouping, *Fronte Democratico Popolare* – the Popular Democratic Front – would defeat the *Democrazia Cristiana* – the Christian Democrats. Both the United States and the Soviet Union channeled millions of dollars into the campaign that pitted Alcide De Gasperi against Palmiro Togliatti.

De Gasperi had visited the United States in January 1947, where he obtained loan monies for his nation. More importantly, his visit – which had been organised by Henry Luce, the owner of *Time* magazine, and his wife Clare Boothe Luce, a future Ambassador to Italy – received favourable attention from the US media. The visit cemented De Gasperi into the US led, western orbit against the Soviet comiform.

Time magazine echoed western fears, describing the election as "more important to the US than its own presidential election next November." Noting the door-to-door campaign in which the Christian Democrats were working to get supporters out to vote while the communists talked about the high cost of living, the magazine warned:

> A Communist-dominated Italy would be far more dangerous than a Communist Czechoslovakia or than a Red threat to Greece or Turkey

against which President Truman had issued a dramatic warning a year ago.

A week later, the magazine observed that "Italy was taut with the danger of civil war." Violence erupted in many places; the military staged a massive parade through Rome, as the Interior Minister, Mario Scelba, announced that the armed forces would be used if the communists tried to make trouble on Election Day. Italian-American celebrities such as Frank Sinatra were enlisted to send messages of support for the Christian Democrats. A *Time* correspondent reported:

> Rome's aged brown walls are heavy with garish tapestries – purple, green, red, black elections posters, shrieking at the people. (If you want jobs and bread, some land to till, some peace to enjoy, vote Communist; if you believe in God, fear Communism, hate tyranny, vote Christian Democrat.)

The historian, Gianni Corbi, observed that the campaign was "the most passionate, the most important, the longest, the dirtiest, and the most uncertain electoral campaign in Italian history."

The US Central Intelligence Agency, which was involved in seeking the defeat of the communists, had secret plans for military intervention, should it prove necessary. In the last two weeks, the mood favoured De Gasperi. Togliatti was booed at Lecce when he denounced the Marshall Plan. Even if the Christian Democrats won, many feared that the Communists would provoke violence and a civil war (on the Greek pattern) immediately after the election, or permit a non-communist government to take over, but then try to wreck it through strikes and sabotage. The concerns were not fanciful: tens of thousands of communist partisans had never surrendered their arms with which they had fought the Germans; and the country's Labour unions had demonstrated their capacity for a national strike during the long campaign.

Time, owned by the ardent anti-communist, nationalist Republican, Henry Luce, and which featured De Gasperi on its cover, summarised the Western view of the looming election:

> What happened in Italy in the days just ahead would answer one vital question: Can Communists capture a nation where there is neither Red army nor Red police? The result would decide whether Italy would take her place with Western Europe (and Western Union) or

with the satellite East. And that decision, in turn, would affect the worldwide question of war and peace. For it was a simple fact that Italy formed a precarious bulge in the West's defenses: if this battle of the bulge were lost, Communism would stand at the Alps and reach deep into the Mediterranean.

Those, in addition to the immediate fate of 50 million Italians, were the stakes involved in the Italian elections.

That the result could even for a moment be in doubt was a bitter comment on the West's terrible uncertainty. It was in the Italian peninsula that the West's Christian faith, bearing a cross and strange new hopes, had begun its conquest of the world. Was it to be defeated now, on the soil on which it had been strongest, by the new tyrannical faith of Communism?

In the end the Christian Democrats won convincingly, scoring 48 per cent of the vote to the Popular Front's 31 per cent. The vote gave the party an absolute majority in both chambers of the Italian Parliament and founded rule by the Christian Democrats for the subsequent 48 years. From 1946 until 1994, the *Democrazia Cristiana* was the largest party in the Italian Parliament, governing in coalition. The unlikely De Gasperi became Italy's fifth longest serving Prime Minister, holding office until 1953.

It is unsurprising that Italy's two greatest cyclists were drawn into the political maelstrom. Gino Bartali was not only linked to Catholic Action; he was a friend of Alcide De Gasperi. The Communists sought Coppi's endorsement, but he declined. According to others, he privately supported the Christian Democrats. Nonetheless, both riders were deployed in the campaign. Coppi's biographer, William Fotherington, writes:

> Bartali was '*De Gasperi in bicicletta*', Coppi 'the Togliatti of the road'. There were posters too: 'Up with Coppi the Communist, down with Bartali the Christian Democrat'.

As Italians went to the polls on April 18, the focus of both Bartali and Coppi was elsewhere: the 31st edition of the Giro d'Italia was only three weeks away from starting in Milan. It was the most anticipated Giro for a long time – and would become one of the most controversial.

A little help from friends

The *tifosi* seemed more excitable than ever as the riders rolled out of Milan on the first stage of the 190-kilometre ride to Turin. The leading riders, who allowed a break including the consistent Wilier-Triestina team member, Giordano Cottur, to ride away, did not match their eagerness. Cottur was a good climber who came to notice as an amateur winning the Bassano-Monte Grappa race twice in 1935-36, then claiming stages of the Giro d'Italia in 1938-39 and again in 1946-47. He had a top ten finish in both the Giro and the Tour de France the previous year, marking him as one of the better riders in the post-war peloton.

It was thought that Bartali and Coppi had agreed to wait until the final stage in the Dolomites to battle for supremacy, coasting into Turin seven and a half minutes behind the stage winner and two other riders. Usually the peloton are watchful of whom to allow a break, and by what margin. Team leaders will permit riders who pose no threat to the General Classification to escape, but usually combine to reel them back, or limit the margin by the end of the stage. In 1948, there was no separate classification for the sprinters: the green jersey, so coloured because it was initially sponsored by the lawn-mower producer, *La Belle Jardinière* was introduced at the 1952 Tour de France to provide an incentive for the fast men to contest the entire event, rather than abandon once the steep ascents commenced. It wasn't until 1966 that a sprinter's points classification was introduced to the Giro d'Italia.

The complacency of Legnano and Bianchi continued day after day as the route took them south. On stage nine over the Apennines to Naples, the two teams allowed another break including Vito Ortelli, Ezio Cecchi, Fiorenzo Magni and Aldo Ronconi to gain more than 13 minutes on the group of Bartali and Coppi. It was either supreme confidence – or supreme arrogance – on the part of Bartali and Coppi to allow their adversaries to steal such a commanding advantage. Not that much changed in the next few stages as the Giro headed north: the stages were claimed by the *gregari*, as the 'heads of state' waited for the mountains.

If the *tifosi* had been eager at the start of the tour, they were now agitated. Vito Ortelli led Magni by a minute and a half until he flatted on the stage from Bologna to Udine, giving the powerful Tuscan a narrow lead over Cecchi as the peloton headed to the mountains. Coppi and Bartali were facing a massive challenge to even make the podium with just three -mountain stages before the final charge from Trent to Milan. The record million-lire first prize, sponsored by the betting agency, Totip, and RAI, appeared to be slipping from their grasp.

Coppi was undaunted. As the road from Auronzo to the mountain town of Cortina d'Ampezzo ascended steeply over the Monte Croce pass, Fausto attacked, taking three and a half minutes from the chasers including Bartali. Even then, Coppi was more than eight minutes behind the leaders, Cecchi and Magni. The following stage 17 is one of the most talked about in the history of the Giro. Coppi attacked again on the steep climbs over the Falzarego and the Pordoi passes, taking time from the chase group, including Magni. Bartali's prospects were dealt a mortal blow when he suffered two punctures, and the race leader, Cecchi couldn't hold the Magni group. Fausto was just one minute 20 seconds in arrears of Magni. He had ridden with wings beneath his saddle, but what he didn't expect was the assistance that Magni received from Wilier fans on the Pordoi, who pushed their hero at every opportunity. Coppi's six minute advantage early on the climb was reduced to less than three minutes by the time the two riders reached the summit.

Coppi protested and officials penalised Magni two minutes, not accepting that the Wilier rider had organised the assistance that the *tifosi* regularly offered their heroes, despite the fact that many fans had been bussed in by the sponsor. No doubt the effect of the controversy on sales of *La Gazzetta* played a part in the decision. The outcome enraged Fausto, and the whole Bianchi team quit the race. Magni, who eventually defeated Cecchi by just 11 seconds, later said that he didn't believe the penalty was why Bianchi abandoned; putting the poor reception he received in Milan down to the fans' letdown. "I was Coppi's friend, as with Bartali, nothing changed between us after this episode." Coppi was suspended for a month for quitting.

Coppi was still seething a week after the Giro, and refused to join the Italian team for the Tour de France. At least that saved the Italian cycling officials the Herculean task of endeavouring to reconcile Coppi with teammates for the event. Instead captaincy of the team went to the seasoned Bartali, who had managed to finish eighth in the Giro despite a string of mechanical problems at key points. At 34, the odds were stacked against the Tuscan. It was a decade since Gino had conquered the French and only two riders had won the Tour when older than 33 – Firmin Lambot in 1922 and Henri Pélissier in 1923 – and only one since – Cadel Evans in 2011. The Italian public held high expectations for their national team, the first to contest the three-week race since the war. The previous year a team of Italians residing in France competed, but lingering post-war tensions precluded an official national squad.

The 1948 Tour was to show glimpses of a future star of the sport, not that many would have thought so at the time. Twenty-three-year-old Louison Bobet was starting his second tour, having abandoned the 1947 edition in tears after eight stages. The young Breton was noticed by the cycling world when he claimed the French Amateur Road Race in 1946, but his abandonment of the 1947 Tour left many wondering if he was too soft for the unforgiving world of the professional peloton.

Jean Robic, the victor in 1947, was back to defend his crown in Paris. Standing just 161 centimetres, this pocket-sized dynamo from Brittany won the national Cyclo-Cross championship in 1945, and would claim the world title five years later. The 1947 race involved an epic battle between René Vietto, and the Italians, Pierre Brambilla and Aldo Ronconi for much of the event. Robic, riding for a regional squad after being neglected by the national team, was a pugnacious, but unpopular member of the peloton. In the final stage, he attacked with race leader, Brambilla, and Eduoard Fachleitner. The two then dropped the *maillot jeune*. Robic offered his compatriot 100,000 francs to secure the win in Paris. Knowing that he could not win himself, being almost seven minutes down on the General Classification, 100,000 francs was a handy reward for Fachleitner to help Robic take the three minutes from Brambilla to claim victory. Hence the Breton became first winner of the Grand Tour not to wear the yellow jersey until the final presentation. It would be another 21 years before the Dutch rider, Jan Jansen, repeated the feat.

Robic was in good form in 1948, finishing third to Fachleitner in the traditional multi-stage, mountainous hit-out for the Tour, the Critérium du Dauphiné Libéré. The field also included Alberic 'Briek' Schotte, the strong Flandrian who had dominated Paris-Tours for the previous two seasons, as well as winning Paris-Brussels. Schotte would go on to win the World Championship in 1948 and 1950, and after retiring from the peloton, coach the dominant Flandria team. The multiple Tour stage winner, both before and after the war, and runner-up in the 1939 edition, Rene Vietto, was also vying for the elusive victory, although, at 34, his best years were probably behind him.

Gino Bartali flew the flag for the Italy in the rain-sodden 237-kilometre opening stage from the capital to Normandy. But there his luck ended. The Italian was delayed by a crash in the next stage, finishing four minutes behind the new leader, Belgian Jean Engels and Louison Bobet. With another year's experience, Bobet was a stronger rider, physically and mentally. He made breaks in the early stages as the tour raced south towards the Pyrenees to lead the Belgian, Roger Lambrecht. In the meantime, Bartali was languishing in the peloton, 20 minutes behind the young leaders. It looked like Gino's best days were well and truly behind him.

Perhaps the destination for the seventh stage, Lourdes, motivated the devout Bartali, as he led both Robic and Bobet over the Aubisque to claim a narrow win. According to Catholic belief, Mary, the mother of Christ, appeared on some 18 occasions to a local peasant girl, Bernadette Soubirous, in 1858. As he demonstrated with his visit to a Marian shrine in Paris after winning the 1938 Tour, Gino had a devotion to Mary. At Lourdes, he visited the famous shrine, praying not to crash as he did in his ill-fated 1937 Tour. Whether motivated by prayer or otherwise, Bartali was finding his legs:

> Guys, I said to my team-mates Corrieri, Bevilacqua, Pasquini and the others, the French are going to attack us today, we have to show that we don't fear anybody. It's necessary to ride fast from the beginning to tire them, then I'll take care of the situation. I drank a coffee and I smoked half a cigarette that gave me some energy, and we arrived all togather at the starting point.

Gino led a select group of 24 cyclists over four major cols, the Tourmalet, the Aspin, the Peyresourde and the Ares, to win the stage. Despite Gino's efforts, Bobet continued to lead the race, with more than 20 minutes advantage over the Italian as the race passed the half way mark and headed north again into the Alps. A repeat of 1938 seemed impossible, as Bobet, a decade younger than Bartali, continued to duel for the lead with Roger Lambrecht, who was having his best year in the professional ranks.

In the meantime, events in Italy reached a crescendo, seriously placing in danger the fledgling republic.

Saving the Republic

While the Christian Democrats had won the election convincingly, the tensions and antagonisms of the long, partisan and sometimes violent campaign simmered. The Popular Front was a coalition of different interests with often varied objectives. Although Palmiro Togliatti was the political head, his grouping included Luigi Longo, the general of Italy's wartime communist partisans; Giuseppe Di Vittorio, boss of the unions; and the socialists of Pietro Nenni. A coalition, especially in defeat, can easily splinter into its constituent parts.

Togliatti's inclinations were conciliatory. He was a believer in Gramsci's 'long march' rather than precipitous revolutionary action. But controlling the disparate groups that comprised his political coalition was demanding and uncertain. These tensions unexpectedly came to a head on July 14, 1948, just 12 weeks after the national election.

As Togliatti was leaving the Parliament, a fervent anti-Communist, Antonio Pallante, shot him three times, causing life-threatening injuries. Pallante seems to have been a mentally disturbed lone wolf who feared a Soviet invasion of the Eastern block. News of the asassination attempt quickly spread by radio across the country. Within hours, workers went on strike and inundated city squares as protests spread from Rome to Genoa, Florence, Turin, Venice and elsewhere. Doctors operated on the stricken Togliatti, saving his life. The Communist leader called for calm, but the demonstrations intensified, with some protesters resorting to violence. The country was on the brink of widespread civil conflict.

As these events played out across Italy, the Tour de France peloton was resting on the Côte d'Azur at Cannes before tackling the the major climbs in the Alps. Despite better form in the recent stages, Gino Bartali still trailed the leaders by 20 minutes. While at his hotel, Gino received a call from his friend, Alcide De Gasperi. The Prime Minister had an idea: if Gino could win another stage of the Tour, it might divert attention from the brewing troubles in Italy – and even unite the fraying nation. Although not recorded, the conversation proceeded:

"Gino, we need you," stressed De Gasperi.

"But what can I do? I am here to race the next stage of the Tour de France, not come home to Italy," replied Gino.

"Exactly, you can do a lot by just winning stages," said the Prime Minister. "If you win a few, it will create a diversion. It will motivate Italian people towards happier feelings. A distraction, believe me we need it."

Gino paused before responding. Perhaps it was the phone call from the Prime Minister. Perhaps it was the inspiration of having visited Lourdes. Perhaps it was bravado, but the response, according to some reports, was astonishing.

"Listen, I will do even better than that. I will win the whole tour!" proclaimed Gino.

Six of the most daunting climbs in the Alps faced the peloton over the next two stages. There would be nowhere to hide; the slightest weakness would be exposed on the relentless ascents and the perilous descents. Even Gino reflected on his promise to De Gasperi and the field left the comfort of Cannes. Ahead of the riders was a massive 274-kilometre ride to Briançon, tranversing the Col d'Allos, Col de Vars, and Col d'Izoard along the way. Robic led Bobet and Bartali over the first two cols, before the Italian attacked on the Izoard. By the time he cycled into Briançon, Gino had an 18 minute lead on Bobet, leaving the young French rider with a precarious hold on the *maillot jeune*. On the next stage he would hand the coveted yellow leader's jersey to Bartali after another inspired ride over the Col du Galibier and the Col de la Croix de Fer. Gino attacked on the Col de Porte. By the time he reached the finish in Aix-les-Bains, Gino had a six minute lead on his nearest rival. Bobet could not match the power of the Italian, finishing seven minutes behind Bartali. "The yellow shirt was finally on my shoulders," recalled Gino, "I was as happy as a kid."

The Italian consolidated his lead in the final Alps stage from Lausanna to Mulhouse. It had been one of the most dominant performances in the Tour de France. Mesmerised Italians followed Gino's exploits on their crackly radio broadcasts and eagerly consumed the reports in their daily newspapers. Tensions in the streets eased; by the time Bartali rode to his second victory in the Tour, the third oldest winner ever, and coming a decade after his first win, he was a national hero. A recovering Palmiro Togliatti called for calm. Sport had transcended politics.

Championship farce

Coppi and Bartali had a Grand Tour each for the season, but their achievements did little to dim the rivalry between them. Their mutual suspicion and distrust spilled into farce at the World Championship Road Race, often referred to simply as 'the Worlds'. Italians had taken great pride in their successes at 'the Worlds': Alfredo Binda, then the national team manager, had claimed the inaugural title, and won two more global crowns; and Italians had been victors in four of the 13 contested since 1927. Only the Belgians had won more titles. There was enormous pride amongst the Italian *tifosi* to have a countryman wearing the famous rainbow striped jersey of the World Champion. It was a mark of national superiority in the competitive psyche of European rivalry.

Four weeks after Bartali's stunning victory in the Tour, the national teams journeyed to the historic castle town of Valkenburg in the Limburg Provence of The Netherlands for the World Championships Road Race. A reported 200,000 fans turned out for the 267-kilometre title chase, many of them lining the famous Cauberg Hill, which the peloton had to climb 27 times. When the race was first conducted at Valkenburg a decade earlier, only eight contestants completed the grueling challenge. The 1948 Worlds was to become an even more controversial edition of the earlier race.

With the two Grand Tour winners, Coppi and Bartali, in the Italian team, the *tifosi* were anticipating fireworks on the Cauberg. Tens of thousands of Belgians had crossed the border to line the short 1.2 kilometre cobblestoned climb that maxed out at 12 per cent. They were there for their national team, which had won six of the 14 Worlds raced until then. The Belgians were the renowned 'hard men' of cycling, growing up in the windy fields of Flanders and the mountainous terrain of Wallonia. Racing for the first time in the now familiar black, gold and red stripes on a light blue jersey, the team was headed by Alberic Schotte, the runner-up to Bartali in the Tour.

Schotte was at home on the roads of Belgium and the Netherlands. He claimed his second Tour of Flanders earlier that year, having also won two Paris-Tours and a Paris-Brussels. Nick-named 'Iron Briek', the Flandrian was one of the best cyclists of the era, especially in the great one-day races. The 1948 Worlds was to become a tale of two races – or more accurately, a race and a non-race – as the action unfolded around Valkenburg.

Schotte was in the early action, forming a break with four other riders, including the Frenchman, Apo Lazarides and the champion Swiss competitor, Ferdi Kübler. Kübler couldn't hold the pace of the other two, leaving Schotte to sprint clear of the Frenchman to claim the first of two World Championships. The rowdy Belgians were ecstatic.

The Italians were crestfallen – and angry. Two of the best riders in the world, Coppi and Bartali, had played a cat and mouse game, fearful that the other would gain an advantage if they chased the escapees. With 70 kilometres to race, they abandoned. The *tifosi* jeered their former heroes, for having disgraced the famous *Azzurra* jersey. The French cycling historian, Pierre Chany, recorded Coppi's version of the farce:

> "When we learned that our gap was more than ten minutes, Bartali was remorseful," Coppi said.
>
> "We must save our honour. Are we going to Fausto?"
>
> "I'm going to bed!" I replied.
>
> "Well," said Gino. "Me too under these conditions."
>
> And we turned around together, without exchanging a word, not very proud of ourselves. . ."

They were suspended for two months "because of a lack of a willingness to compete," a penalty that was subsequently waived after appeal by the professional cyclists' association.

Briek Schotte's World Championship was no fluke: he was the dominant rider of the season, winning not only the Worlds, but the inaugural Challenge Desgrange-Colombo, a world cup series of the eight most prestigious races, named after the directors of the Tour and the Giro. He would repeat his World's win at Moorslede, Belgian two years later, joining his compatriot, Georges Ronsse, as twice winner of the rainbow stripes.

Back in Italy, Coppi rode an 80 kilometre solo breakaway to smash the 'race of the falling leaves' – the Giro di Lombardia. The year that commenced with freezing weather on the continent would conclude with the beginnings of a Cold War that shaped the history of the world for the next half century.

14

A World Made New

There's only one man in the lead: his jersey is celeste and white; his name is Fausto Coppi
-- RAI radio commentator, Mario Ferretti, during the 17th stage of the 1949 Giro d'Italia.

When Fausto won and you wanted to check the time gap to the man in second place, you didn't need a Swiss stopwatch. The bell of the church clock tower would do the job just as well
-- Raphaël Géminiani.

The 1948 election of Alcide De Gasperi's Christian Democrats gradually sidelined the Italian communists, a pattern replicated across Western Europe, although they retained a large membership on the peninsula. The new leaders on the continent represented stability when the populace sought certainty and continuity. Schuman in France, De Gasperi in Italy and Adenauer in Germany were Christian Democrats, the new political movement that would dominate much of Western Europe for the following decades. They represented cautious progress, not the radical departures that followed the Great War.

As Tony Judt writes in his history of postwar Europe, "it may seem rather odd that so much of the rehabilitation of postwar Europe was the work of men who reached maturity and entered politics many decades earlier." Alcide De Gasperi had been born in 1881, five years after Konrad Adenauer, the postwar Chancellor of West Germany. They were not alone: Winston Churchill in Britain, and Léon Blum and

GREAT RIVALRIES

Old friends: Gino Bartali and Alcide De Gasperi.

Cycling and the Story of Italy

Robert Schuman in France were born in the previous century. This is unsurprising, given the destruction of a whole generation in the Great War.

Like Adenauer and Schuman, De Gasperi was formed by Catholic social doctrine. Although the formal church still had significant sway in postwar Europe, as the Italian elections demonstrated, De Gasperi and the other leaders of the Christian Democrats maintained an independence from it, having experienced the abandonment by the Vatican of previous Catholic parties in various countries in the first half of the century. Each man also brought the perspective of the outsider to their polity: De Gasperi from Tyrol in the former Austrian-Hungarian Empire, Adenauer from the Rhineland, and Schuman from Luxembourg and the Lorraine. Together with the French economist, Jean Monnet, they are regarded as the founders of modern Europe.

At 67, and in frail health, De Gasperi, the son of a petty Austrian official, was an unlikely leader of the new republic. Yet, this was the man around whom the anti-communists rallied. "This tall, lanky man with chilly blue eyes, aggressive nose, a wide, grimly compressed mouth, was the bearer of Christian Democracy's standard – a Red Cross on a white shield with the legend: 'Liberty'," reported *Time*. A humble man, who lived with his wife, Francesca, in a simple Roman apartment, De Gasperi had a reputation for compromise. But it was Catholic Action, stirred into action by its leader, Luigi Gedda, after the Communist victories that proved decisive in the 1948 elections. The *Time* correspondent wrote:

> As the campaign drew to a close. . . It became more and more apparent that the force which might well decide De Gasperi's fate was not his own party, nor even his own stubborn courage. That force was Catholic Action. It had the zeal, the positive approach and the missionary skill which the Christian Democrats lacked. It's 3,000,000 lay members, probing into every village and every house, urged the people first of all to vote (a big turnout would be bad for the Reds), and secondly to vote for the Christian Democrats or other anti-communist parties (but Catholic Action does not support Italy's budding neo-Fascists).
>
> Catholic Action was the first political force that knew how to best the Communists at their own game of zealously serving the people's simple, urgent needs.

The result established the Christian Democrats as the party of government for the next three decades, with De Gasperi Prime Minister until 1953. Addressing those "simple, urgent needs" was the key to ongoing success as the nation rebuilt from the devastation of the war.

The new campionissimo

Fausto Coppi's domination of the last great race before winter, the Giro di Lombardia, was to be repeated in the *Primavera*, the chase from Milan to San Remo in March 1949. Once again, Coppi's trademark solo breakaway was on show. By the time he cycled into the seaside resort, Fausto had stolen a four-minute break over the chasing group, including Fiorenzo Magni and Vito Ortelli. Bartali was languishing 10 minutes behind.

Coppi had a cracking start to the 1949 season. Not only did he dominate, Milan-San Remo, he won the Giro del Veneto, the Giro della Romagna and the National Championship Road Race. Adolfo Leoni out-sprinted Fausto and Magni in the Giro del Piemonte, while the great Belgian, Rick Van Steenbergen defeated his compatriot, Ward Peeters, and Coppi at Liege in the Flèche Wallonne. Fausto had also played a major role in his brother, Serse, being declared the joint winner of the world's toughest one-day race, Paris – Roubaix. First conducted in 1896, the monument of cycling is a gruelling race over country lanes and rough cobblestone sectors from the French capital. Fausto urged his younger brother to join a break, but having been dropped by them; Serse nonetheless rode to victory after the leaders were sent on a misdirected route. The French were furious. In the end, both Serse, and the French rider, Andre Mahe, were jointly awarded the victory.

By contrast, Bartali had an ordinary start to the season, finishing well behind his young rival in the early one-day races. Gino had also left the Legnano team, to ride for the new Bartali-Gardiol team on bikes constructed by the Santamaria brothers in Milan and named after the champion rider. It was an international squad, including Belgian and Swiss riders, the most notable being Ferdi Kübler, who would become one of the greatest riders of the early 1950s. Kübler finished second to his team leader in the Tour de Romandie at Geneva a few weeks before the start of the Giro d'Italia. With Bartali's form improving, the *tifosi* were excited by the prospect of another classic showdown in the three-week Giro.

The Giro d'Italia appeared a race in two, with Fiorenzo Magni, the rising star of Italian cycling, opting to ride the Tour de France instead. Magni was in superb form, having won the first of three consecutive Ronde van Vlaanderen in April, defeating Valare Olliver, who would go on the claim the Belgian Championship, and the reigning World Champion, Briek Schotte.

The 1949 Giro d'Italia would reveal the full destruction of the war on the country, as the peloton wound their way north from Sicily. It had been almost two decades since the race had toured the southern island, necessitating a ferry trip for the entourage from Rome and Naples. The early stages were grist for the opportunists who could chance a break in the hope of a stage victory – even possession of the *maglia rosa* for a few days of glory before the race ascended the mountains. One of them was Mario Fazio, a native Sicilian, who was motivated to claim the first stage in the town of his birth, Catania. Riding for the Bottecchia team, the well-travelled journeyman had two victories in France the previous season, including the Tour of Lorraine. Fazio outsprinted another member of the successful break, the Bianchi rider, Andrea Carrea, to claim a popular local victory and the early leadership of the Giro.

But it was the third place getter in the opening stage, Giordano Cottur, who would carry the pink jersey to the mainland after the first two stages in Sicily. Cottur was the Wilier Triestina team captain, but at 35 was coming to the end of his career. He had first come to attention by winning successive Bassano-Monte Grappa races as an amateur in 1935 and 1936, and two stages of the Giro d'Italia after turning professional, but like many riders of the era, was at the height of his ability when racing was interrupted by the war. Returning to the sport after the conflict, he finished 8th in the 1947 Tour de France and third in the 1948 Giro d'Italia to his team-mate, Fiorenzo Magni.

Cottur was in a break on the second stage with Sergio Maggini and the young Swiss rider, Fritz Schaer, who would go on the win many races in the 1950s. Riding for Atala, Maggini claimed the stage at Messina, but Cottur led the General Classification on time, and claimed the race leader's pink jersey, which he would wear for the next five stages as the peloton wound its way north through Salerno, Naples, Rome and Pesaro.

The two main protagonists, Bartali and Coppi, were content in the first week of the race to sit in the peloton, although Coppi did claim the fourth stage into Salerno from Leoni and Bartali, and stole a break with Cottur on the following stage when the Tuscan wasn't paying attention to the flow of the peloton. With time bonuses for intermediate sprints having been introduced, the race favourites had to be more attentive to breaks going away, something Gino wasn't always good about.

Cottur lost the *maglia rosa* on the seventh stage from the capital to Pesaro, a massive 298-kilometre trek across the Apennines from the Tirreno to the Adriatic coasts. Mario Fazio, having made the break without Cottur, regained the pink jersey for the next two stages to Venice and Udine. Adolfo Leoni, previously a *gregario* for Bartali, demonstrated his ability by winning the next stage for Legnano before the first of the mountain climbs, as race over the Rolle, Pordoi, Campolongo and Gardena passes in the Dolomites.

Bartali was the first to attack on the Rolle, distancing all his younger rivals except Coppi, Cottur and Aldo Ronconi. It was a display of awesome climbing from the rider they called *Il Vecchio* – the old man. But success is fickle; no sooner had Bartali and the leaders regrouped in the valley before the climb of the Pordoi, Coppi attacked when Gino started to eat. The 'old man' chased but then suffered a puncture and lost more time deciding which geared wheel to swap over. Coppi dropped the other leaders, cresting the Pordoi five minutes ahead of his main rival. He gained more time on the Gardena, winning the stage by seven minutes. Leoni clung to the *maglia rosa* by just 28 seconds over Coppi, with Bartali and Cottur 10 and 13 minutes behind him.

Coppi had a commanding lead over Bartali, but his opponent had one more chance to outpace his young rival: an even tougher climb over five Alpine passes, the Maddalena, Vars, Izoard, Montgenevre and the Sestriere. At 254 kilometres in length, the riders faced a gruelling stage that would determine the outcome of the tour. The accounts of the stage vary greatly, but the facts are stark: Coppi, either chasing down an attack by Primo Volpi on the first climb, or taking advantage of Bartali's mechanical problems, crested the Maddalena alone, and then soloed over the next four climbs to carve almost 12 minutes from Bartali, who also alone, was seven minutes ahead of the next group including Cottur. Many followers of the sport regard stage 17 of the 1949 Giro as the greatest ever performance in the greatest ever Tour of Italy.

Despite a 23-minute gap, Bartali tried again on the last stage, cresting the famous Ghisallo climb above Lake Como ahead of the peloton, only to have the group rejoin on the descent. Coppi was safely third. Bartali, then 35, had ridden a superb Giro, distancing every other rider, but Coppi was at the height of his ability. He had now equalled Bartali and Brunero as the thrice winner of the Giro d'Italia. He would eventually equal Binda's record of five victories. But in 1949, he was ready to attempt a feat never before achieved; to win the Giro-Tour double in the same year.

Winning the Giro d'Italia and the Tour de France was almost impossible. First, the three-week, physical and mental sapping events were just a few weeks apart. It can take even the most fit cyclist weeks to recover from a Grand Tour. Secondly, the events are run under very different conditions. The stage that Coppi won in the Alps was raced in cold, freezing conditions but the Tour is usually conducted at the height of summer.

A far more serious challenge was to ensure that Coppi and Bartali both worked for the Italian team, and not against each other, as occurred in their farcical World Championship race at Valkenburg. The Tour was then conducted as a competition between national teams. With Gino the defending champion, and Fausto the Giro winner, Italy had a powerful combination, provided the two antagonists could work together. Just getting them to the start was a major achievement for the Italian manager, Alfredo Binda. Days of negotiations resulted in an arrangement that each star would have five *gregari*, with Coppi's group on Bianchi bikes, while Bartali and his *domestiques* were on his own branded machines. Binda managed to get Coppi and Bartali to reluctantly agree to follow his team orders, but neither was happy with the situation, accusing the other of a lack of trust and cooperation. It wasn't a great foundation for a tilt at the Tour de France.

While Coppi and Bartali, along with Magni, formed the core of a very strong team, they faced tough competition in the 4,808-kilometre marathon. Louison Bobet, René Vietto and Raphaël Géminiani were in the French squad, while the Belgians were headed by Rick van Steenbergen and Stan Ockers, who would subsequently win and place in the World Championship Road Race. The race was becoming one of the most anticipated in cycling history.

The early stages of the Tour through northern France and Belgium were to prove an anticlimax for the fans expecting fireworks from the beginning. Coppi and Bartali were content to sit back in the peloton, allowing lesser-known riders to revel in the glory of stage wins. One of them, the 24-year-old Jacques Marinelli, riding for the secondary Ile de France team, in only his second year as a professional, had finished second on two stages and wore the *maillot jeune*. It would be his best year as a cyclist, eventually finishing on the podium ahead of some of the greatest riders of the era.

Coppi's rivalry with Bartali exploded on stage five, a 293-kilometre race from Rouen to Saint Malo, but not in the way expected. Sensing his opportunity, Marinelli powered into a small break of seven riders, including Coppi. But misfortune in the form of an over-enthusiastic spectator brought down both the *maillot jeune* and the Giro champion. Marinelli and his bike were unscathed, but Coppi was left seething on the side of the road, his Bianchi unridable. To add insult to injury, the following team car didn't have Coppi's replacement bike, and he refused to ride the one they had. When Bartali caught up, he waited with his adversary until Binda arrived in the second team car with Coppi's bike. The two Italians then raced off in pursuit of the escapees, but Coppi, without sufficient food, slowed so much that an exasperated Bartali finally rode away from him. Coppi struggled into the seaside finish 18 minutes behind the winner, the Swiss champion Ferdi Kübler. Exhausted and angry, Fausto threatened to abandon the Tour, believing that Binda had favoured his nemesis. The second *campionissimo* eventually calmed the man who would replace him as the 'champion of champions', but Coppi was then a massive 36 minutes behind the race leader, Marinelli, on General Classification. His first tilt at the Tour seemed in significant trouble.

Yet once Fausto had recovered his mental equilibrium, his 'never say die' attitude kicked in. He smashed the crack field in the 92-kilometre time trial, taking 7 1/2 minutes from Marinelli, and cut the deficit to less than 15 minutes in just one stage in the Pyrenees. But for a flat tyre towards the end, he would possibly have claimed the stage that Jean Robic won. In the meantime, Fiorenzo Magni claimed the yellow leader's jersey for the Italians after winning the last stage before the mountains. He would hold it on the intermediate stages between the Pyrenees and the Alps.

Two massive stages through the Alps covering 534 kilometres would rewrite the Tour – and the history of cycling. Almost 10 1/2 hours after departing Cannes on the Côte d'Azur, having ascended the Allos, Vars, and Izoard, Bartali and Coppi rode into Briançon five minutes ahead of Jean Robic. They had put their intense rivalry aside, Coppi having waited for Bartali when he flatted, and then allowed his older companion to celebrate his 35th birthday with a victory and the *maillot jeune* in France's highest city.

Two days later, the Italians dominated again, breaking away from the peloton. When Bartali suffered a fall, Binda allowed Coppi his wings. Fausto rode the final 40 kilometres alone, finishing nearly five minutes ahead of his compatriot. To cheering Italians waiting the finish at Aosta, *Forza Italia* reigned supreme. Coppi took the yellow jersey to lead Bartali on General Classification by almost four minutes. He would extend his lead in a 137-kilometre time trial from Colmer to Nancy, before finishing the final 340-kilometre stage in the midst of the peloton at Paris behind Rick Van Steenbergen and Stan Ockers. Coppi had turned a 36 minute deficit into an 11 minute lead over Bartali, who was another 14 minutes ahead of the next finisher, Jacques Marinelli. Italy had triumphed; Coppi and Bartali had proven themselves the best riders in the world; and Fausto had emerged as the new *campionissimo*.

Four weeks later, Coppi attempted to cap off an incredible season by adding the World Championship Road Race to his tour double. Alfredo Binda had won the Giro and the Worlds in 1927, and Learco Guerra had finished second to the Belgian, Karel Kaers, in 1934, after claiming the Giro, but no rider had won the Triple Crown. Conducted at Copenhagen for the third time since 1927, the 290-kilometre race for the Rainbow Jersey attracted 35 starters. Being an almost flat course, it favoured the sprinters and the strong one-day *rouleurs*. Coppi got himself into an early break with Rick Van Steenbergen and Gerrit Schulte, a multiple national track champion in the pursuit, and the winner of that year's Tour of the Netherlands. The Swiss riders Ferdi Kübler and Ernst Stettler joined them, making a bunch sprint the more likely outcome of the race. Coppi tried as he might to gain a break on the others, but Van Steenbergen clung to his rear wheel with sheer determination. Van Steenbergen, the superior sprinter, slipped off Coppi's wheel in the sight of the finish to claim the first of three World Championships, while Kübler, riding in the Belgian's slipstream, snatched the second placing from the Italian.

Four years later, on a hilly course at Lugano, Switzerland, Fausto Coppi would win the World Championship. It would be another quarter of a century before any cyclist won the triple-crown – the great Eddy Merckx in 1974, having previously claimed both tours in 1972 but only managing fourth at the Worlds that year. Only one other cyclist would claim the triple-crown to date, the Irishman, Stephen Roche in 1987. Miguel Indurain went close in 1993, winning both tours, but finishing in second placing, 19 seconds behind Lance Armstrong at Oslo in the Worlds.

Fausto Coppi capped a magnificent 1949 season by winning the World Pursuit Championship on the track in Denmark and defeating Ferdi Kübler in the 'race of the falling leaves'. He had won the two grand tours, two monuments of cycling, a world track championship and finished third in the World Road Race Championship in just one year. He was the greatest cyclist of his time – and arguably the best ever.

The party of government

While Fausto Coppi was establishing his ascendency over the postwar peloton, the Christian Democrats were cementing their place as the party of government in Italy. Winning the 1948 election was a significant victory, but without a program to address the nation's ongoing challenges and to cement the coalition of anti-communist voters and groupings, the Party risked only a short term in government. The challenges were not new: how to industrialise successfully and grow the economy, and how to address the endemic problems of land ownership and poverty, especially in the south, and the continuing regional differences and rivalries. Solutions had proven elusive in the past: industrial progress had been significant at various stages, but the queues of the postwar unemployed, the excess of farm labourers, and the demands for a more equal distribution of land were exacerbated by the war. Democratisation had compounded the political challenges. The workers in the industrial north were always a fertile field for the socialists and communists; the millions of peasants in the south could not be ignored at the expense of the landowners.

Ultimately, industrialisation and economic growth prospered in the north. Like the United Kingdom, France and Germany, Italy had a larger stock of machine tools at the end of the war than at the beginning. Major engineering firms in the north – apart from the air and ship building industries – had not suffered during the war. By 1949, Italy's industrial and agricultural production exceeded the 1938 levels. The Marshall Plan had aided the reconstruction in the late 1940s. Initially the aid to Italy benefitted the imports of coal and grain, and the rebuilding of the textile industry. Tony Judt observes:

> But thereafter 90 per cent of Italian counterpart funds went directly to investment: in engineering, energy, agriculture and transportation networks. In fact, under Alcide De Gasperi and the Christian Democrats, Italian economic planning at the end of the forties rather resembled its east European counterpart, with consumer goods deliberately disfavoured, food consumption held down to pre-war levels and resources diverted to infrastructure investment. This was almost too much of a good thing: American observers became nervous and tried unsuccessfully to encourage the government to introduce more progressive taxes, relax its austere approach, allow reserves to fall and avoid bringing about a recession.

The European Payments Union, established with US credit, encouraged levels of cooperation between Continental nations, assisted the expansion of trade, and slowly engendered a new confidence across Western Europe. The US objective was being fulfilled: to prevent economic collapse, stimulate trade, and preclude further Soviet expansionism. By forcing the Europeans to work together for their mutual benefit, a remarkable period of peace and stability emerged. But this was not at all clear in the late 40s and early 50s.

The south in particular remained a challenge. A series of land reform laws in the 1950s broke up almost three-quarters of a million hectares, benefitting more than 100,000 peasant families. While politically popular, the measure helped only a very small proportion of the landless peasants. The scheme covered a little more than two per cent of Italy. Many landowners avoided the laws by divesting to family members or making the minimim improvements required to retain their property. Worse, many of the beneficiaries were left with landholdings too tiny to be economically viable, with poor roads and lacking adequate water. The number of small allotments of less than 10 hectares actually increased in the decade following the war. Many people were forced to move to the North for jobs and economic security.

Another political solution was required for the South. The answer lay in financial and economic programs, administered by local party affiliates that established a widespread system of patronage. Loans, jobs and a program of state welfare underpinned the economy and entrenched the Christian Democrats. This program, with its feudal echoes, political pragmatism and strands of social justice ideology, enabled the Christian Democrats to maintain their political advantage in the South.

The Swiss domination

Although he was to subsequently repeat his Giro-Tour double in 1952, and win the World Championship the following season, Fausto Coppi was possibly at the height of his ability during 1949 and early 1950. Yet the man now nicknamed *Ginaccio* – tough, old Gino – outfoxed him in the *Primavera*. At nearly 36-years of age, Bartali was still competitive with the best in the world, defeating Nedo Logli, Oreste Conte and Fiorenzo Magni at San Remo. Coppi, along with Ferdi Kübler, Louison Bobet and 39 others were in a bunch designated as equal ninth.

The peloton moved north for the Spring Classics – the great one – day races in France and Belgium – as the European winter receded. It was there that Coppi demonstrated his ability to win not just on the velodrome and in the mountains, but also in the rough cobblestones of the region. It was another Italian, Fiorenzo Magni, who first raised the green, white and red tricolour in winning his second successive Ronde van Vlaanderan in early April. A week later, Coppi, having survived the wet sludge and slippery cobblestones with the help of his team, made a break with the French rider, Maurice Diot as the peloton slowed at a feed station in Paris-Roubaix. With 45 kilometres to race, Coppi attacked, leaving Diot more than three minutes behind, and the next finisher, Rick Van Steenbergen, another nine minutes in arrears.

Three weeks later, Fausto repeated the feat in La Flèche Wallone, the arduous race through the Ardennes. Once again, he made a break then simply rode away from the others to win by over five minutes. But fame and fortune in cycling are fickle. In the Giro d'Italia, Fausto fell heavily when another rider shifted in on him, breaking his pelvis in three places. His season was all but over. It was to be the year of the Swiss. Hugo Koblet, with the aid of time bonuses and the assistance of Coppi's *gregari*, defeated Bartali in the Giro, while his compatriot, Ferdi Kübler, claimed the Tour after the Italians quit the race. Magni had been leading the Swiss rider by 2 1/2 minutes when Bartali and Jean Robic crashed into a photographer near the summit of the Col d'Aspin. In the resulting melee, riders were punched and kicked, and Bartali claims he was attacked with a knife.

When the melee ended, Bartali and Magni chased down the leaders, Bobet, Géminiani and Ockers, reeling in an incredible 12 minutes to allow Fiorenzo to take the yellow jersey, two and a half minutes ahead of Ferdi Kübler.

Bartali was furious about the actions of the French fans and insisted on both Italian teams quitting the race, despite Magni being in the *maillot juene*. The Italian riders were of mixed views about the idea, with some wanting to help Magni to victory, but Bartali was resolute, and Binda and the Italian Federation agreed with him. The Italians went home, Kübler was victorious in Paris and Magni never won a Tour de France. Asked many years later about the incident, Magni replied:

> Of course I felt bad about that but I believe that there are bigger things than a technical result, even one as important as winning the Tour de France . . . In my life I have never pretended to have a role that was not mine. When they decided to withdraw I didn't pretend that I would go on in the race alone. That wouldn't be my style.

GREAT RIVALRIES

It was a mark of Coppi's dominance that having broken his pelvis and been off the bike for many weeks, he returned to racing in October to finish third in the Giro di Lombardia behind the young Legnano rider, Renzo Soldani, and Antonio Bevilacqua, the winner of both the National Road and Pursuit championships that season.

Just as Europe was beginning to exhibit the first signs of a more integrated, cooperative existence, road cycling adopted a more international flavour. In the pre-war years, a handful of riders had competed in the tours and classics outside their homeland, but this became commonplace in the 1950s. "If the 1950 peloton burned brightly with star riders, the 1951 roster was a nova," wrote Bill and Carol McCann in their *Story of the Giro d'Italia*. "The start list for the 1951 Giro d'Italia has to be considered the race's finest so far, and perhaps the best ever. It was deep, with superb talent from all over Europe." Amongst them were the Swiss stars, Kübler and Koblet, Louison Bobet, Rick Van Steenbergen and Fiorenzo Magni.

Ferdi Kübler

The Swiss cyclist was the star of 1950 and 51. He had been a successful track cyclist before finding triumph on the road. Born into a poor farming family as the Great War ended, Kübler found a job as a delivery rider. Tall in statute, Kübler developed considerable strength riding many kilometres on the delivery bike each day. Beginning his professional career in 1940, Kübler had become the complete cyclist in a decade. He became the Swiss National Champion in the track pursuit, the cyclocross and on the road numerous times. In 1948 and 1949, Kübler won the Tour de Suisse and finished second in the then unofficial World Time Trial Championship, the Grand Prix des Nations.

Known as 'the madman' because of his habit of talking to himself while riding, Kübler was the dominant rider of 1951 and 1952. Fate had intervened in 1949 when leading the Tour de France: he suffered three punctures on one stage and lost the *Grand Boucle* to Fausto Coppi. With the withdrawal of the Italians in 1950, Kübler outrode the Belgian, Stan Ockers, and Louison Bobet, to claim the yellow jersey in Paris. He continued to star in the next two seasons, winning the two Ardennes Classics, La Flèche Wallone and Liege-Bastogne-Liege, over the one weekend in both 1951 and 1952. In 1951, he also showed up the Italians at home, when he defeated Magni and Bevilacqua at Varese in the World Championship. He was still competitive when at the age of 35 finished second to Bobet in the Tour de France.

Hugo Koblet

If Ferdi Kübler was the dour, sometimes mischievous giant of the peloton, his Swiss rival, Hugo Koblet, was the opposite. Born into a middle class family at Zurich, the young Koblet worked in the family bakery, sweeping floors and delivering produce. He took up track riding, winning the national amateur Pursuit title at 20 years of age before turning professional. Koblet became one of the best endurance riders on the velodrome, winning numerous popular six-day races, including at Chicago and New York in the US, and at Frankfurt, Brussels and Dortmund.

With his ready smile and blonde hair, Koblet was the darling of cycling fans. He was reputed to carry a small bottle of cologne, and a comb to brush his hair after finishing a race before blowing kisses to his female fans and being interviewed by journalists. The French paper, *L'Equipe*, described him as 'Apollo on a bike'. Having won the 1950 Giro, when Coppi crashed and his Bianchi team rode for the Swiss champion (and a share of the prizemoney), Koblet was to claim the other grand tour the following year. He would defeat the two of the best French riders of the era, Raphaël Géminiani and Lucien Lasarides by more than 20 minutes, winning five stages along the way, including a 135-kilometre solo victory and a dominant individual time trial. Koblet also won the 140-kilometre Grand Prix des Nations by 1 minute 42 seconds over Coppi and finished second to his great nemesis, Ferdi Kübler, in the Tour de Suisse. He would win the Swiss tour in 1955, but it was 1950 and 1951 that his star shined the brightest. Koblet reired in 1958, but suffered from unwise investments and a failed marriage. Six years later, he drove his Alfa Romeo into a tree near Zurich, dying four days later.

GREAT RIVALRIES

The third man

One of the most iconic images of professional cycling is of Fiorenzo Magni in the 1956 Giro d'Italia. It depicts a grimacing Magni with a length of tyre tube gritted between his teeth, the other end tied to his handlebars. Magni had fallen and broken his clavicle – so the team mechanics had rigged the tubing to allow him to apply pressure to the handlebars lacking in his left arm because of the injury. He had refused a plaster cast and discharged himself from hospital to continue the tour. It was stage 12 of the Giro, and Magni was in contention for his fourth Grand Tour.

Fiorenzo Magni was one of the hard men of the peloton. He rode in the shadows of Bartali and Coppi, but his achievements place him high in the pantheon of cycling's greats. Born in December 1920 to Giuseppe and Giulia Magni at Vaiano, Fiorenzo had taken over his father's business after his death in 1937, before being conscripted into the Italian armed forces three years later. His military service was to prove both a blessing and a curse.

Like many young men of the era, life was interrupted by the war. Fortune smiled on Magni when he was allowed to contest a race rather than embark with his battalion to the Albanian front, as the ship sank without survivors. Magni subsequently served in Rome until recalled to Florence and subsequently into the armed forces of Mussolini's puppet state, the Republic based at Salò on Lake Garda. He was later accused of killing a partisan leader in a battle at Valibona in 1944, but was released on the testimony of Alfredo Martini, who was to stand on the podium in the 1950 Giro d'Italia, and who had finished second to Magni in their first race as teenagers.

Married in 1947, Magni won the Tre Valli Varesine that year before his unexpected win in the 1948 Giro when Coppi abandoned. But it was to the north – in Belgium – that Magni made his mark, winning three consecutive Ronde van Vlaanderen – the Tour of Flanders. Like many of Europe's great races, the Ronde was conceived as a promotion for a newspaper, *Sportwereld*, in 1913 by Karel Van Wijnendaele, its then editor-in-chief. For many years, the race was conducted on the same day in March as Milan-San Remo, but in the early 1930s moved to a week before Paris-Roubaix. The changed date, and the inclusion of the race in the unofficial World Cup, the Challenge Desgrange-Colombo, began to attract competitors from beyond Belgium. Only one foreigner, Heiri Suter from Switzerland in 1923, had won the Ronde prior to the Second World War, but that was to change markedly afterwards.

Magni was in good form at the start of the 1949 season, winning the Giro della Toscana and finishing third to Coppi in Milan-San Remo. He had ridden in the Grand Prix des Nations time trial in France in the two previous seasons, but never in Belgium. The change of date, his good form, and the prospect of having the reigning Giro champion attracted Magni to start in the Ronde. It would be a prescient decision.

Magni prepared well for the challenge:

> I had never been to Belgium, but I had heard and read in the newspapers that the roads were very tough, much harder than those in Paris-Roubaix. . . So I thought it would be a good idea to use wooden rims, which are less rigid than the traditional [aluminium] ones. It was hard to find those rims . . . Then I had a special kind of tubulars (tyres), larger and heavier than the normal ones, made. And I put foam rubber all around the handle bar to cushion the blows.

The efforts paid off for the Italian, who won the 260-kilometre race from the in-form Valare Olliver and the reigning Flanders and World Champion, Briek Schotte. Magni repeated the bike set-up to defeat Schotte the following year. In 1951, he equalled Achiel Buysse's three victories, although Magni is the only rider to have claimed victory in the Ronde in three consecutive years, each in cold, wet and miserable weather. He had become the 'Lion of Flanders'.

Magni was in sparkling form at the beginning of 1951, winning a series of other races, including Milan-Turin and the Italian Championship in addition to the Ronde. By contrast, Coppi had a disastrous start to the season. The rising French star, Louison Bobet, won Milan-San Remo; and Coppi broke his clavicle in March when he crashed in Milan-Turin, interrupting his preparation for the Giro.

The 1951 Giro turned into an epic battle between Magni and Rick Van Steenbergen, with some great stages from Coppi in the time trial, Kübler who would go on to win the Tour de France, Bobet who claimed the climber's Classification and the young Giancarlo Astrua, who would finish third in the 1953 Tour De France. Bartali crashed early in the three-week event, losing significant time.

Four years later, the then 35-year-old Magni would defeat the 36-year-old Coppi by a mere 13 seconds in the 1955 Giro after the race leader, Gastone Nencini, suffered a series of mechanical issues in the penultimate stage from Trent to San Pellegrino. Magni later remarked:

> During the break I first saw signs saying 'Viva Nencini!' Then people quickly changed them to 'Viva Coppi!' and 'Viva Magni!' After the radio had reported our break, with 80 kilometres to go, the roads were overflowing with people. Thousands of people were waiting for this couple of 'elderly' champions. When today I hear that a 35-year-old athlete is considered old, I smile. It depends on the way you reach this age!

Despite winning his third Giro in 1955, Magni considered his second placing to Coppi the following year as his 'greatest win' as a cyclist. It was the race which the iconic photograph reveals the passion and perseverance of Fiorenzo Magni, racing his last season as a professional, and defending the *maglia rosa* he had won the year before.

After crashing and breaking his clavicle, on stage 12, Magni, without any strength in his left arm, even to brake, crashed again on stage 16, fracturing his humerous. Waking up in an ambulance, he insisted on it stopping and getting back on his bike, finishing with the peloton, which had slowed for him. Magni pressed on, including a freezing stage through the snow from Merano to Trent where 60 riders abandoned. The great Luxembourg rider, Charly Gaul, made up 16 minutes on the stage to don the *maglia rosa*. Magni never gave up, trying to attack the leader, and eventually finishing second in the Giro. It was a fitting end to his great professional career.

15
The Transition Years

Age and treachery will overcome youth and skill

-- Fausto Coppi.

Cycling, the sport of the century, triumphs over time and space

-- La Gazzetta dello Sport.

Italy in the early 1950s was little changed from the interwar years. Two-in-five working people were employed in agriculture, many of them peasants. Only one child-in-nine attended school past the age of thirteen. More than a million homes had been destroyed in the war, and housing remained a significant challenge. A quarter of Italian families lived in poverty. Yet within a decade – and more so by the end of the 1960s – the national economy had changed markedly. Italians abandoned agriculture in vast numbers; millions migrated internally and elsewhere in Europe for work; and the tertiary, service sector of the economy boomed.

Alcide De Gasperi's Christian Democrat administration was partially the architect of these changes, but largely the beneficiary of the economic transformation of Europe. At the heart of the government's architecture was the *Cassa per il Mezzogiorno* – the Fund for the South. Created with a loan from the World Bank, the scheme funded major infrastructure projects including land reclamation, electrification, water supply to towns, irrigation for farms and road building through financial and taxation incentives for investment by private enterprise. Sixty per cent of investment was directed to the South under the scheme, but its outcomes were mixed. Coastal regions benefitted at the expense of

GREAT RIVALRIES

Gino Bartali with Pius XII.

the interior, many of the projects created few jobs, and others were established because of patronage rather than a sound business case.

The more direct impact of De Gasperi's program was the creation and expansion of large State-owned enterprises that employed hundreds of thousands of Italians. The Institute for Industrial Reconstruction alone provided work for more than 200,000 Italians at the beginning of the decade, and a few years later three-in-five of all of the country's public employees were in the provinces of the *Mezzogiorno*. In a little over a decade, agriculture's proportion of national production halved. In a generation, many families, including an increasing number of older women, were employed in the service sector. The South continued to remain the poorest region of Italy, but significant advances occurred in income, consumption and infant mortality.

But it was a combination of other developments that changed the well-being of Italians significantly. In the North, the great industrial expansion was based on tens of thousands of small enterprises, mostly employing less than 100 workers. As the Cold War developed, military expenditure soared across Europe, benefitting industry. But it was the combination of freer trade and a more integrated European economy, including the mobility of labour that lifted the standard of living of Western Europeans.

These developments, which ultimately resulted in a European Economic Community, eased ancient national jealousies, and harnessed a rivalry of purpose. Although political in resolve – to constrain an emerging Germany by establishing an authority to control French and German coal and steel production – Jean Monnet's scheme became the foundation of Europe's post-war economy. Named after the French Foreign Minister, Robert Schuman, the plan established the European Coal and Steel Community. Six European nations, all governed by Christian Democrats, signed the formal Treaty at Paris in 1951.

The economic progress and stability that the Paris Treaty helped to engender had another major outcome for Italy. Southern Italians had moved to the north of the country in their millions following World War II, as well as overseas to the new world nations such as Australia. But the massive emigration to America had fallen to a trickle as a result of restrictions imposed by the US Congress. The first great

Inter-Europe migration commenced soon after the war, as thousands of Italian workers travelled to Belgium to work in the coal mines of Wallonia. The Paris Treaty, and the consequent boom in the German economy, expanded the emigration. By the mid-1950s Germany had entered agreements with many countries to attract guest workers. In a quarter of a century, seven million Italians were to move from the peninsula, many of them elsewhere in Europe. The reduced demand for local jobs and the flow of remittances benefitted Italy considerably. These developments, along with improvements in education, changed the prospects for many Italians from the 1950s.

A changing sport

The economic and cultural transformation that had started to sweep Western Europe had parallels in the world of cycling. The sport had already started to internationalise in the early post-war years although it would be another quarter of a century before it truly became global. The campaign of Bartali, Coppi and Magni in France and Belgium, and the usurpation of the Grand Tours by the Swiss in the early 1950s was an omen of more changes to come. The Vuelta a España had first been conducted in 1935, but it was interrupted by the Spanish Civil War and World War II, and not run annually until 1955. In 1956, Miguel Poblet and Federico Bahamontes, two of the greatest Iberian cyclists of the era, contested the Giro d'Italia.

Cycling enjoyed a golden era in Europe in the early 1950s. It often attracted more spectators than football, both to the roads and the velodromes, filled more columns of the newspapers, and featured extensively on radio. While the postwar economic boom would see millions of cars manufactured over the decade, demand outstripped supply, and the bicycle and the motor scooter remained popular modes of transport.

But it was in more basic aspects of cycling that significant changes occurred in the postwar decade: equipment improved, training methods were modernised, and the role of teams developed. These aspects, together with the gradual improvement in the roads resulted in a generational change in the sport.

Multiple gears had been invented in the 19th century, but their use was restricted in professional racing until 1937. Although early, crude versions of the modern derailleur were in use, including by the independent competitors in major races, the professionals were restricted to stopping and physically changing the rear gearing, usually by flipping over the wheel to use a smaller or larger cog on the other side. This action became more efficient after Tullio Campagnolo invented a quick-release mechanism in the 1920s, a device used to this day.

Campagnolo subsequently invented a mechanism that allowed the rider to select one of four gears on the rear hub by the use of two levers while still riding. Another former racer, Oscar Egg invented a variation of the gear changing mechanism that Roger Lapébie used to win the 1937 Tour de France.

Campagnolo continued to experiment with gearing for many years, finally producing a superior updated version of his Corsa system in the early 1950s. Other advances included the change from heavier steel cranks to a lighter aluminium version, the use of lighter steel in frames, more efficient brakes, and the mounting of the gear levers on the down tube. By the end of the 1950s, the professionals in the peloton had far superior bikes than a decade before.

But it was in diet, training and the approach to teams racing that more significant developments occurred. 'Eat, drink, smoke and ride', seems to have been the dietary motto of the earliest endurance cyclists. The unexpected winner of the second Tour de France – after the first four finishers were disqualified for cheating – Henri Cornet, had a daily food supply of 11 litres of hot chocolate, four litres of tea, champagne and 1.5 litres of rice pudding. The Champion French cyclist, Lucien Petit-Breton, was reported to have been chomping on a chicken when he crashed in the first stage of the inaugural Giro d'Italia.

Cyclists would stop to eat at wayside cafes. A heavy meal of steak was regarded as *de rigueur* in the early peloton. Consuming alcohol and smoking was commonplace. Indeed, rules were introduced after complaints by cafe owners that riders would takes drinks, including alcohol, without paying. In *Fiesta: The sun also rises*, Ernest Hemingway recounts an encounter with a group of competitors over dinner after the penultimate stage of the 1928 Tour du Pays Basque at San Sebastian:

In the dining room, at one side, there was a long table of bicycle riders, eating with their trainers and managers. They were all French and Belgians, and paid close attention to their meal, but they were having a good time... The bicycle riders drank much wine, and were burned and browned by the sun.

Coppi once quipped of Bartali: "If I had drunk just part of the wine Gino has, I'd be dead." Smoking was routine in the peloton. It was said to 'open the lungs'. Photos of Gino Bartali smoking were common. It was his way of dealing with anxiety.

Gino Bartali was one of the early students of performance nutrition. As a young cyclist, he religiously followed a physical training regimen devised by a Dutch scholar. He recorded his regime in notebooks, a practice that led to his early nickname, 'the accountant'. He experimented with different foods, but was a product of the wisdom of his age: as much meat as possible, lots of coffee, and dozens of eggs, usually eaten raw! But he also tried a new approach. His *gregario*, Bruno Gianeli, recalled:

> During training Gino used to bring a sandwich (frittata) filled with spinach and omelette. Before the 1950 San Remo – breakfast with tea, bread and butter, honey and biscuits. The others who ordered spaghetti and steak all stopped at half race. Because, as Gino said, "it is not today's food that makes us run, but that of yesterday."

Raw egg yolks, and a bottle containing watered down egg custard or sugar and water were a staple for the Tuscan during a race. After the war, Gino increased his coffee intake, having up to 28 expressi in a day, continued to enjoy drinking wine, often partying late into the night. His training was also traditional: long endurance rides, usually at a solid speed, but without the variations of interval training, and rest days that are now common.

The younger Fausto Coppi was also imbued with decades-old wisdom about nutrition and training, especially through his coach and mentor, Biagio Cavanna. Yet he turned the old approach on its head. Instead of heavy meals of steaks, chicken hoops worth of raw eggs, with wine to wash it down, Coppi experimented with smaller, lighter meals of fruit, vegetables and grains, either lightly cooked or raw. He replaced steaks with carbohydrates, and eating smaller amounts more often during races.

Decades before the Team Sky's 'marginal gains' strategy, Fausto Coppi revolutionised professional cycling. In his biography of the

Italian Champion, *Fallen Angel*, William Fotheringham wrote:
> Since the war, Coppi and the Bianchi team had perfected the way a squad raced, with the help of the selfless *gregari* and the bike company's financial power. This was to be the blueprint for future greats. The Bianchi way was emulated by Louison Bobet and Jacques Anquetil – winners of eight Tours between them between 1953 and 1964 – and also by the Red Guard of Rik Van Looy, who dominated one-day racing in the late 1950s and 1960s. The same team principles were applied by Eddy Merckx, Bernard Hinault, Miguel Indurain and Lance Armstrong, to name but the best. This was, just one area in which Coppi was laying down the foundations on which professional cyclists and their teams would build an entire sport.

It was the team that Coppi built around him, and the training methods they adopted, that stood apart from his contemporaries. The long, steady rides of old were replaced with both endurance and speed training. The team trained together, simulating racing conditions; interval training and motor pacing were introduced to the regimen. Extra attention was given the bikes to ensure that they were in the best condition. And success was rewarded with the financial backing of Bianchi to afford whatever was required to generate even more success. Cavanna's house at Novi Ligure became the nursery for future *gregari*. Team presentation, being punctual and being – and looking – professional were preconditions for participation. In short, Fausto Coppi, together with Cavanna, his *gregari*, his mechanic, Pinella di Grande, and Bianchi, transformed the sport of professional road cycling.

Nothing was left to chance – and this included doping. Drug use had been a feature of endurance cycling from the outset. The vast distances that were cycled in the early years, starting in the very early hours of the morning, and finishing late in the afternoon, having traversed rough gravel roads and almost impossible mountain passes, induced the riders to employ any and every competitive advantage, drugs included.

Daniel Oakman writes in his biography of Hubert Opperman, the great Australian cyclist who finished a credible 18th in the 1928 Tour de France and who won the 1,200 kilometre Paris-Brest-Paris in 1931:
> Since the first Tour of 1903, racers looked for anything that might ease their suffering and perhaps give them the edge over their competitors. Tour riders were known to use cocktails of alcohol, caffeine, chloroform, ether, cocaine, arsenic, nitroglycerin and strychnine ...

the use of tonics, drugs, medicines, tinctures – whatever they might be called – was so normal that by 1930 the Tour rule book stated that stimulants had to be supplied by the competitors themselves and would not be provided by the race organizers.

'Oppy' as he was known, seems to have resisted any admonitions to use drugs, but by the 1950s, the cocktail of medications utilized by the riders in the peloton included amphetamines. They had been used by some pilots in their long distance aerial missions during the war, and were readily available. Norman Ohler in his book on the use of drugs in Nazi Germany, records that by the mid 1920s, Germany was the largest morphine-producing state and a 'global dealer' in heroin and cocaine. A decade later, the methamphetamine, Pervitin, was mass-produced for the army and used extensively.

It was an open secret in the peloton that riders and teams experimented with different medications and tonics. Bartali once searched for a vial that Coppi had thrown on the roadside only to discover it was a harmless substance readily available. On another occasion, his team searched Coppi's hotel room after the riders had departed for the race start, looking for evidence of what the champion cyclist was using. The line between readily accepted stimulants and other more dangerous concoctions was often blurred. Bartlali later recalled:

> We know how these things go. Having heard endlessly about the miraculous results achieved with 'bombs', I was convinced to try myself. If I did it just once, I told myself, it certainly wouldn't be the end of the world.

With Cavanna's assistance, Coppi and his teammates perfected the type and dosage of amphetamines taken at various times of the day – with meals, and at different stages during a race. The champion Australian rider of the 1950s, Russell Mockridge, who rode in the 1952 and 1955 Tours, vividly recounted the mayhem caused by the extreme heat and doping on the ascent of Mount Ventoux in the '55 Tour de France:

> Jean Mallajac, third in a previous Tour, and a member of the French team, was making a crazy zig-zag across the road near the summit. With only one foot firmly clamped to a pedal, he dragged his other foot on the road, continued for a few yards, then slumped in a heap by the roadside.
>
> When Dr Dumas [tour doctor Pierre Dumas] arrived, he was almost dead and only a quick injection of soluble camphor and an

oxygen mask brought some life back into his body. The doctor shouted for a police guard to keep everyone away from the stricken rider as he lay by the roadside, grey-faced, mouth foaming, eyes bulging. On his way to hospital Mallejac was in an absolute frenzy of delirium. The temperature was now more than 120 degrees [48.8 C].

But he was not the only one affected, although he was by far the worst. There were other riders collapsing or pedaling drunkenly on in the trial by fire. With some it was too much dope; with others it was the heat. Charly Gaul had to have an injection and Ferdi Kübler, the big Swiss who had attacked the Ventoux like a lunatic, at one point looked in a similar condition to Mallejac. But somehow he stayed on his machine past the summit, down the descent, only to collapse less than a mile from the finishing banner at Avignon.

Weeping, Kübler refused the help of his team-mate Bovay, who tried to assist him to pedal the last few yards. It took Ferdi over 20 minutes to snap out of his semi-comatose condition and pedal into Avignon, where he told the journalists, 'Ferdi est trop charge. The Tour is finished for him. He is too sick, too old. Ferdi will never start again. He killed himself on the Ventou.'

Mockridge also referenced Louison Bobet, who completed three consecutive victories in that year's Tour. With the innocence of an outsider, Mockridge wrote:

> Dope, apparently, is the bomb that will send a rider romping home miles ahead of everyone else in the race and have such a bad effect that he will never ride well again. Stimulants, according to Bobet, are the milder type of drugs in more common use which, if used wisely, have definite advantages without being harmful. . . Whatever the rights or wrongs of their uses, it is standard practice for a rider in Europe who wants to take the sport seriously to find himself a trainer who is an expert in their use.

Coppi had such a trainer in Cavanna. It was reported that the veteran mentor had put Coppi on a course of strychnine for a week before the World Championship Road Race, and consumed pure caffeine on the day. Asked about drug use after his career was over, Coppi was candid: "I only used drugs when necessary." When pressed about how often that was, he replied: "almost always." His undoubted successor as the world's best rider, Jacques Anquetil was even blunter:

> Leave me in peace, everybody takes dope. You'd have to be an imbicile or hypocrit to imagine that a professional cyclist who rides 235 days a year can hold himself together without stimulants.

GREAT RIVALRIES

Long before the EPO era, the Festina Affair and Lance Armstrong, drugs were a significant feature of road cycling.

Fears and stability

Although unanticipated at the time, the 1950s heralded unprecedented peace and stability in Europe. The settlement of the German issue, the developing economic dependency of western nations, the gradual evolution of the European political community, the shift of global tensions, especially between the USSR and the US elsewhere – to the Korean Peninsula and, later, Cuba, the death of Stalin in 1953 and the denunciation of his 'errors' by Khrushchev three years later and the slow demise of the Communist Party as a political force in Western Europe (except Italy) all contributed to the new era of stability. Even Italy and Yugoslavia finally resolved their dispute over Trieste – the city would be in Italy and the hinterland in Yugoslavia, now Slovenia.

Paradoxically, the anticipation of another great conflict aided peace and prosperity. The scars of two great wars were still raw, and they drove a level of cooperation, often reluctant at first, but ultimately with renewed confidence about Europe itself. Nonetheless a great cultural conflict was waged between the east and the west. The West's Congress for Cultural Freedom countered Stalin's Peace Initiative in the early 1950s. But the culture of prosperity ultimately prevailed, as the new consumerism and the impact of American culture had its impact in Europe. In an age of movies and television, global influences had a significant impact on the culture of Europe.

Triumphs and tragedies

Fausto Coppi looked forward to the 1951 season in anticipation of a better year than his previous one. He had recovered from his broken pelvis at the Giro to finish on the bottom step of the podium in the Giro di Lombardia, an indication that he was still amongst the best cyclists in Europe. His great rival, Gino Bartali, by then 36, had a good start to the season, splitting Ferdi Kübler and Jean Robic for second placing at La Flèche Wallone. There was still life in the 'old man' of cycling.

But then tragedy struck for Coppi in one of the first races for the season, the Milan-Turin, in early March when he fell and broke his collarbone. Fiorenzo Magni, who went on to have a stellar season – probably his best – won the race. He also claimed his third consecutive Ronde van Vlaanderan, the Giro d'Italia, and finished second to Ferdi Kübler in the World Championship at Varese.

Coppi lost valuable training and racing opportunities while his clavicle recovered, and was not in his best form for the Giro. Fiorenzo Magni eventually won the race from Rik van Steenbergen and Ferdi Kübler. Fausto was fourth, just over 4 minutes down on the winner.

A few days before the Paris departure of the Tour de France, an even greater tragedy struck. Fausto's younger brother, Serse, died of head injuries after falling from his bike at the end of June during the Giro del Piemonte in Turin. He had caught his front tyre in a tramline, fell and hit his head. At first, he seemed OK, getting back on his bike and riding to the finishing line with others. That night, Serse complained of a headache. His condition worsening, he was taken to hospital where he died of a cerebral haemorrhage. It was in the days when most cyclists rode without any head protection. The padded leader straps that became fashionable – more so the modern helmet – might have cushioned the blow and lessened the trauma. There was no MRI scanning in those days; indeed an operation was delayed because of a lack of blood supplies.

Fausto was devastated. Although three and a half years younger, Serse had been the balancing influence on his famous sibling. They had ridden and lived together on tour for years. Serse countered Fausto's intensity. He was more than a brother; he was in part a confidant and mentor for the champion cyclist. The death of a cyclist hits the entire peloton. The professional peloton is a close knit group: riders, mechanics, *soigneurs* and team directors share a life on the road together for months of the year. They have ridden for and against each other. They share the triumphs and the tragedies, knowing that an accident can befall any of them. Gino Bartali was particularly affected: it brought back the nightmares of the loss of his own brother, Giulio, in a cycling accident 15 years before.

There was little time for mourning and reflection. With the start of the Tour de France just a few days away, the funeral was quickly conducted before Fausto and the other riders made their way to Paris, having been paid 500,000 francs to race. The Tour was a triumph for Hugo Koblet, who defeated the leading French riders Raphaël Géminiani and Lucien Lazarides. Gino Bartali rode a fine race, just off the podium in fourth position. Fausto Coppi showed glimpses of his brilliance, but lost more than 30 minutes on stage 16, a relatively easy 192-kilometre race from Carassonne to Montpellier in the south of France.

The death of Serse Coppi robbed Fausto of an important, balancing influence in his life. Already quiet, he became more introspective. It also affected his marriage. His wife, Bruna, endured rather than enjoyed cycling, although she did attend some of his races. Serse's death worried her more. Could not the same happen to Fausto? He had already had a series of major injuries. He had achieved fame and fortune. They didn't need the money and they now had a young daughter, Marina, to think of. Although the team shared the winnings from races, the endless series of criterium and *kermesse* events were money-spinners for the top professionals. Then there were the winter track events, where thousands of people were happy to pay to see their heroes in action on the banked velodromes.

There are many reasons why marriages breakdown. As Tolstoy famously observed in *Anna Karenina*, "each unhappy family is unhappy in its own way." There are also a variety of reasons why people start affairs, amongst them the confluence of long periods of separation from family, and the power and attraction of celebrity. It is not entirely clear when Fausto Coppi began an affair with Giulia Occhini, the wife of Enrico Locatelli, a doctor in Varano Borghi, a small village on the shore of Lake Camabbio, north-west of Milan. Locatelli was a fan of the *campionissimo*; Giulia became infatuated with him. Coppi spent time with the couple after they became friendly, visiting them at their home and going out with them. Over time, the bond between Fausto and Giulia grew, just as the relationship with Bruna was cooling. Nor was Fausto about to give up his life as a cyclist. The will to succeed, to best his rivals, Gino Bartali principle amongst them, still burnt strongly in his heart.

Fall from grace

The great rivalry between Coppi and Bartali was on display again in 1952. Bartali was still a force to be reckoned with, despite being one of the oldest riders in the peloton. Coppi had had two ordinary seasons, punctuated by injury. Perhaps 1949-50 had been the climax of his career. But Coppi had a plan to repeat his remarkable Giro-Tour double in 1949. After a promising start to the season, including a second to Rik van Steenbergen in Paris-Roubaix, Coppi concentrated on being prepared for the Giro.

Bianchi and Coppi revolutionized the way in which professional road racing was conducted in the 1952 season. It came at the culmination of Fausto's consideration of diet and training methods, and a new regime for the team during races. Coppi had always ridden with his head and his legs, knowing that success is as much a mental pursuit as physical. Knowing how to read the unfolding race, closely observing the smallest signs of strain or fatigue in competitors, and having your teammates ready to assist were already the hallmarks of a champion. But Coppi and Bianchi took this to a level higher in 1952. He planned which races he would enter with much more thought, rather than ride the season. More significantly, they planned each race with care, orchestrating the moves and attacks to tire or decimate the opposition. Central to this strategy was the decision to hire Raphaël Géminiani to ride for Bianchi.

Géminiani was a rising star of the sport. French, but of Italian ancestry, Raphaël first came to prominence by winning the National Junior Road Championship before the war. Since resuming after the conflict, he had claimed four stages of the Tour, and finished second to Hugo Koblet in 1951, winning the mountains classification along the way. Géminiani was hired to be what teams today call a 'super domestique' – a *gregario di lusso* in Italy's cycling idiom.

Géminiani's task was simple: he was to launch breaks in the stages, forcing the other teams to chase him down, while Coppi, protected by his *gregari*, conserved his energy for the critical times. By the early 1950s, the Grand Tours had assumed their modern character. The 1952 Giro consisted of 20 stages, averaging 192 kilometres, with two rest days. The following Tour was 23 stages of an average of 209 kilometres, again with just two rest days. It was also the first Giro in which Australian cyclists participated.

GREAT RIVALRIES

Géminiani earnt his salary in the Queen stage of the Giro, a 272-kilometre ascent of the Falzarego, Pordoi and Selle Passes in the Dolomites. The Frenchman went away on the first climb, while Coppi outstayed his rivals, eventually joining Géminiani on the Pordoi. Coppi eventually rode clear of his teammate, his signature long solo on display once again. Coppi had an eight-minute lead over Magni, Bartali, Donato Zampini and Kübler when he rode into Bolzano. Coppi returned the favour in the last stage, allowing Géminiani to lead over the ascents, and deny Bartali the climber's competition.

The Tour was an altogether different challenge. Still raced by national teams, it meant that Raphaël Géminiani could not ride for the Italians. But worse, the rivalry between Coppi and Bartali resurfaced, leading to *Gazzetta dello Sport* to arrange for mediation between the warring rivals. The compromise was even more complex than the previous one: Coppi, Bartail and Magni would be co-leaders of the team, each with their own *gregari*. The *Gazzetta* even paid for the cyclists to compete! Getting Coppi and Bartali to the start line was one thing; encouraging them to assist each other was another. Coppi, in particular, never really trusted Bartali in a race. The Italians were favoured in the absence of Kübler, Koblet and the rising Bobet, but internal warring could easily derail their campaign.

In the end, Coppi was too strong in the mountains. On the first ever ascent of l'Alpe d'Huez, the famed 13-kilometre, 1000-metre climb up 21 switchbacks, only Jean Robic could stay with the Italian, but even he was dropped four kilometres from the summit. If there was any doubt about the final victor of that year's tour, it was put to rest in stage 11, the climb over four cols – the Croix de Fer, the Galibier, the Montgeneve, and the Sestriere. Italians flocked to the last climb in their thousands, as the stage finished at the Italian ski resort. Coppi demolished the peloton – the Tour was his for losing. In fact the organisers doubled the prize money second and third placings to maintain interest amongst the other competitors. The Belgian, Stan Ockers eventually finished second, 28 minutes behind Coppi, with the Spanish rider, Barnardo Ruiz and further 6 minutes astern, just ahead of Bartali, Robic and Magni. Bartali had even put his rivalry for Coppi aside, assisting him on the final stages.

Coppi had achieved the 'double double'. He never rode the Tour de France again. Only one major race eluded him: the World Championship Road Race. That he was to achieve the following season. Along the way he defeated Hugo Koblet in the Giro. He missed the Tour to concentrate on his preparation for the Worlds, going to Lugano, Switzerland, with his *gregario*, Michele Gismondi from Bianchi three weeks prior to the event. The 270-kilometre race comprised 18 laps of a course around the town, with especially constructed sectors of cobbled climbs. Two-thirds of the way through the event, Coppi stretched his legs, but it was on the 17th lap that he powered away from the great Belgian one-day racer, Germain Derycke to win by more than six minutes, with Stan Ockers a further minute behind him. Ockers was to win the title at Frascati two years later, a race in which four previous winners of the rainbow jersey, Louison Bobet, Ferdi Kübler, Briek Schotte and Fausto Coppi, all abandoned.

An estimated 30,000 fans that had flooded into Lugano were delirious with joy. Amongst them was Coppi's wife, Bruna, and also the woman who had become his mistress, Giulia Locatelli, who was photographed next to him. Fausto returned home with Cavanna, Gismondi and Bruna, but the cracks in his personal life were soon to rip apart. Crowds turned out to see their hero race on the road and the track. But fame was about to be replaced by notoriety. While the relationship was an open secret in the peloton, his teammates ensured that it remained as private as possible. It came to the ultimate, inevitable conclusion at the 1954 Giro, won by the unlikely Carlo Clerici. The Giro descended into farce when Coppi contracted food poisoning, and the other riders essentially went on strike after the organizers failed to honour a promise of more prizemoney to make the race competitive. Clerici, a little known *gregario*, joined an escape on stage six with Nino Assirelli and gained a 13-minute lead on the field. Coppi's mood darkened as the race continued. He had a fight with the Swiss *gregario*, Emilio Croci Torti, as the press turned against him and the peloton.

Friends of Coppi, even the Pope, urged him to return to Bruna after an annulment was sought. Italy was a conservative country. Sixty-nine percent of Catholics still attended mass in 1956. The Church had retained its influence in relation to marriage in the settlement with

Mussolini, and the Christian Democrats supported the family.

The media pounced. Photos of Coppi with Giulia – named the *Dama Bianca* (the White Lady) for a coat she wore at a stage finish at St Moritz – were published and the press reported that Bruna had filed for divorce. Dr Locatelli also filed for divorce against Giulia. The following months were messy, with prurient reporting by the media, invasive searching of the couple's home, the jailing of Giulia for four days, and a very open trial, all before a public that had turned against their former hero. Then as now, the public will endure only so long sportspeople who substitute personality and character with arrogance, and neglect modesty and integrity.

The adultery action was settled with a 50-million lire payment by Coppi to Bruna, but the public trial dragged on, with the magistrate condemning both the cyclist and Guilia, although her the most, which reflected both contempory public morality and a law that was not changed until ruled unconstitutional in 1968. They were sentenced to three months imprisonment for leaving their spouses, but the sentences were suspended. In the meantime, Giulia was expecting their child who was born in Argentina where he could be registered to unmarried parents. Named Faustino, he was born while his father was riding in the 1955 Giro d'Italia, a race that he lost by just 13 seconds to Fiorenzo Magni. It was to be his last podium in a Grand Tour. He had won the Italian Championship that year and finished second in Paris-Roubaix, despite the travails of his private life and his age.

Epilogue

The future will not be built through force, nor the desire to conquer, but by the patient application of the democratic method, the constructive spirit of agreement, and by the respect for freedom
-- Alcide De Gasperi.

The race is no respecter of reputations; you're only as good as now
-- Phil Liggett.

By the mid 1950s, Italy was well into the journey to post-war recovery, a stable political structure, and a system of government that worked despite institutional arrangements that had not changed greatly from the previous pre-war period. As Tony Judt observes in his postwar history of Europe:

> The country lacked a stable majority in favour of any one party or program, and the complicated electoral system of proportional representation generated parliaments too divided to agree on substantial or controversial legislation: the post-war Republican constitution did not acquire a Constitutional Court to adjudicate its laws until 1956, and the much discussed need for regional autonomy was not voted upon in Parliament until 14 years later.

Alcide De Gasperi's Christian Democrats successfully navigated the shoals of Italian politics through the 1950s, winning more than 40 per cent of the vote in both 1953 and 1958. They formed coalitions with minor parties – of the centre until 1963 and thereafter of the non-communist left until the late 1970s. This was the first legacy that De Gasperi, the unlikely Prime Minister of postwar Italy, left. Three years after he died in 1954, the Treaty of Rome established the European

GREAT RIVALRIES

The 'Lion of Flanders', Fiorenzo Magni during the 1956 Giro d'Italia.

Economic Community, the forerunner of the European Union three decades later.

De Gasperi's success in establishing a party that maintained broad popular support on the conservative, centre-right of Italian politics stands in contrast to the experience on the left. While the communists under Palmiro Togliatti became the second most popular party after the war, the vote for the left was split with other parties, including the socialists. A year before Togliatti's death in 1964, the communists won 25 percent of the vote, a proportion that rose to over a third in 1976. But national government eluded the communists, which were more successful in local and regional elections. Togliatti remained a Stalinist throughout his decades-long leadership of the Italian communists, even after the Soviet leader had died, and was denounced in Moscow. The party was disbanded in 1991, with most of its members transferring to the *Partito Democratico della Sinistra* – the Democratic Party of the Left. History was moving against Togliatti's view of the world. The irony is that the Italian Communist Party had remained the largest non-ruling communist party in Europe partially because many of its members rejected the totalitarian insistence that the political realm transcended every other sphere of human activity.

But that didn't mean that the culture of the west was not also changing. How institutions deal with change is a key to their success and their longevity. As the oldest, continuous political institution in the world, in particular the West, the Roman Catholic Church was the prime example. It had survived oppression and ascendency, favour and disfavour. It had been at the centre of the secular, political regime of various eras, and on the periphery. Over the centuries it had been led by good and godly men, and by vain and venal princes. Yet it had survived. At its core, it represented a creed that was based on love that sought to uphold the dignity and liberty of the individual, which at times had been forgotten or neglected, nonetheless remained central to its message. And it had gone through many difficult, challenging transitions over the centuries, by reverting to its central philosophy that spoke to the hearts of men and women across cultures and generations.

It was also the Roman Catholic Church, synonymous with the eternal city for almost 2,000 years. The issue of the Papal States had been resolved only recently by Mussolini, but the idea within the Church that it was a major power in world affairs remained potent. No one believed this more than Eugenio Pacelli, subsequently Pius XII, who re-established the church as a political force in Italy.

Although personally a humble, ascetic and caring man, Pacelli was the last of the great 'Princes of the Church'. He was an intellectual, who brought the dispassionate scholar's attention to the problems facing the world. His grand vision of concordats with various nations, especially those hostile to Christian principles, was noble in intent, but naive in application. Hitler, Mussolini and the leaders of Eastern Europe honoured many of these agreements in their breach. The experience of the Church in Hungary in the 1950s is the most obvious example. The later disciples of this approach, namely the leaders of the *Ostpolitic* regime of the 1970s, and the recent kowtowing to the Chinese communists, maintain this tragic legacy, despite the efforts of John Paul II and Benedict XVI.

Pacelli's death in 1958 marked a turning point for the Church. It is Catholic tradition that the Cardinals of the Church, guided by the Holy Spirit, elect the new Pope. While this may be theologically true, it also means the College of Cardinals, humans all, and subject to all the pressures, challenges and aspirations of each age, not to mention internal political currents, elect the next leader of the Catholic Church. In 1958, they chose Angelo Giuseppe Roncali, who took the title Pope John XXIII. It took 11 ballots to choose the new Pope, and then a man, who at the age of 76, might be expected to remain in the position for only a short period, and to do little. It was a transitional measure. Roncali, the fourth son (of 14 children) of sharefarmers from the village of Sotto il Mare near Bergamo, was a distinct contrast to the aristocratic Pacelli. His relatively short Pontificate will be recorded as one of the most significant in church history. As if understanding the great transition that the world – Europe in particular – was undergoing, John XXIII or *Il Papa Buono*, as he was known, sought to engage the Church in an epochful dialogue, which he announced just three months after becoming the pontiff. It became known as the Second Vatican Council – the first having been conducted in the late 1800s, but prematurely ended because of war. The second Council lasted from

1962-1965, concluding under John XXIII's successor, Paul VI.

Throughout his reign, John XXIII – who had served as nuncio to Bulgaria during the war and helped Jews to escape persecution – sought to redefine the relationship between the Church and the Jewish people. It was one of the significant changes to arise from the Council.

The end of an era

While major political, economic and cultural currents were reshaping both Italy and the world, the professional careers of three of the country's greatest cyclists were coming to an end.

Gino Bartali's last podium was to be a second placing to Hugo Klobet on the penultimate stage of the 1954 Giro d'Italia. Mounting the podium for the last time at Sankt Moritz-Dorf, Gino was just shy of his 40th birthday. His days on the bike had been numbered after being badly injured in a car crash the previous October. He was rushed to hospital in Milan where his wife, Adriana, found him with fractured vertebrae and internal damage to his bowels and intestine. During his recuperation, an old friend, Alcide De Gasperi, visited the great cyclist. Gino would officially retire in 1955. He went into business, investing in bicycle manufacturing when scooters and cars were replacing the humble vehicle. It was not the most successful venture. In later years, he commentated on cycling and appeared on a down-market television show in Italy.

Fiorenzo Magni followed his 1955 Giro triumph with a number of minor wins the following season, a second to Charly Gaul in the Giro and a third placing at the Giro di Lombardia. He had already been planning his post cycling career, opening a motorcycling dealership near Monza, and later a car dealership.

Fausto Coppi's last significant season was 1955, in which he claimed the Italian Road Championship, wins in a series of other Italian races, as well as second placing at Paris-Roubaix and second in the Giro. Coppi rode on for the next three years, winning and placing in some minor races, including a six-day race on the track at Buenos Aires in 1958, but his sporting star was fading.

The French historian of the sport, Pierre Chany, recalls Coppi's last years, observing he was

"a magnificent and grotesque washout of a man, ironical towards himself; nothing except the warmth of simple friendship could penetrate his melancholia. But I'm talking of the end of his career. The last year! In 1959! I'm not talking about the great era. In 1959, he wasn't a racing cyclist any more. He was just clinging on."

In December 1959, Fausto joined a group of French cyclists – Raphaël Géminiani, Roger Riviere, Jacques Anquetil, Henri Anglade and Roger Hassenforder – to contest a couple of races in Upper Volta. The races were an excuse to go hunting in Africa, which Coppi, an avid outdoor sportsman, looked forward to. Indeed, the last entry on his *Palmares* is second placing to Jacques Anquetil, who would dominate the Tour de France in the early 1960s, in the GP Ouagadougou, contested in the capital of the former French colony of Upper Volta in West Africa subsequently renamed Burkina Faso in 1984.

Tragically, a number of the group contracted malaria, from which Coppi died in early February 1960, his doctors initially unable to discover the cause of his illness. Thousands of the *tifosi* attended his funeral at Castellania. In death, Coppi became an object of myth and legend that continues to this day in Italy.

In an intriguing footnote, the newspaper, *Corriere dello Sport*, reported in late 2001 that Coppi had been poisoned while competing in Burkina Faso as an act of revenge against the death of a local cyclist during a race against the foreigners. The assertions had been made to a visiting French Benedictine priest during a confession. While the claims are doubtful –and subsequently dismissed by an Italian court – Coppi remains as fascinating in death as he was in life.

The golden age

The settlement of the question of Trieste largely completed the hopes for the *Risorgimento*. Italy was a united nation. A long period of peace and stability, beginning at the end of the war, and interrupted only by the civil unrest and terrorist activities of the Red Brigades in the 1970s and early 80s – who assassinated Prime Minister Aldo Moro and Legnano owner, Emilio Bozzi, amongst others – has ensured. As Tony

Cycling and the Story of Italy

Judt observes, Italy evolved its own distinct form of government:

> Italy was in practice run by un-elected administrators working in central government or one of many para-state agencies. This distinctly un-democratic outcome has led historians to treat the Italian political system with some disdain. The opportunities for graft, bribery, corruption, political favouratism and plain robbery *were* extensive and they worked above all to the advantage of the virtual one-party monopoly of the Christian Democrats. Yet under the umbrella of these arrangements, state and society in Italy proved remarkably resilient in the face of inherited challenges and new ones ahead.

Italy also shared in the great economic post-war boom, that generated businesses, created employment, facilitated vast new infrastructure and lifted millions of people out of poverty. The volume of global exports increased sixteenfold over the next four and a half decades, bringing unimagined prosperity to many.

Progress meant change. The humble bicycle, which had helped to shape the future and the culture of the nation, was losing its relevance. Forty-seven million Italians owned just 342,000 private cars in 1950. A decade later, the 50 million Italians owned 2 million vehicles; and by 1970, the 54 million people had more than 10 million vehicles. Companies like FIAT produced thousands of small cars that more and more families could afford. And many people who could not afford a car were able to purchase the motor scooters like the Vespa that became ubiquitous on the streets of the nation's cities. While the bicycle remained popular, especially in the early years after the war when poverty and unemployment remained high, it was being replaced quickly by motor vehicles. This in turn, had a lasting impact on cycling as a sport.

As sales fell for bicycles, manufacturers had less money to spend on teams and sponsorship. Until the early 1950s, bicycle manufacturers sponsored teams; hence the great squads such as Atala, Bianchi, Legnano and Wilier in Italy; and Alcyon, Thomann-Dunlop and J.B. Louvet in France. The changing economics of cycling meant that teams had to look elsewhere for sponsorship. Fiorenzo Magni was at the forefront of this change, asking his personal sponsor Nivea to take over the team's sponsorship, signing a deal with the Swiss manufacturer, Fuchs, in 1954.

It was a radical move for the times. Nivea made moisterizers, not bikes. Outrage ensued in some quarters. Jacques Goddet, who had replaced Henri Desgrange as the Director of the Tour de France after four decades, was insistent that only bike companies sponsor teams. Economics ensured that Magni prevailed: within a decade, the team sponsors included the musical company EMI, the car maker Peugeot, the Belgium margarine manufacturer, Solo, and, perhaps, the most famous of all, Molteni, an Italian salami manufacturer from Arcore on the outskirts of Milan.

The economics of the bicycle industry also led to the demise of the national teams in the Tour de France in 1962 after three decades. Once again Goddet reluctantly had to agree. The sponsors, especially the remaining bike manufacturers could not afford to pay their teams to ride the Tour, yet gain no publicity from the event. Increasingly the rider's kit, especially the jersey, became a mobile billboard. In the early part of the century when only bike manufacturers were sponsors, it mattered less as the company name adorned the frames, but the changes in sponsorship wrought a new approach.

The early 1950s were truly a golden age for professional cycling. Not only were the greatest cyclists of a generation competing with each other, they were paid more than at any other time up until about the mid 1980s. The 1955 Tour de France, for example, offered the mean rider (ie the total prize money divided by the number of riders) € 5,923, compared to just € 4,735 a quarter of century later in 1980. As the team shared the prize money in the major races, most professional cyclists also raced the lucrative criterium and *kermesse* circuit where they kept their winnings, as well as the winter track carnivals.

Cycling authorities also started to react, albeit very slowly, to the scourge of drugs in the sport. When Roger Riviere broke his back after the heavy use of amphetamines in 1960, and the Dutch track cyclist, Knut Jensen, died in the Olympic team time trial, also after doping, the UCI finally introduced regulations. But changing the culture of the sport was slow: in the 1966 Tour de France, the peloton went on strike after urine tests were introduced. Drugs would continue to damage the sport for decades into the future.

Cycling and the Story of Italy

Great rivalries

More than anything, the post war decade was a golden age for Italian cycling because of two men, Gino Bartali and Fausto Coppi. A library of books has been written about them, as the *Bartaliani* (Gino foremost among them) and the *Coppiani* vied to create a lasting legacy. In reality, they were neither saints nor sinners. Gino 'the pious' was a devout Catholic, who was subsequently named as one of the Righteous among the Nations by Israel for helping to save Jews from the holocaust. Despite being generous to his *gregari*, he had a reputation in the peloton for welshing on deals with his competitors. Coppi may not have displayed his religion overtly like Bartali, but insisted that it was a personal matter for him and was disgusted at being described as an atheist. Following his 1949 Tour victory, Coppi presented his *gregari* and the team manager, Alfredo Binda, with gold medals depicting the Madonna del Ghisallo, the patron saint of cyclists. He scandalized conservative Italy by leaving his wife for Giulia Locatelli, yet considered reconciliation in his last years.

Despite being great rivals, Bartali and Coppi often displayed acts of generosity and kindness towards each other. Fausto first showed a photograph of his new son to Gino. Just before his death, Coppi signed a contract with a small team, San Pellegrino, which was managaed by Bartali. Neither would have been as great without the other, and they knew that.

Cycling was a significant part of the culture of Italy in its first century. It reflected the grand passions of the people as they fashioned a nation; a nation born of, and shaped by, great rivalries.

Riders at the 1952 Giro d'Italia, including the Australians, Dean Whitehorn and John Beasley (in sunglasses at the right).

Australian Cyclists in Italy

Many of those who raced in Europe in the 70's and 80's are the ones who've made enormous efforts to make it possible for young riders to get effective support in trying to establish themselves as professional cyclists now
-- Garry Clively, the first Australian to complete the Giro d'Italia.

I had nothing left in the legs but as a cyclist, you just keep going until the finish
-- Cadel Evans on the 2002 Giro d'Italia.

To be an athlete at this level you have to be self-centred, driven, hungry (literally and figuratively) and spend most of your life tired
-- Mathew Hayman, the super-domestique who rode four Giro d'Italia and won Paris-Roubaix.

The 1950s was a golden era for Australian sport. As the sporting capital of the nation, Melbourne, having won the bid to host the 1956 Olympics, was the home of many great contests: the Australian Tennis Open, the Melbourne Cup, a major cricket Test, and the highly popular Australian Rules Football competition. It was also the location of two of the country's most prestigious cycling races. First conducted in 1887, the Austral Wheel Race is the oldest, continuing track race in the world. Eight years later, the Melbourne-Warrnambool Cycling Classic was first contested – initially in the opposite direction as a 270-kilometre race to the capital of Victoria from the seaside city. Each of the events followed the peculiar Australian style: they were handicaps. Over time, other major races were established as cycling gained popularity. Tens of thousands of people flocked to the wooden velodromes. International stars of the track, like Marshall 'Major' Taylor and Floyd MacFarland, battled with the local champions on the banked tracks.

Track racing boomed in the first few decades of the 20th century. A trio of Australians, Alf Goullet, Alfred Grenda and Jackie Clark, became stars of the sport in the US, eventually settling there. Others, such as Cecil Walker, raced for many seasons on the popular American velodromes such as Madison Square Garden in New York before returning to Australia.

Yet very few were attracted to the European road races, even though similar events were being conducted in Australia. In 1914, two intrepid Victorians, Duncan 'Don' Kirkham and Iddo 'Snowy' Munro, were part of a six-man Australian team that had ventured to Europe the previous year. They became the first Australians – indeed the first non-Europeans – to contest the Tour de France after impressive performances earlier in the season, including the Milan-San Remo in Italy, Paris-Roubaix in France, and the Tour of Belgium. Kirkham finished an outstanding ninth to Ugo Agostini at San Remo, while Munro was 26th. A week later, Munro was 37th in the gruelling Paris-Roubaix. Their performances won them a start in the Tour, riding as *domestiques* for Georges Passerieu on the Phebus/Dunlop team. Passerieu abandoned, leaving the Australians best placed for the team, with Kirkham 17th and Munro 20th. As the 1914 Tour was getting underway, the events that resulted in the Great War were playing out. It would be another 14 years before Australians rode again in the Tour de France.

A team of three Australians, Ernie Bainbridge, Percy Osborne and Hubert Opperman, and a New Zealander, Harry Watson, sailed to France in 1928, expecting to be part of a larger French team, only to find themselves racing the Tour alone against ten-man squads. All but Bainbridge completed the Tour, with 'Oppy' 18th, Watson 28th and Osborne 38th. Opperman became a national hero in France, winning the famous 24 hour Bol d'Or, covering an amazing 909 kilometres, before riding on to claim the world 1,000-kilometre record to boot! Oppy returned to France in 1931, racing there and in Switzerland, before finishing 12th in the Tour and winning the 1,200-kilometre Paris-Brest-Paris

Cycling and the Story of Italy

In the early 1950s, encouraged by Opperman, who had retired from racing and had been elected to the Australian Parliament – later serving as the Minister for Immigration – the Melbourne *Sporting Globe* helped fund another group of Australians to race in Europe. They would become the first Australians to ride the Giro d'Italia. The newspaper proclaimed in January 1952:

> The *Sporting Globe*-sponsored International Jubilee Cycling Trust has selected John Beasley, Peter Anthony, Eddie Smith and Don Williams as Australia's team to contest European road cycling classics, including the Tour of Italy and the Tour de France.

Dean Whitehorn replaced Williams before they team set off on the European venture. Gino Bambagiotti, an Italian six-day cyclist who had travelled to Australia to race in Sydney prior to the war, managed the team. Bambagiotti had won a stage of the 1937 Tour of Poland, and a second placing in the Buenos Aires six-day. He was also a runner-up in the Sydney six-day in 1938.

Beasley, the youngest at 21, was the reigning Australian road champion. He had a good start to the European visit, finishing 55th in the world's oldest one-day classic, Liege-Bastogne-Liege. The *Sporting Globe* reported on May 21:

> Footscray cyclist John Beasley earned the plaudits of the French Press and world top ranking as a road rider for his magnificent fourth in the Criterium Polymultiple (154 kilos) in France . . . Beasley finished only 19 seconds behind the winner, Jean Robic, who out-sprinted Wagtmans and Martinez.

Two weeks later, the Australians joined some of the greatest cyclists of the era in Milan for stage one of the 1952 Giro d'Italia. Alongside them were the stars of the sport including Fausto Coppi, Gino Bartali, Fiorenzo Magni, Ferdi Kübler, Hugo Koblet, Rik Van Steenbergen and Stan Ockers. It was a crack field, which Coppi would conquer before going on to win the Tour de France.

The Australians, who were hoping for a ride in the Tour, joined the Nilux team for the Giro. It was a tough introduction to a Grand Tour, the first time that the young Aussies had experienced a three-week event with the world's best. Beasley was in the best form, but others were struggling after the first week. Having agreed to an all or none pact, the quartet abandoned after the eighth stage to Ancona. Eddie Smith's 14th in the third stage was the best result for the Aussies.

Beasley returned to Australia to finish fourth behind the Rowley brothers, Keith and Max, and the 1950 World Amateur Road Champion, Jack Hoobin, in the unaugural *Sun* Tour. Now the *Herald Sun* Tour, the race reflected the growing interest in cycling in the early 1950s and the work of many supporters, incluiding Iddo Munro, and Nino Borsari, the 1932 Olympic Pursuit Team gold medalist at the Los Angeles Olympics, who had ridden in the 1934 Centenary Tour of Victoria before returning in 1940 and eventually settling in Melbourne.

Beasley returned to Italy in 1955, where he joined Arthurs Julius, Russell Mockridge and Jim Taylor for the World Championships at Frascati. Mockridge had finished 14th in the five-stage Rome-Naples-Rome tour. They also raced in France, with Beasley in 15th placing on the last stage of the Dauphiné Libéré when a broken chain and a fall dashed his chances of an even higher finish. Nonetheless, the Australians had impressed the Europeans. Mockridge and Beasley joined the Luxembourg team of Charly Gaul for the Tour de France, but Mockridge had a bad knee infection, and a bout of food poisoning afflicted both he and Beasley. Beasley had to withdraw after the third stage, while Mockridge struggled on to finish 64th to Louison Bobet who claimed his third straight win in the world's greatest race.

It would be another two decades before an Australian finished the Giro d'Italia. An 18-year-old Australian amateur cyclist, Garry Clively, journeyed to Italy in 1975 with the dream of riding for a local team. In an interview with the cycling website, *veloveritas*, Clively later explained his journey to Italy:

> It could have been Belgium, but circumstances directed me to Italy. I was a besotted teenager who absolutely had to race in Europe. It was something a lot of young riders from Australia were beginning to think of doing. Young David Allan and I had heard a rumour that a few Aussies were going to head for Italy in early 1974 to try and join an amateur team called Siapa in northern Italy. We found out they would be looking for a man by the name of Harry Luther who was a rep for Shimano and was somehow linked to the team. All we knew was that he lived in a small town south of Ravenna and that he might be able to help us.

Cycling and the Story of Italy

On our arrival there we found out that he was somewhere in Spain and we later learned he'd had a fall out training there and was in hospital. We had very little money and no plan B, so we hunted down the Siapa team director in Ravenna and introduced ourselves. The poor guy just had to laugh at us; David was 17 and I was 18, both with a bike and tiny suitcases and wanting to join his team.

Mr Luther had not been in a position to hear about us coming so to them we were a complete surprise. They didn't know about anyone coming from Australia except Clyde Sefton who was due after the Christchurch Commonwealth Games road race. They wanted to turn us away, but I asked if we could just go training with the team a couple of times to see what it would be like to experience at least that much.

It was all a bizarre joke to them and they must have thought it would be a laugh to lose us both on some climb out in the middle of the countryside and then forget all about us. Of course, we had other plans, this being our only chance to make an impression and get our foot in the door there.

They weren't a bad lot and the team generally dominated the regional races. However, they had no idea just what kind of a rider David Allan was. He was really a unique talent. I wasn't going too badly either and so between the two of us we gave the *Directeur Sportive* – who followed the run that first day – something to think about by dropping them all, much to our own surprise.

Being only 17, David was too young for the Siapa team, but they kindly found him a team a little south of Ravenna, where he raced that year (winning 18 races no less), while they found a place for me in a cheap hotel and let me join the team, giving me a jersey and a pair of shorts.

The owner of the team was very kind to me and welcomed me in the most friendly manner, although it was always clear that I had no contract and no income whatsoever except prize money. I couldn't wait for the team to gather and drive to races because there wasn't much to eat in that hotel and at least we ate well on the road.

Clively finished fourth in the World Amateur Road Race Championship at Namur, Belgium, and claimed a series of podium finishes in Italy to become the country's leading amateur cyclist. The considerable success with Siapa led to an offer to ride for the professionl Magniflex team. Clively contested the 1976 Giro, a race that included two of the greatest riders of the era, Francesco Moser and Eddy Merckx. He finished 44th in the tour won by Felice Gimondi. Clively's best result was in 1977, when still a 21-year-old, he finished 7th in the Vuelta a España, just seven minutes down on the great Flandrian winner, Freddy Maertens. Despite his talent and results, Clively departed Europe, and gave up racing, only to return a decade later to win the Australian Road Championship and a series of other races in 1989-90.

Michael Wilson was the first Australian to win a stage of the Giro in 1982 when he defeated the dual Tour de France winner, Laurent Fignon, in the third stage to Cortona, Tuscany. He also finished 8th on General Classification in 1985, and had three other stage podiums. A few other Australians competed in the 1980s, including Shane Bartley, John Trevorrow, David MacFarlane and Neil Stephens. Phil Anderson won stages in 1989 and 1990, as did Allan Peiper in the latter year.

It wasn't until 1990 that an Australian wore a race leader's jersey when Phil Anderson claimed the *maglia azzura* – an award made between 1989 and 2015 for the cumulative leader at the midpoint of each stage, named the intergiro.

The trickle of Australians during the 1990s – Stephen Hodge, Eddie Salas, Pat Jonker and Matthew White – became a flood after the turn of the century. More than 60 Australians have now ridden the Giro. More than a dozen have won stages, including Robbie McEwen with an amazing 12 wins (as well as nine seconds and four thirds), David McKenzie, Brad McGee, Brett Lancaster, Michael Rogers, Simon Gerrans, Cadel Evans, Mark Renshaw, Matthew Goss, Matthew Lloyd , Adam Hansen, Michael Matthews, Rohan Dennis and Caleb Ewan (including being members of a winning Teams Time Trial team).

No Australian has won the overall Giro d'Italia: Cadel Evans was the first to wear the leader's pink jersey and has come the closest with a third placing in 2013. Six riders have finished in the top ten: Michael Wilson, Phil Anderson, Brad McGee, Michael Rogers, Richie Porte and Cadel Evans. Secondary jerseys have been won by Matt Lloyd (mountains), Cadel Evans (points) and Richie Porte (best young rider).

Australians have also starred in other major Italian races. Matt Goss and Simon Gerrans have won Milan-San Remo, and Stuart O'Grady, Allan Davis, Heinrich Haussler and Caleb Ewan have finished on the podium.

Simon Gerrans, who won not only Milan-San Remo, but also Liege-Bastogne-Liege, the only Australian to win two of the monuments of cycling, also claimed both an individual and a team's stage of the Giro d'Italia, and wore the *maglia rosa*.

Phil Anderson finished third in the Giro di Lombardia twice, and Rohan Dennis, Matt Goss, Robbie McEwen, Michael Wilson, and Phil Anderson (individually) and Baden Cooke, Cameron Meyer, Stuart O'Grady and Mark Renshaw (Teams Time Trial) have won stages of Tirreno-Adriatico.

Australians have also won the race named in honour of Italy's two great cyclists, *Settimana Internazionale di Coppi e Bartali* – the International Week of Coppi and Bartali – a five-day stage race first conducted in 1984: Phil Anderson in 1991, Cadel Evans in 2008, and Lucas Hamilton in 2019.

Timeline

Mazzini's Young Italy movement formed.	1831	
	1839	The mechanical bicycle invented.
Proclamation of the Kingdom of Italy with Piedmont King Emmanuel II the monarch of the new nation.	1861	
Defeat of the Papal States; Rome becomes the new capital of Italy.	1870	
	1876	The Milan-Turin race first conducted.
Francesco Crispi appointed Prime Minister.	1885	Edoardo Bianchi starts manufacturing bicycles in Milan.
Rerum Novarum published by Leo XIII.	1891	
Italian forces routed in the Battle of Adwa, Ethiopia.	1896	*La Gazzetta dello Sport* first published in Milan. The first modern Olympics are conducted in Greece.
	1899	Bicycles first used by troops in the Second Boer War.
King Umberto assassinated by anarchist, Gaetano Bresci.	1900	
Giovanni Giolitti appointed Prime Minister.	1901	
	1902	Victoria Rossi (later Legnano) bicycles first manufactured.
	1903	The first Tour de France is conducted.
	1905	Giovanni Gerbi wins the inaugural Giro di Lombardia.
	1906	Wilier bicycles first manufactured at Bassano del Grappa.
	1907	Lucien Petit-Breton wins the first Milan-San Remo.
	1909	Luigi Galetti wins the first Giro d'Italia.
	1910	Carlo Galetti wins the first-of-three Giro d'Italia, one as a team time trial member.
Italy defeats the Ottoman Empire in Libya.	1911	
	1913	Costante Girardengo starts his first Giro d'Italia, won by Carlo Oriano.
Italy suffers the 'Red Week' of strikes.	1914	Costante Girardengo wins the first of nine Italian road race championships. Gino Bartali is born at Ponte a Ema, Florence. The first Australians ride in Italy.
Italy declares war on Austria-Hungary, entering the Great War on the side of Britain, France and Russia.	1915	

GREAT RIVALRIES

The Russian Revolution.	**1917**	Costante Girardengo wins the first of six Milan-San Remo classics.
The Great War ends.	**1918**	
Treaty of Versailles signed.	**1919**	Girardengo wins the first Giro after the war, leading the GC for the entire race and is named the first *campionissimo* – Champion of Champions. Fausto Coppi is born at Castellania, Piedmont.
	1921	Giovanni Brunero wins the first-of-three individual Giro d'Italia.
Benito Mussolini launches the *Fasci di Combattimento* movement. Fascist march on Rome and Mussolini is appointed Prime Minister.	**1922**	
	1924	Ottavio Bottecchia becomes the first Italian to win the Tour de France after leading the GC for the entire race. Alfonsina Strada becomes the only woman to ride the Giro d'Italia, which was won by Giuseppe Enrico, who had been born in Pittsburg, Pennsylvania to an emigrant family.
Mussolini becomes *Il Duce*.	**1925**	Alfredo Binda wins the first-of-five Giro d'Italia.
	1927	Binda wins the inaugural World Road Race Championship at Nurbergring, Germany, the first of three victories, and becomes the second *campionissimo*. Ottavio Battecchia is killed in mysterious circumstances.
The Lateran Treaty signed.	**1929**	
Pope Pius XI attacks fascism in *Non Abbiamo Bisogno*.	**1931**	The *maglia rosa* (pink jersey) is first awarded to the race leader of the Giro d'Italia, Learco Guerra.
Concordat with Germany signed by the Vatican.	**1933**	Alfredo Binda wins his fifth Giro d'Italia.
Austrian Chancellor Englebert Dollfuss assassinated by the Nazis.	**1934**	
Spanish Civil war breaks out.	**1935**	Gino Bartali wins the first of four national championships.
	1936	Bartali wins the first-of-three Giro d'Italia. The Olympics are held at Berlin.
Mit brennender sorge published	**1937**	
Kristallnacht *Manifesto of Racial Scientists* published in Italy	**1938**	Bartali wins the Tour de France.

Cycling and the Story of Italy

Eugenio Pacelli elected as Pope Pius XII. World War II begins when Germany invades Poland. Italy signs a 'Pact of Steel' with Germany. Italy enters WWII by invading Greece and Albania.	**1939**	
	1940	Coppi, aged 20, wins his first Giro d'Italia, the last before the war. Gino Bartali marries Adriana Bani.
Allied forces occupy Sicily. Mussolini dismissed and imprisoned; and an armistice is signed with the Allies. German troops move into northern Italy and free Mussolini.	**1943**	Coppi called-up for service, is posted to Africa, captured and imprisoned. Bartali helps to rescue Jews in Italy.
Mussolini is executed by partisans. Alcide De Gasperi is appointed Prime Minister of Italy.	**1945**	Fausto Coppi marries Bruna Ciampolini.
Marshall Plan proposed. Civil unrest grips Italy.	**1947**	Coppi wins his second Giro d'Italia.
Italians vote to become a republic and the Constitution is adopted. The Christian Democrats headed by De Gasperi win the national elections. Communist leader Palmiro Togliatti shot and injured. *Il ladri di biciclette (The Bicycle Thieves)* is first shown. Italy joins NATO	**1948**	Fiorenzo Magni wins his first (of three) Giri d'Italia. Gino Bartali wins the Tour de France, a decade after his first victory. Bartali and Coppi abandon the World Championship Road Race.
	1949	Coppi becomes the first cyclist to win the Giro d'Italia - Tour de France double. He becomes the third *campionissimo*.
Italy is a founding member of the European Coal and Steel Community.	**1952**	Coppi wins his second Giro-Tour double. First Australians compete in the Giro d'Italia.
De Gasperi retires as Prime Minister.	**1953**	Fausto Coppi wins the World Road Race Championship at Lugano, Switzerland, and his fifth Giro.
	1954	Coppi's relationship with Giulia Occhini revealed.
	1955	Gino Bartali retires from professional cycling.
The Treaty of Rome establishing the European Economic Community is signed.	**1957**	
Pius XII dies and Angelo Roncali elected as Pope John XXIII.	**1958**	
	1960	Fausto Coppi dies from malaria. The Olympics are held in Rome. Jacques Anquetil wins the first-of-two Giri d'Italia.

Select Bibliography

Anderson, Philip, with Christi Valentine-Anderson (1999) *Philip Anderson – Cycling Legend* [Lothian, Melbourne]

Applebaum, Anne (2017) *Red Famine: Stalin's War on Ukraine* [Doubleday, New York]

Austin, Ronald J (2008) *Cycling to War* [Slouch Hat Publications, McCrae, Australia]

Bartali, Gino with Nario Pancera (1958) *La mia storie* [Stampa Sportive, Milan]

Bartali, Gino (1979) *Tutto sbagliato, tutto di rifare* [Mondadori, Milan]

Bartali, Gino with Romano Beghelli and Marcello Lazzerini (1992) *La leggenda di Bartali* [Ponte Alle Grazie Eitori, Florence]

Belbin, Giles (2017) *Chasing the Rainbow* [Aurum Press, London]

Blainey, Geoffrey (2000) *A Short History of the World* [Pengiun, Melbourne]

Boardman, Chris (2015) with Chris Sidwells, *The Biography of the Modern Bike* [Cassell, London]

Bobet, Jean [Adam Berry, trans] (2008) *Tomorrow, we ride* [Mousehold Press, Norwich]

Bouvet, Philippe et al (2010) *The Spring Classics – Cycling's Greatest One-Day Races* [Velopress, Boulder, Colorado]

Campbell, Ian (2017) *The Addis Ababa Massacre: Italy's National Shame* [Oxford University Press, New York]

Chany, Pierre (1979) *La Fabuleuse Historie des Classiques at des Championnats de Monde* [Editions EDIL, Paris]

Coppi, Fausto (1950) *Le Drame de Ma Vie* [Editions France-Soir, Paris]

Craven, John (2015) *The 'Warrnambool'* [Bas Publishing, Dromana, Victoria]

Curtis, Martin (2008) *Russell Mockridge – The Man in Front* [Melbourne Books, Melbourne]

Dalin, David G (2005) *The Myth of Hitler's Pope – How Pope Pius XII Rescued Jews from the Nazis* [Regnery, Washington DC]

Duggan, Christopher (1994) *A Concise History of Italy* [Cambridge University Press, Cambridge]

Emerson, Maureen (2018) *Riviera Dreaming: Love and War on the Cote d'Azur* [I.B Taurus, London]

Evans, Cadel, with Rob Arnold (2009) *Close to Flying* [Grant Hardie, Prahan, Australia]

Farren, Paul and Charlie (2013) *Bicycling through Time* [Images Publishing, Mulgrave, Vic]

Fitzpatrick, Jim (2011) *Major Taylor in Australia* [Star Hill Studios, Kilcoy, Australia]

Fitzpatrick, Jim (2013) *Wheeling Matilda – The story of Austalian cycling* [Star Hill Studio, Kilcoy, Qld]

Fotherington, William (2002) *Put me back on my bike - In search of Tom Simpson* [London, Yellow Jersey Press]

Fotherington, William (2003) *A century of cycling – The classic races and legendary champions* [Mitchell Beazley, London]

Fotheringham, William (2009) *Fallen Angel – The Passion of Fausto Coppi* [Yellow Jersey Press, London]

Foot, John (2011) *Pedalare! Pedalare!* [Bloomsbury, London]

Gallagher, Brendan (2017) *Corsa Rosa – A History of the Giro d'Italia* [Bloomsbury, London]

Gilbert, Martin (2003) *The Righteous: The unsung heroes of the holocaust* [Black Swan, London]

Gilbert, Martin (2006) *Kristallnacht – Prelude to Destruction* [Harper Collins, New York]

Guinness, Rupert (2018) *Power of the Pedal* [NLA Publishing, Canberra]

Harris, Bret (2017) *Tour de Oz* [Harper Collins, Sydney]

Hemingway, Ernest, (1927) *Fiesta: The Sun Also Rises* [Vintage, London, 2000]

Hemingway, Ernest (1929) *A Farewell to Arms* [Vintage, London, 2005]

Hochhuth, Rolf (1964) *The Deputy* [Grove Press, Balitmore, 1997]

Isitt, Tom (2019) *Riding in the Zone Rouge* [Weidenfield & Nicholson, London]

Judt, Tony (2005) *Postwar – A history of Europe since 1945* [Penguin, London]

Johnson, Paul (2001) *Modern Times: The World from the Twenties to the Nineties* [Harper Perennial, New York]

Lapide, Pinchas E (1967) *The Last Three Popes and the Jews* [Souvenir Press, London]

Lehnert, M. Pascalina (2014) *His Humble Servant* [St Augustine's Press, South Bend, Indianna]

Liggett, Phil & Doug Donaldson (ed) (2005) *Dancing on the Pedals: The found poetry of Phil Liggett, the voice of cycling* [Breakaway Books, Halcottsville NY]

McCann, Bill & Carol (2006) *The Story of the Tour de France* Vol 1: 1903-1964 [Dog Ear Publishing, Indianapolis]

McCann, Bill & Carol (2011) *The Story of the Giro d'Italia* Vol 1: 1909-1970 [McCann Publishing, Cherokee Village, Arkansas]

McEwen, Robbie & Edward Pickering (2011) *One Way Road* [Ebury Press, North Sydney]

McConnon, Alli & Andres (2012) *Road to Valor* [Broadway, New York]

Molony, John (2016) *Don Luigi Sturzo: the Father of Social Democracy* [Connor Court, Redland Bay, Qld]

Mulholland, Owen (2003) *Uphill Battle – Cycling's Great Climbers* [Velo Press, Boulder, Colorado]

Murphy, Paul, with R. Rene Arlington (1983) *La Popessa* [Warner, New York]

Noel, Gerard (2008) *Pius XII – The Hound of Hitler* [Continuum, London]

O'Brien, Colin (2017) *Giro d'Italia – The story of the world's most beautiful bike race* [Pursuit,

London]

O'Grady, Stuart with Reece Homfray (2014) *Battle Scars* [Hardie Grant Books, Melbourne]

Ohler, Norman (2018) Shaun Whiteside trans. *Blitzed: Drugs in Nazi Germany* [Allen Lane, London]

Olliver, Jean-Paul (Richard Yates trans) (1980) *Fausto Coppi: The true story* [Bromley Books, London]

Olliver, Jean-Paul (1993) *Le pedaleur de charme – Hugo Koblet* [Glenat, Grenoble]

Opperman, Hubert (1977) *Pedals, Politics and People* [Haldane Publishing, Sydney]

Peiper, Allan, with Chris Sidwells (2005) *A Peiper's Tale* [Mousehold Press, Norwich]

Phillips William D & Carla Rahn Phillips (2010) *A Concise History of Spain* [Cambridge University Press, Cambridge]

Picchi, Sandro (2013) *Gino Bartali* [Pacini Editore, Ospedaletto, Pisa]

Procktor, Richard (1970) *Nazi Germany* [Bodley Head, London]

Ramati, Alexander (1978) *The Assisi Underground: The Priests who Rescued Jews* [Stein & Day, New York]

Rowley, Max (1990) *The Rowleys – Golden Years of Cycling* [Caribou Publications, Melbourne]

Sarfatti, Michele [John & Anne C Tedeschi Trans] (2006) *The Jews in Mussolini's Italy: From Equality to Persecution* [University of Wisconsin Press, Madison, Wisconsin]

Schindler, John R (2001) *Isonzo: The Forgotten Sacrifice of the Great War* [Praeger, Westport, Connecticut]

Schofield, Ben (2014) *Wheel Life - Cycling recollection of the 1950s and 1960s* [Ben Schofield, Melbourne]

Sidwells, Chris (2018) *The call of the road* [London, William Collins]

Sidwells, Chris (2016) *The Art of the Cycling Jersey* [Rodale, New York]

Sykes, Herbie (2011) *Maglia Rosa* [Bloomsbury, London]

Thomas, Gordon (2012) *The Pope's Jews* [Thomas Dunne Books, New York]

Thompson, Christopher S (2006) *The Tour de France - A cultural history* [Berkeley, University of California Press]

Van Reeth, D, and DJ Larson [eds] (2016) *The economics of professional road cycling* [Switzerland, Springer International Publishing]

Vanwalleghem, Rik (2014) *100x The Tour of Flanders* [Pinguin, Belgium]

Woodland, Les (2017) *The Inside Story – Cycling's World Championships* [McCann Publishing, McMinnville, OR]

Websites:

Historic Palmeres and Race Results: www.cyclingarchives.com

Giro d'Italia: www.giroditalia.it

Glossary

Belle Epoque: (French 'Beautiful era') The period preceding the Great War.

Breakaway: A group of riders who have surged ahead of the main field – the peloton.

Campionissimo: Champion of Champions, an Italian designation only ever awarded to three riders, Costante Girardengo, Alfredo Binda and Fausto Coppi.

Classics: The most significant one-day races in Europe.

Corsa Rosa: The pink race – another name for the Giro d'Italia.

Criterium: A road race around a short circuit – each lap usually from 1 – 2 kilometers in length.

Domestique: See *Gregario* below

General Classification (GC): The overall leader of a tour, usually the rider who has cycled the cumulative distance at the end of each day in the least time, but some events have time bonuses for certain achievements, such as winning a stage, a sprint, or a hill climb.

Gregario: (*Domestique* in French). Origin: A soldier in the Roman Legions, hence a support rider for a team.

Gregari di Lusso: a super *domestique*

Grand Boucle: (French 'The great circle') – The Tour de France

Grand Tour: The great three-week races – the Giro d'Italia, the Tour de France and the Vuelta a España.

Head(s) of State: An expression coined by the cycling commentator, Phil Liggett, to refer to the leading riders in the peloton.

Il Duce: The Leader

Irrendenta: A territory cuturally, historically or ethnically linked to one nation, but under the control of another country.

Isolato: Independent (non-team) riders in a race.

Kermesse: A road race around a longer circuit, each lap often 10 – 15 kilometres in length.

Maillot Jeune: The yellow jersey worn by the leader on General Classification (overall leader on time) of the Tour de France. Coloured yellow after the tint of the paper on which the original organizer of the race *L'Auto* was printed. It was first worn in the 1919 Tour.

Maglia Rosa: The pink jersey worn by the leader on General Classification (overall leader on time) of the Giro d'Italia. Coloured pink after the tint of the paper on which the organizer of the race, the newspaper *La Gazzetta dello Sport*, is printed. The pink leader's jersey was first worn in the 1931 Giro by Learco Guerra.

Monuments: Five of the earliest and most prestigious one-day classics: Milano-San Remo, Ronde van Vlaanderen (Tour of Flanders), Paris-Roubaix, Liege-Bastogne-Liege, and the Giro di Lombardia.

Mur: A short, steep climb (literally 'a wall')

Nuncio: Ambassador of the Holy See.

Ostpolitic: a Wetern foreign policy of détente towards the Soviet East; and more generally, a policy of détente towards totalitarian states.

Palmares: A cyclist's record of results in major races.

Peloton: The main (and usually largest) group of riders in a race.

Primavera: The first one-day classic of the season, Milan-San Remo. It is also known as *La Classicissima*.

Prime: Prizemoney for intermediate sprints in a race.

Prologue: A (usually) short individual time trial first stage of a Tour.

Puncheur: A strong cyclist on short steep climbs.

Queen stage: The highest mountain stage of a tour. In the Giro d' Italia, this stage is known as the Cima Coppi.

Rouleur: (French 'to roll') A good all round cyclist.

Soigneur: (French 'caretaker') Team helper and masseuse

Tifosi: Italian fans of the sport.

UCI: Union Cycliste Internationale – the international governing body of cycle racing.

Index

Aagne, Antonio & Pierre, 82,
Abraham, 175
Adenauer, Konrad, 225,
Adwa, Battle of,
Aerts, Jean, 84,
Agostini, Ugo, 270,
Alavoine, Jean, 106
Alfonso XIII, King, 111,
al-Husseini, Hajj Amin, 175,
Alighieri, Dante, 18,
Ali, Mohammed, 208,
Allan, David, 272,
Altenburgen, Karl, 105
Ambrosio, Vittorio, 177,
Anderson, Phil, 274,
Andrews, Ben, 12
Anglade, Henri, 264,
Anna Karenina, 254,
Anquetil, Jacques, 106, 190, 249, 251, 264,
Anthony, Peter, 271,
Archambaud, Maurice, 108, 109, 124, 190,
Armstrong, Lance, 234, 249, 252,
Assirelli, Nino, 257,
Astrua, Giancarlo, 241,
Aucouturier, Hippolyte, 37, 38,
Augustus, 138
Azzini, Ernesto, Giuseppe & Luigi, 46
Badoglio, Pietro, 167, 177,
Bahamontes Frederico, 246,
Bailo, Osvaldo, 139, 150, 187,
Bambagiotti, Gino, 271,
Bainbridge, Ernie, 270,
Bani, Adriana, (Adriana Bartali) 155, 157, 167, 180, 181, 183, 263,
Barral, Luigi, 119
Bartali, Andrea, 180,
Bartali, Anita & Natalini, 88,

Bartali, Gino, 13, 24, 28, 29, 44, 56, 85, 87, 89, 96, 99, 100, 101, 103, 106, 108, 113, 114, 115, 116, 119, 120, 123, 124, 126, 128, 129, 131, 133, 135, 136, 139, 140, 141, 143, 147, 149, 152, 153, 154, 155, 156, 167, 171, 180, 182, 185, 186, 187, 188, 191, 192, 193, 195, 197, 199, 200, 201, 202, 207, 208, 211, 215, 216, 217, 218, 219, 220, 221, 222, 223, 226, 228, 230, 231, 232, 233, 236, 237, 241, 244, 246, 248, 250, 252, 253, 254, 256, 263, 267, 271,
Bartali, Giulio, 88, 89, 99, 100, 115, 116, 117, 131, 253,
Bartali, Torello & Giulia, 87, 88, 89, 90, 96, 97, 99, 100, 104, 116, 117, 142,
Bartley, Shane, 274,
Bartolini, Luigi, 187,
Bautz, Erich, 125, 126,
Beamon, Bob, 208,
Beasley, John, 268, 271, 272,
Beaugendre, Omar, 48,
Belloni, Gaetano, 60, 61, 65, 66, 67, 76, 106, 208,
Benedict XV, Pope, 92, 158, 162,
Benedict XVI, Pope, 262,
Beni, Dario, 41, 43,
Benac, Gaston, 107,
Bergamaschi, Vasco, 106, 109, 129, 139, 140,
Bestetti, Pierino, 65,
Bevilacque, Antonio, 200, 211, 238, 239,
Bianchi, Edoardo, 23, 35,
Bicycle Thieves, 187,
Bidot, Marcel, 82
Binda, Alfredo, 12, 24, 25, 28, 61, 64, 66, 67, 68, 69, 71, 76, 80, 82, 85, 105, 107, 108, 109, 113, 114, 118, 144, 145, 196, 222, 230, 232, 233, 267,
Binda, Primo, 64
Bini, Aldo, 14, 106, 114, 127, 129, 139, 149, 189, 193,
Bismarck, Otto von, 21, 110, 111, 164,
Bizzi, Olimpio, 122, 149, 150, 151, 152, 153, 187, 191,

GREAT RIVALRIES

Blum, Léon, 139, 225,
Bobet, Louison, 218, 219, 220, 221, 236, 232, 236, 237, 238, 239, 241, 249, 251, 256, 257,
Bolis, Enrico, 105,
Bongrani, Primo, 36,
Bonhoeffer, Dietrich, 173,
Bonomi, Ivanoe, 75, 194,
Bordin, Lauro, 59,
Borg, Bjorn, 208,
Borsari, Nino, 11, 121, 272,
Bottecchia, Ottavio, 53, 61, 63, 70, 80, 83, 124, 139,
Bozzi, Emilio, 264,
Braun, Eva, 183,
Brambilla, Cesare, 46
Brambilla, Pierre, 218,
Bresci, Gaetano, 21
Brizi, Luigi, 181,
Brocco, Maurice, 47, 48,
Brunero, Giovanni, 65, 66, 67, 76, 86, 196, 230,
Bugno, Gianni, 61, 76,
Buse, Herman, 106
Buysse, Achiel, 241,
Buysse, Lucien, 60, 63,
Buysse, Marcel, 60, 106,
Cadorna, Luigi, 54,
Caesar, Julius, 138,
Calzolari, Aflonso, 51, 56, 59, 61,
Campagnolo, Tullio, 103, 247,
Camellini, Fermo, 200, 212,
Campolini, Bruna, (Bruna Coppi), 194, 258,
Camussso, Francesco, 85, 125, 126,
Cañardo, Mariano, 84
Canavesi, Severino, 122, 139, 140,
Canera, Primo, 124,
Cancia, Cesare Del, 121,
Cappello, Anthony, 12
Carita, Mario, 183,
Carrea, Andre, 229,
Casamonti, Oscar, 99, 100, 104,
Casartelli, Fabio, 29
Cavanna, Biagio, 57, 71, 82, 147, 149, 168, 196, 212, 248, 249, 250, 251, 257,

Cavour, Camilo Benso di, 18, 138,
Cecchi, Ezio, 151, 207, 216, 217,
Chesi, Pietro, 80
Chiappini, Pietro, 139,
Christophe, Eugène, 45,
Churchill, Winston, 203, 225,
Ciampolini, Bruna, (Bruna Coppi), 168, 195, 209, 254, 257,
Ciapelli, Augusta, 104,
Cimalli, Marco, 121,
Cinelli, Cino, 137, 139, 140, 187, 189, 190, 191,
Cinelli, Giotto & Arrigo, 191,
Cipriani, Mario, 106
Cipollini, Mario, 9, 23, 68,
Clark, Jackie, 270,
Clemens, Mathias, 132,
Clerici, Carlo, 257,
Clively, Garry, 269, 272, 273,
Colombo, Emilio, 53, 61, 76, 84,
Communist Manifesto, 159,
Contador, Alberto, 209,
Conte, Oreste, 236,
Cooke, Baden, 275,
Coppi, Dominica & Angiolina (Boveri), 143, 144, 168,
Coppi, Fausto, 13, 23, 24, 25, 28, 29, 33, 44, 56, 57, 61, 108, 126, 143, 145, 146, 147, 149, 150, 151, 152, 153, 154, 167, 168, 169, 187, 190, 192, 193, 193, 194, 195, 196, 198, 199, 201, 207, 208, 211, 212, 215, 216, 217, 222, 223, 224, 228, 230, 232, 233, 234, 235, 236, 237, 238, 239, 240, 241, 242, 243, 246, 248, 250, 251, 252, 253, 254, 256, 257, 258, 263, 264, 267, 271,
Coppi, Faustino, 258,
Coppi, Maria, Dina & Livio, 143,
Coppi, Marina, 254,
Coppi, Serse, 143, 145, 193, 196, 199, 228, 253,
Corbi, Gianni, 214,
Cornet, Henri, 38, 247,
Corno, Ulisse, 28,
Corriere della Sera, 33, 35, 36, 40, 57, 76,
Corriere della Sport, 264,
Cosson, Victor, 132,
Costa, Elia Dalla, 121, 155, 157, 179, 180,

Cycling and the Story of Italy

Costamagna, Emilio, 35, 49,
Cottur, Giordano, 199, 200, 216, 229, 230, 231,
Cougnet, Armando, 29, 30, 35, 41, 42, 43, 44, 50, 51, 108, 198,
Crippa, Salvatore, 200,
Crispi, Francesco, 20, 21, 110, 111,
Cuniolo, Giovanni, 41,
Dannecker, Theodore, 178,
Davis, Allan, 274,
Decaup, Maurice, 40
Delegazione Assistenza Emigrati Ebrei (Delasem), 172,
Demuysere, Joseph, 107, 108,
Dennis, Rohan, 274,
Derycke, Germain, 257,
Desgrange, Henri, 33, 37, 38, 39, 47, 53, 59, 63, 82, 83, 125, 126, 131, 266,
Deruyter, Charles, 55
Didier, Christophe, 149, 151,
Diggelmann, Walter, 149, 151,
Diot, Maurice, 237,
Dittenbrandt, Karl, 45
Dortignacq, Jean-Baptist, 45,
Drexler, Anton, 165,
Duboc, Paul, 32, 51,
Dollfuss, Englebert, 111, 138,
Dumas, Pierre, 250,
Egg, Oscar, 247,
Eichmann, Adolf, 175,
Engels, Friedrich, 159,
Engels, Jean, 219,
Enrici, Giuseppe, 65, 139,
Evans, Cadel, 152, 218, 269, 274,
Ewan, Caleb, 274,
Faber, François, 54,
Fabiani, Callisto, 104
Fachleitner, Eduoard, 218,
Facta, Luigi, 75,
Farinacci, Roberto, 78, 193,
Faure, Antoine, 38
Favalla, Pierino, 121, 149, 150, 187, 189,
Fazio, Mario, 229, 230,
Ferdinand, Franz, 87,

Ferrett, Eugène, 29
Ferretti, Mario, 225,
Fignon, Laurent, 208, 274,
Finzi, Aldo, 172,
Fontan, Victor, 82
Foreign Affairs, 185,
Franco, Francisco, 112, 127, 173,
Frantz, Nicolas, 53,
Galen, Clemens von, 173,
Galetti, Carlo, 31, 40, 42, 43, 45, 46, 47, 48, 49, 50, 51, 56, 58,
Galton, Francis, 19
Ganna, Luigi, 31, 34, 37, 41, 42, 43, 44, 45, 47, 48, 40, 51, 56,
Garibaldi, Giuseppe, 17, 18, 33, 138,
Garin, César, 38,
Garin, Maurice, 37, 38,
Garrigou, Gustave, 30, 31,
Gasparri, Pietro, 95,
Gasperi, Alcide De, 94, 197, 199, 206, 210, 211, 213, 214, 215, 221, 225, 226, 243, 245, 259, 261, 263,
Gasperi, Francesca De, 95, 163, 227,
Gatti, Angelo, 35,
Gaul, Charly, 242, 251, 263, 272,
Gedda, Luigi, 227,
Géminiani, Raphaël, 225, 232, 237, 239, 254, 255, 256, 264,
Gentile, Giovanni, 93
Gentiloni, Vincenzo Ottorino, 92,
Georget, Emile, 301,
Gerbi, Giovanni, 16, 26, 27, 28, 31, 37, 39, 40, 48, 50, 51, 76,
Gerini, Rinaldo, 105
Gerrans, Simon, 10, 12, 274,
Gervasini, Randolpho, 105
Ghirardelli, Alberto, 121,
Giacobbe, Luigi, 84, 85,
Gianeli, Bruni, 248,
Giolitti, Giovanni, 20, 21, 25, 71, 75, 77, 78, 88, 91, 92,
Giornale d'Italia, 137,
Girardengo, Costante, 23, 28, 46, 51, 52, 53, 56, 57, 59, 60, 64, 65, 66, 67, 68, 76, 80, 82, 83, 105, 106, 124, 129, 143, 145, 149, 189, 196,

Girardengo, Carlo and Gaetana, 56
Girmondi, Felice, 274,
Gismondi, Michele, 257, 257,
Giuliano, Salvatore, 210,
Gobbo, James, 11
Goddet, Jacques, 125, 126, 130, 266,
Goddet, Victor, 125,
Goebbels, Joseph, 120,
Goering, Herman, 175,
Goss, Matthew, 274,
Goullet, Alf, 270,
Gramsci, Antonio, 94, 206, 220,
Grande, Pinella di, 249,
Graziani, Rodolfo, 128,
Grenda, Alfred, 270,
Grynszpan, Herschel, 174,
Guerra, Ivano, 81
Guerra, Learco, 57, 68, 80, 81, 82, 83, 85, 106, 108, 113, 122, 134, 196, 233,
Guidi, Rachele, 93
Gullo, Fausto, 210,
Hamilton, Lucas, 275,
Hampsten, Andy, 65,
Hansen, Adam, 274,
Hassenforder, Roger, 264,
Haussler, Heinrich, 274
Hayman, Mathew, 269,
Heller, Henry, 40
Hemingway, Ernest, 54, 247,
Herald Sun, 11, 272,
Hesjedal, Ryder, 209,
Heydrich, Reinhard, 174, 175,
Himmler, Heinrich, 175, 183,
Hinault, Bernard, 249,
Hitler, Adolf, 113, 119, 128, 137, 138, 148, 157, 165, 166, 167, 171, 172, 175, 176, 177, 178, 179, 182, 183, 262,
Hoare, Samuel, 128,
Hodge, Stephen, 12, 274,
Hoobin, Jack, 272,
Idea Ricostruttive, 207,
Il Popolo d'Italia, 74, 124, 135, 138,
Italia Libera, 97
Indurain, Miguel, 234, 249,

Jansen, Jan, 218,
Jensen, Knut, 266,
John XXIII, Pope, (Angelo Roncali), 262, 263,
John Paul II, Pope, 160,
Jonker, Pat, 274,
Julius, Arthurs, 272,
Kaers, Karel, 233,
Kesselring, Albert, 177, 179,
Keynes, John Maynard, 173, 205,
Khrushchev, Nikita, 252,
Kint, Marcel, 124, 130, 132, 137,
Kirkham, Duncan 'Don', 270,
Koblet, Hugo, 211, 212, 234, 237, 238, 239, 254, 255, 256, 257, 263, 271,
Kristallnacht, 174,
Kübler, Ferdinand (Ferdi), 197, 223, 228, 232, 234, 236, 237, 238, 239, 241, 251, 252, 253, 256, 271,
La Dottrina del Fascism, 93,
Ladri di Biciclette, 187,
La Gazzetta dello Sport, 26, 28, 29, 30, 33, 34, 36, 39, 40, 44, 48, 49, 50, 57, 61, 63, 67, 68, 83, 84, 198, 199, 217, 243, 256,
Lambot, Firmin, 218,
Lambrecht, Roger, 219, 220,
Lancaster, Brett, 274,
Landra, Guido, 137,
Lapébie, Roger, 103, 126, 247,
Lapize, Octave, 54,
Lasarides, Lucien, 239,
Laval, Pierre, 128,
Lazarides, Apo, 223,
Lazarides, Lucien, 254,
L'Auto, 33, 38, 83, 107, 125,
Leducq, André, 82, 107, 109, 130, 131, 132, 143, 212,
L'Equipe, 239,
Lefèvre, Géo, 38,
Le Greves, Rene, 124,
Lehnert, Pasqualina, 163, 182,
Le Mond, Greg, 208,
Lenin, Vladimir (Ulyanov), 161,
Le Petit Journal, 55

Cycling and the Story of Italy

Liggett, Phil, 117,
Leo XIII, Pope, 91, 159, 163,
Leoni, Adolfo, 140, 150, 152, 153, 188, 189, 192, 193, 195, 228, 230,
Locatelli, Enrico, 254, 258,
L'Union Vélocipédique de France, 38
Le Velo, 33
Liggett, Phil, 143, 259,
Liston, Sonny, 208,
Livy, Titus, 17,
Lloyd, Matthew, 274,
Locatelli, Giulia, 267,
Longo, Luigi, 220,
Looy, Rik Van, 249,
L'Osservatore Romano, 182
Lucotti, Luigi, 59
Logli, Nedo, 236,
Louie, Jakes, 130,
Louviot, Raymond, 107
Luce, Clare Boothe, 213,
Luce, Henry, 213, 214,
Luzzatti, Luigi, 138,
Machiavelli, Niccolo, 18,
McEnroe, John, 208,
McEwen, Robbie, 274,
McGee, Brad, 274,
MacFarland, Floyd, 270,
MacFarlane, David, 274,
McKenzie, David, 274,
MacMillan, Kirkpatrick, 23
Madonna del Ghisallo, 28,
Maertens, Freddie, 83, 274,
Maes, Romain, 124,
Maes, Sylvère, 124, 126, 129, 131, 207,
Maggini, Sergio & Luciano, 207, 229,
Maglione, Luigi, 175, 176,
Magne, Antonin, 84, 107, 124, 129, 130, 131, 132,
Magni, Fiorenzo, 44, 189, 207, 216, 228, 229, 231, 233, 236, 237, 238, 239, 240, 241, 242, 246, 253, 256, 258, 260, 263, 265, 266, 271,
Magni, Giuseppe & Giulia, 240,
Magretti, Paolo, 25

Mahe, Andre, 228,
Malavasi, Letizia, 81,
Mallajac, Jean, 250,
Malthus, Thomas, 19,
Manifesto of the Racial Scientists, 137, 138,
Mara, Michele, 84,
Marabelli, Diego, 119
Marchisio, Luigi, 84, 85,
Marshall, George C, 203, 204, 213,
Mariano, Giuseppe, 105
Marinelli, Jacques, 232, 233,
Martini, Alfredo, 240,
Marx, Karl, 74, 159, 161,
Mattano, Giuseppe, 129,
Matteotti, Giacomo, 78, 97, 134,
Matthews, Michael, 274,
Mazzini, Giuseppe, 18, 19, 138,
Mein Kampf, 174,
Menlik, Emperor, 110,
Merckx, Eddy, 60, 61, 68, 76, 83, 190, 234, 249, 274,
Merlano, Domenico, 146,
Meulenberg, Eloi, 130,
Meyer, Cameron, 275,
Micheletto, Giovanni, 50,
Mit brennender sorge, 174,
Mockridge, Russell, 250, 251, 272,
Molin, Pietro Dal, 23,
Mollo, Enrico, 105, 106, 123, 150, 151, 152, 153,
Monnet, Jean, 227, 245,
Montero, Ricardo, 84
Moore, James, 190,
Morello, Ambrogio, 109, 124,
Morgagni, Tullo, 26, 35,
Morgenpost, 176,
Moro, Aldo, 264,
Moser, Francesco, 190, 273,
Motta, Michele, 201,
Munro, Iddo 'Snowy', 270, 272,
Mussolini, Arnaldo, 79,
Mussolini, Benito, 19, 73, 74, 75, 76, 77, 78, 79, 80, 83, 85, 87, 92, 93, 94, 96, 97, 109, 110, 111, 112, 113, 117, 119, 121, 123, 124, 127,

128, 129, 135, 136, 137, 138, 139, 142, 148, 149, 155, 167, 169, 171, 172, 173, 177, 178, 179, 183, 192, 193, 206, 262,
Mussolini, Bruno and Vittorio, 85
Negrini, Antonio,105
Nencini, Gastone, 242,
Nenni, Pietro, 220,
Nicolas II, 161
Niccacci, Rufino, 181,
Non Abbiamo Bisogno, 96,
Nulli, Edmondo, 188,
Occhini, Giulia, (Giulia Locatelli), 254, 258, 267,
Ockers, Stan, 232, 233, 237, 238, 256, 257, 271,
O'Grady, Stuart, 274,
Oliveri, Guiseppe, 76
Olliver, Valare, 229, 241,
Olmo, Giuseppe, 106, 114, 122,
Opperman, Hubert, 249, 250, 270, 271,
Oriani, Carlo, 41, 44, 50, 51, 54, 56, 58,
Orlando, Vittorio, 73, 78,
Ortelli, Vito,189, 195, 200, 216, 228,
Osborne, Percy, 270,
Owens, Jesse, 120
Pacelli, Eugenio (Pius XII),
Pact of Steel, 148,
Pallante, Antonio, 220,
Pantani, Marco, 9, 23
Paret, Henri, 37,
Parri, Ferrucio, 194,
Paris-Soir, 107
Parvesi, Attila, 115
Passerieu, Georges, 270,
Pavesi, Eberardo, 45, 47, 48, 50, 51, 56, 64, 113, 143, 147, 151, 152, 153, 195, 196, 198,
Paul VI, Pope, 263,
Payan, Ferdinand, 38,
Pedretti, Paolo, 121,
Peeters, Ward, 228,
Peiper, Allan, 274,
Pélissier, Charles, 82, 83,
Pélissier, Francis, 63,
Pélissier, Henri, 32, 62, 63, 64, 218,
Pesenti, Antonio, 107,

Petacci, Claretta, 183,
Petit-Breton, Lucien, 30, 31, 39, 41, 45, 48, 49, 51, 54, 69, 247,
Petrarch, Francesco, 18
Piccini, Alfonso, 64
Pilati, Gaetano, 97,
Pius IX, Pope, 18
Pius X, Pope, (Giuseppe Sarto), 91, 92, 120, 158,
Pius XI, Pope, (Achille Ratti), 93, 96, 121, 158, 162, 174, 175,
Pius XII, Pope, (Eugenio Pacelli), 158, 162, 163, 164, 166, 175, 178, 179, 182, 199, 203, 244, 262,
Poblet, Miguel, 246,
Porte, Richie, 274,
Pothier, Lucien, 37,
Pottier, André, 40
Prevost, Charles, 38,
Referendum Istituzionale, 197,
Renshaw, Mark, 274,
Rerum Novarum, 91, 159,
Ricci, Mario, 151, 188, 193, 195, 200,
Riefenstahl, Leni, 120
Rimoldi, Puerto,
Ritter, Arno, 45
Rivera, Jose Antonio & Fernandez, 112
Rivera, Miguel Primo de, 111, 112,
Riviere, Roger, 264, 266,
Robic, Jean, 218, 221, 233, 237, 252, 256, 271,
Roche, Stephen, 234,
Rogers, Michael, 274,
Roghi, Bruno, 198,
Rommel, Erwin, 168,
Ronconi, Aldo, 200, 216, 218, 230,
Ronsse, Georges, 67, 223,
Roosevelt, Franklin D, 203,
Rosello, Vittorio, 212,
Rossi, Jules, 125, 129,
Rossignoli, Giovanni, 42, 43, 48, 49, 51, 56,
Roth, Ernst von, 174,
Rowley, Keith, 11, 272,
Rowley, Max, 11, 272,
Ruiz, Bernardo, 256,

Cycling and the Story of Italy

Salandra, Antonio, 71, 77, 78, 92,
Salas, Eddie, 274,
Salassie, Haile, 128,
Sarfatti, Margherita, 79, 172,
Scelba, Mario, 214,
Schaer, Fritz, 229,
Scheda Peronale, 193,
Schlek, Andy, 209,
Schotte, Alberic 'Briek', 219, 223, 229, 241, 257,
Schulte, Gerrit, 234,
Schuman, Robert, 225, 227, 245,
Segato, Guglielmo, 115
Servadei, Glaudo, 189, 191,
Sherwen, Paul, 203,
Sici, Vittorio De, 187,
Sinatra, Frank, 214,
Sizzi, Armando, 89,
Smith, Eddie, 271,
Soldani, Renzo, 238,
Soubirous, Bernadette, 219,
Speicher, Georges, 124, 129, 131,
Spencer, Herbert, 19
Sporting Globe, 271,
Sportwereld, 240,
Starace, Achille, 123, 193,
Stalin, Joseph, 162, 203, 205, 213, 252,
Stampfl, Franz, 11
Steenbergen, Rick Van, 228, 232, 233, 234, 237, 238, 241, 253, 255, 271,
Stephens, Neil, 274,
Stettler, Ernst, 234,
Stopel, Kurt, 107
Strada, Alfonsina, 65, 102
Sturzo, Don Luigi, 77, 94,
Suter, Heiri, 241,
Taylor, Marshall 'Major', 103, 270,
Taylor, Jim, 272,
Teisseire, Lucien, 195, 196,
Time, 213, 114,
Titian, 208,
Toccaceli, Quirino, 189,
Togliatti, Palmiro, 95, 194, 206, 210, 211, 213, 214, 220, 222, 261,

Tolstoy, Leo, 254,
Tomaselli, Gian Fernando, 23, 35,
Tommasello, Giovanni,
Torriani, Vincenzo, 198,
Torti, Emilio Croci, 257,
Tosi, Franco, 24
Trevorrow, John, 11, 274,
Trousselier, Louis, 40, 41, 42,
Truman, Harry, 214,
Umberto I, King, 21
Umberto II, King, 197,
Union Cycliste Internationale, 67,
Valetti, Giovanni, 122, 123, 128, 139, 140, 141, 142, 149, 150, 196,
Varetto, Angelo, 113
Vervaecke, Félicien, 124, 129, 131, 132, 137,
Vervaecke, Julian, 107
Vicini, Mario, 125, 126, 129, 132, 139, 140, 141, 149, 150, 152,
Victor Emmanuel II, King, 18, 21,
Victor Emmanuel III, King, 171, 177, 197,
Vietto, Rene, 130, 218, 219, 232,
Ville, Maurice, 63,
Vinci, Leonardo di, 23
Vittorio, Giuseppe Di, 220,
Vissers, Edward (Ward), 125, 130, 132,
Vissers, Louie, 130,
Voice of America, 213,
Volpi, Primo, 230,
Walker, Cecil, 270,
Watson, Harry, 270,
Weckerling, Otto, 126,
White, Matthew, 274,
Whitehorn, Dean, 268, 271,
Wijnendaele, Karel Van, 240,
Wilhelm, Kaiser, 164,
Williams, Don, 271
Wilson, Michael, 274,
Zampini, Donato, 256,
Zanazzi, Renzo, 208,

www.ingramcontent.com/pod-product-compliance
Lightning Source LLC
Chambersburg PA
CBHW070755230426
43665CB00017B/2369